Praise for **their end is our beg**

"Their End Is Our Beginning is a passionate, clear-eyed analysis that tackles the roots of policing and boldly envisions a future without it. . . . Bean's position is crystal clear: The end of policing and the end of capitalism are intertwined, and from their end can emerge our beginning as a truly free society." —**Hossam el-Hamalawy**, *Middle East Eye*

"brian bean lays out a brilliant, thoroughly persuasive case for why capitalism needs cops and why a genuine socialist future is impossible with police and prisons. Abolition is the first step toward liberation. So what are we waiting for?" —**Robin D. G. Kelley**, author of *Freedom Dreams*

"Their End Is Our Beginning powerfully exposes the comprehensive entanglement of policing and capitalism, revealing how these two forces bolster, feed, and necessitate each other. With bold prose and deep research, brian bean chronicles these institutions' twin evolutions: a story of intertwined economic, structural, physical, and social violences. He also illuminates a path to a world without them. At a time when policing is wielded to enforce rising authoritarianism, this is the book we need." —**Maya Schenwar**, coauthor of *Prison by Any Other Name*

"brian bean pulls no punches in this provocative and compelling analysis of the police as an institution. A new generation of activists, suspicious of 'reform' and inspired by the ideas of abolition, will find big ideas here about the origins of the police and what it means to imagine a world without them." —**Brian Jones**, author of *Black History Is for Everyone*

"Five years after Minneapolis shook the world, political and economic elites are unified around a single message: We were wrong. Wrong to demand abolition, wrong to suggest that communities can take care of themselves, wrong to imagine alternatives to racist fear, capitalist greed, and colonial genocide. But brian bean is here to remind us that they are the ones who are wrong: The police are little more than glorified guardians of whiteness and wealth, and they will be the first to go when these twin systems come crashing down." —**Geo Maher,** coordinator of the W. E. B. Du Bois Movement School for Abolition & Reconstruction and author of *A World Without Police*

"Think the movement for police abolition is over? Think again. In this bold and uplifting work, brian bean shares inspiring examples of people who managed their communities after driving out the police. And he reminds us that the role of police is not to prevent crime but to defend capitalism. *Their End Is Our Beginning* is a much-needed breath of hope as we blaze our path to a better world." —**David McNally** author of *Blood and Money*

"brian bean is NOT afraid! With unapologetic determination and clarity, *Their End Is Our Beginning* pulls no punches in making the case for the abolition of police and prisons. His book should be considered a critical tool in the long struggle to think, talk, and act on our own terms." —**David Omotoso Stovall**, author of *Engineered Conflict*

"With compelling prose and beautiful images, *The End Is Our Beginning* lays out the clear and convincing evidence that any path to real social justice requires eliminating the roadblock of police power." —**Alex S. Vitale**, author of *The End of Policing*

"*Their End Is Our Beginning* is a book about cops—where they come from, what they do, and why they do it. Cops, as brian bean so eloquently writes, hold a capitalist order together, and so this book is also about class, racial capitalism, and the state. The goal, as the title makes clear, is revolutionary abolition, not reform. We don't need a better world; we need another world. But since cops block our way, bean offers us this book as his contribution to the fighting movement we need to get us there." —**David Correia**, coauthor of *Violent Order*

their end is our beginning

COPS, CAPITALISM, AND ABOLITION

brian bean

Haymarket Books
Chicago, Illinois

© 2025 brian bean

Published in 2025 by
Haymarket Books
P.O. Box 180165
Chicago, IL 60618
www.haymarketbooks.org

ISBN: 979-888890-373-5

Distributed to the trade in the US through Consortium Book Sales and Distribution (www.cbsd.com) and internationally through Ingram Publisher Services International (www.ingramcontent.com).

This book was published with the generous support of Lannan Foundation, Wallace Action Fund, and Marguerite Casey Foundation.

Special discounts are available for bulk purchases by organizations and institutions. Please email info@haymarketbooks.org for more information.

Cover and interior artwork by Charlie Aleck.
Cover design by David Gee.

Printed in Canada by union labor.

Library of Congress Cataloging-in-Publication data is available.
Library of Congress Control Number: 2025938100

10 9 8 7 6 5 4 3 2 1

إلى الشهداء
For the martyrs

¡Presente!

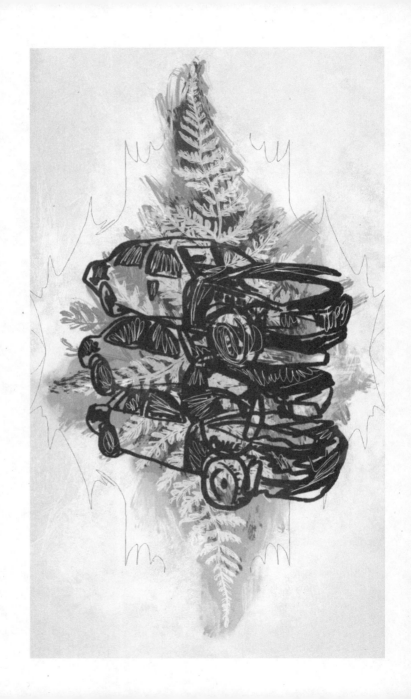

contents

introduction
"A Single Picture of Police Violence and Capitalist Exploitation"   **1**

chapter 1
Origins of a Violent Order: Where Cops Come From   **17**

chapter 2
"Bullies in Blue Suits": What Cops Do   **63**

chapter 3
The Police State and Its Functionaries   **109**

chapter 4
An Ever-Raging Fire: International Revolt and Resistance   **145**

chapter 5
Revolutionary Abolitionism   **181**

acknowledgments   **217**

notes   **221**

index   **261**

¡Presente!

introduction
"A Single Picture of Police Violence and Capitalist Exploitation"

A cop is a cop. He may be a very nice man, but I haven't time to figure that out. All I know is that he has a uniform and a gun and I have to relate to him that way, that's the only way to relate to him at all. Because one of us may have to die.
— **James Baldwin**

The abolitionist mission isn't done until every prison is empty, when there are no more cops, when the land has been given back, that's when it's over.
— **Tortuguita**[1]

It may be strange, though perhaps necessary, to begin with endings. In the writing of this book, new, violent endings are cast upon us every week. They are every day, continuous. With which of these tragically commonplace stories does one begin?

In March 2024, cops in San Bernardino, California, killed Ryan Gainer. Ryan was fifteen, a child. Ryan, his sister says, was "a beautiful soul." Cops put three bullets into his body within seven seconds of seeing him. Ryan was in distress when his family called for help. "Why did you shoot him?" his family screamed at his killers, who then withheld first aid from their victim. "He's dying!" his family can be heard yelling at the cops in the video released of the incident. Their child, their brother, shot down, murdered before their eyes. In remembering Ryan, his loved ones shared on social media a video he made when he was alive: "To all the viewers," he said, "make sure you have a great day, be the spark, and make sure to spread kindness."[2] Cops do not care for beauty, for souls, for kindness.

This book is an argument against the police. For the vast majority of the people in this country, and across the globe, the cops are a dangerous and useless institution. Their primary tool is violence, always threatened and often utilized. As detailed below, they were created to forcibly organize and maintain a social order benefiting the interests of the ruling social group (or class) of the ultrarich. For most working people, that "order" is the chaos and danger produced by this unequal society, which defines our daily life as always on the brink of crisis. The cops hold capitalist order together and hold the people down.

A central tool deployed to maintain this order is racism. Far from a byproduct, racism operates to construct and reconstruct relations essential to capitalism. In the construction of capitalism, racism is not the sawdust left over, but the saw with sharpened teeth. Here in the US, anti-Black racism has been, and is, vital to the origin and maintenance of US capitalism. Its effects are cataloged most starkly in the American gulags where Black men have a one in three chance of being incarcerated, six times more likely than their white counterparts. Black women, while much less likely than Black men to face incarceration, are *sixty-two* times more likely to be incarcerated than white women.[3] The racist system has disappeared 1.5 million Black men from

"A Single Picture of Police Violence and Capitalist Exploitation" 3

the community through incarceration or—per one report—premature death.[4] In some cities, such as Baltimore, the life expectancy gap between white and Black neighborhoods just three miles apart is twenty years.[5] In Chicago, the life-expectancy gap across racialized neighborhoods is thirty years.[6]

Effectively curtailing the violence of police power requires limiting their number, tools, weapons, and ability to act. Reforms that fail to do so can create what Mariame Kaba calls a dangerous "new common sense,"[7] and—as many have pointed out—end up extending police powers.[8] The ruling class's status and position in society depend on the police behaving as designed. Thus, ruling-class politicians and the capitalists behind them are greatly invested in working against and resisting any attempts at reform that would alter the core function of the police. Far from a broken institution, the institution of the police is working well for the ruling class. As an essential tool of violence, this core function is irrevocable. The police cannot be—in the end—reformed.

This book is about abolishing the police. Abolitionist thought and practice have a long history, which reaches back centuries and contains multiple, often conflicting political trends. In recent decades, revolutionary Black women have spearheaded and theorized movements against the prison industrial complex (PIC) in the US. These efforts and their abolitionist politics were brought into broader awareness by the mass protests of the 2020 George Floyd/Breonna Taylor uprising. Simply put, abolition is the idea that we can organize our society to meet all the needs of its participants effectively without armed officials prowling the streets or locking individuals away. We can build a different society without armed deputies escalating simple interactions like traffic violations into deadly violence. We can build a world where situations like mental health crises and domestic violence are managed by communities rather than violent killers. To get there, we need to disarm, defund, disband, and abolish the police. Only in the rubble of police headquarters and prisons will we be able to clear space for parks in which our children can play, skate, explore; where our communities can gather, bond, grow, and watch the sun rise and set.

Tyre Nichols photographed sunsets. "People have a story to tell, why not capture it," he said, describing his photography on his website.[9] Tyre loved to skate. Videos of him jumping curbs and dropping in on ramps on his board, backlit by the California sun, show him smiling, joyful in the feeling of movement, freedom, and grace.[10] On his meal breaks from work, Tyre would visit his mother, whose name was tattooed on his arm. Tyre, like Ryan Gainer, was described as having a "beautiful soul." In January 2023, Memphis police conducted a traffic stop on Tyre, less than a hundred yards from his mother's house. During the course of the stop, Tyre was dragged from his car, tased, punched, kicked, batoned, pepper sprayed, and ultimately beaten to death by a gang of cops for twelve minutes. Held down to the pavement by five cops, Tyre begged for them to stop, calling out for his mom, as he was repeatedly struck in the head with a baton. "I am going to baton the fuck out of you," the killers yelled.[11] "I hope they stomp his ass," a cop cheered on. The cops seem to relish in their destruction of beautiful souls.

This book is about the cops and capitalism. Cops patrol, maintain, recreate, enforce, and repress resistance to a racist capitalist system.[12] Thus, the abolition of the police requires a breaking with capitalism. Abolitionist politics have always been a contested field,

"A Single Picture of Police Violence and Capitalist Exploitation"   5

with anticapitalist politics a prominent, if not dominant, tendency. Angela Davis, one of the more prominent abolitionist figures, explains, "Ultimately we are going to have to dismantle this system and move in a socialist direction."[13] Mariame Kaba states, "We're not going to abolish the police, if we don't abolish capitalism by the way! It ain't going to happen."[14] "Can we abolish prisons without abolishing capitalism?" a podcast interviewer asked Ruth Wilson Gilmore. Her response: "No. It's a short answer."[15] Prominent radical scholar Robin D. G. Kelley opened his remarks at a panel entitled "Abolition Communism" in 2023 by saying, "When I saw the title 'Abolition Communism' it kinda felt redundant and a relief. It shouldn't even be a question, but people actually ask me the question, 'Is abolition possible under capitalism?' The answer is no."[16] Kelley then pointed out that in the *Communist Manifesto*, the word *abolition* was used twenty times, *abolish* nine, and *communism* (when not used as a name or a party) thirteen. It is essentially an adage in the movement that the object of abolition is not just the cops and the cages but the society that produces the social problems to which cops and cages serve as barbaric, false solutions.

This book aims to make concrete this connection between capitalism and the police, going beyond slogans or political common sense. What about capitalism necessitates the police? The institution of police is just one of any number of possible institutions that could be imagined to forcibly maintain private property and an unequal class society. A shopkeeper's store or a capitalist's factory could be secured for them in any number of ways. Yet, with some regional variation, the cops are a universal feature of capitalism. "In basically every country that exists," writes journalist Vincent Bevins, "you can get a cop to beat you up."[17] Why is this particular form of repression the one relied upon? Why, for example, doesn't the military play this role? Why does the ruling class not rely on directly controlled and privately funded security guards or mercenaries—which, today, play only a supplemental role? The cops have emerged as capitalism's favored method of control because they were produced by the special conditions of capitalism, which created police as a discrete and unique social institution. Their formation occurred in lockstep with the development of the capitalist system and its political form in the capitalist state. The timing is not coincidental. This book will show that this connection is essential to understanding how and why the cops function. Grasping their social function will help us better strategize ways for us to abolish the institution.

Focusing on this connection requires that our aims be clear. Fighting to abolish the police and end capitalism necessitates the creation of a new democratic order—that of socialism.[18] A classless, stateless society, free of oppression and exploitation, where we—ordinary people—democratically control and creatively run our entire society. Economic resources and productive capacity would be collectively organized to meet the needs of all. As free people, we would democratically determine what happens with our labor and its fruits. This new order is the antithesis to the one that currently plagues the earth. If we are to, as abolitionist Ruth Wilson Gilmore says, "change everything," then we must prepare to win, which means being "ready for the morning after."[19] An explicit suture of the politics of revolutionary socialism to that of abolitionism, this book argues, is necessary for the success of both. It is a red sun that will dawn on the first morning of a cop-free world. Readers will encounter a good deal of quotes from the socialist tradition, including figures like Marx, Lenin, Stuart Hall, and others.

This book will also make clear that any strain of the socialist movement that does not hold as central the general politics of

"A Single Picture of Police Violence and Capitalist Exploitation"

antiracism and police abolition is incoherent and self-defeating. Socialists should take a cue from Marx, who, in referring to the earlier abolitionist movement that fought chattel slavery in the US, championed it as "the most momentous thing happening in the world today."[20] Lenin, in his foundational work *What Is to Be Done?*, wrote that the task of the socialist revolutionary was to be "able to generalize all these manifestations [of tyranny and oppression] and produce a *single picture of police violence and capitalist exploitation*."[21] A single picture: to abolish the police, we must abolish the capitalist state, achieved through an international revolution for socialism, a path that inevitably passes directly through a police line.

Tortuguita (Manuel Esteban Paez Terán) fell in love with the woods.[22] In an attempt to stop the razing of more than three hundred acres of forest for a ninety-million dollar training facility, known as "Cop City," Tortuguita joined with other defenders in Atlanta's Weelaunee Forest as they camped in the woods. Comrades described Tort as bringing "indescribable jubilance to every moment of their life."[23] Tort was a tireless and committed activist, abolitionist, artist, and ecologist. Eight days after the murder of Tyre Nichols, cops raided Tortuguita's camp and shot them while they were sitting cross-legged in their tent. Fifty-seven bullets tore through their body, killing this joyful defender and lover of the woods. Cruelty and mercilessness are included in cops' role as purveyors of state violence.

This book is about cops, capitalism, and the state. The question of "the state" looms behind many critical, strategic discussions in the movement. Do abolitionists ask for reforms of states? Are states sites of struggle, and what is the role of elected office? Do abolitionist projects mean building small alternatives to policing outside of the current state structures? Can we not just go around the state? Or build islands of abolition and defend them from attack? Is there even an "outside the state" in today's increasingly authoritarian web of surveillance and social control? All these questions lead to the basic one: How will we achieve abolition? If we are demanding, as abolitionists Mariame Kaba and Andrea Ritchie ask, that "a carceral, racial capitalist state disarm itself," then how do we expect to win a confrontation that aims to strip the principal power of violence held by the ruling class?[24]

This book is about that confrontation. I will argue that, rather than capitalist states being sites of struggle that can be perhaps repurposed for our aims, states are the chief obstacle to achieving abolition. Anticapitalists and abolitionists alike must be clear that we need to abolish the state to achieve liberation, even as we build our own networks and institutions to replace it. This horizon does not invalidate the struggle for smaller reforms like cutting their number, funding, and legal immunities, and replacing police duties with alternatives to the police. All these reforms comprise the day-to-day work of abolitionists and socialists and are important to both building a durable, powerful movement and providing some relief from the immediate harms raining down in the capitalist storm. The aim of abolishing the capitalist state does, however, provide direction and scale for the tasks ahead, the compass pointing toward what is ultimately necessary: revolution against the capitalist police state.

The violence unfurls continuously as stories repeat themselves,

"A Single Picture of Police Violence and Capitalist Exploitation"   9

identical in form yet imposed on unique individuals. Barely two weeks after the murder of Ryan Gainer, cops in Queens, New York, murdered nineteen-year-old Win Rozario. Win's family, like Ryan's, called the police because of a mental health crisis. When the cops arrived, Win's mother was holding him. His brother Utsho opened the door and told the officers to "be gentle" with his sibling. Win was shot in his mother's arms six times, according to his family, and killed.[25] The tragedies repeat and repeat and repeat.

And these are stories of those who are typically perceived as more "innocent" victims than people like Korryn Gaines, killed by Baltimore SWAT in 2016 after a long standoff in which she pointed a shotgun at the cops attempting to execute a warrant at her home. The warrant was for missing a court date for a traffic ticket.[26] Dexter Reed was twenty-six when he was murdered by Chicago cops, six days before Win Rozario. The cops pulled Reed over, reportedly for his windows being too tinted. For this innocuous offense, the plainclothes agents leapt out of their unmarked car, ran up and surrounded Reed's vehicle, guns drawn, shouting expletives and commands. Someone shot first, then the cops fired ninety-six bullets in forty-one seconds. Dexter dropped his gun and tried to escape, when he was shot down; at least three more bullets were fired into him as he lay bleeding on the ground. Even if Dexter shot first at police, the situation was the culmination of a repeated routine for police: stop a car on "suspicion"; escalate the situation; end it in a hail of bullets.[27] Common police practice creates conditions of escalation and entrapment that result in impromptu death warrants and extrajudicial executions. We should be wary of the narrative of the "perfect victim." Blame and guilt fall on the cops, full stop.

After so many acts that leave us speechless, there remains only one thing to say: Fuck the police. As the poet says: "And we hate po-po." These words have echoed around us as we marched, and perhaps we have voiced them ourselves. These are words of legitimate rage, rooted in grievances of both the daily trauma and the historical legacy of racism, slavery, genocide, colonialism, and stolen labor, land, and lives. However, they are not merely an emotional epithet but a sensible articulation of conditions from which a guiding political perspective can be derived. The slogan ACAB is scrawled on walls the world over, All Cops Are Bastards, which is not a simple personal aspersion of the character of individuals in uniform but reflects a material analysis of the police as an institution. It is a description of the present that requires translation to an imagined future and the will to fight for it. This book aims to bring out and sharpen this analysis explicitly, with Marxism as a theoretical tool. I began with an ending, and now I end with a beginning. The end of the police is the beginning of a new world. A world free of oppression and exploitation, a world of creativity and real democracy. Let us hasten its coming.

Chapter Overview

In chapter one, "Origins of a Violent Order," I trace the origins of the modern police. The mid-nineteenth-century birth of modern policing corresponds with the development of industrial capitalism, each of which contributed to the production of the other. Capitalism created a new working class, organized in cities, which allowed for the mass extraction of profit but also created problems for the ruling class in managing the conditions of this new order, especially the capacity of the working class for resistance—in

"A Single Picture of Police Violence and Capitalist Exploitation" **11**

crowds. Many histories of policing paint a picture of a linear development, with the police invented out of thin air in nineteenth-century London and exported as a total package, or of slave patrols in the US simply turning into cops wholesale (although some of them did just that). Instead, I will argue that the establishment of the police as the favored method of capitalist states occurred through a period of experimentation among the ruling class globally. In the creation of this new body, different states drew on their own practices of repression in domestic experiences, colonial rule, and control of the enslaved. These earlier institutions of repression, like the slave patrol in the United States, would provide what Ben Brucato describes in their excellent history on the subject as "a core logic of policing that would be a component in the genetic material for centuries of policing in this country."[28]

An assessment of the origins of the police clearly illuminates their primary role as the suppression, prevention, and pacification of working-class resistance. Crucial to that task was the violent imposition of racism, with anti-Black racism as central. In the first chapter, I emphasize the continuity of these core functions throughout the history of policing. Exploring their origin provides a counterargument to reformist positions claiming that police brutality can be limited by legislation or policy, or that the main problem of the police is "militarization" or the "warrior cop." This argument, according to critical police theorist Mark Neocleous, creates "a blockage in critical thinking about police power" because it is based on the assumption that "policing is not about violence but something else, usually security, law and order, peace and tranquility, the good of the community, policing by consent rather than through coercion."[29] Instead, as their history shows, the police are violent by design.

I move on to describe current policing practices in the second chapter, "Bullies in Blue Suits." Here, I explore what cops actually do. I discuss a variety of the most common myths that surround police activity, a central part of which is the concept of crime. As my argument elaborates, the category of crime and its legal articulations are not rooted in the betterment of society but in class control. From their origin to the present, the express mandate of police has been the prevention of crime. However, this chapter traces how the ruling class defines *prevention* as the ordering and managing of working people to best promote conditions for capitalism. While capitalism creates conditions of unemployment, poverty, and accompanying social ills, the police mission is explicitly not to resolve or fix these problems. Instead, police are tasked with keeping these problems under just enough control to allow the wheels of profit to keep turning.

Cops, perhaps ironically to their advocates, are not particularly good at solving crime or preventing it, as this is not their purpose. Cops are also assigned to manage other social problems like mental health crises and intimate partner violence. Often, in these cases, cops make the situations worse, regularly murdering people in need of help. In the end, rather than being an institution of "public safety," the cops are, in many cases, a public danger. This second chapter aims to provide tools and arguments to help disprove that myth.

In chapter three, "The Police State and its Functionaries," I turn from what police do to an exploration of *why* they do what they do. Understanding the purpose of the police involves an exploration of their relationship to the capitalist state. States in capitalism function to generalize the interests of the ruling class and ensure a positive business environment for capital. Police—a special body of armed individuals—are the core of the state, playing

"A Single Picture of Police Violence and Capitalist Exploitation" 13

a central role. I will also discuss racism as a political project of the capitalist state and how cops enact this project spectacularly. The relationship that the police have with the state conditions their relationship with the rest of society, with working people, and the oppressed. Bound to the state in a relationship of antagonism with all other social spheres, the police are established as enemies of working-class and antiracist movements. They invariably play this role despite the fact that many cops may come from working-class backgrounds and, in the present-day US, are also demographically diverse. Seeing the police as a key instrument of the capitalist class, rather than just as a subsidiary, has profound implications for the strategy and tactics of abolition. We can't take on the cops without taking on the state.

Specific implications are addressed in the fourth chapter, "An Ever-Raging Fire." I take us to a series of movements outside of the United States to explore struggles where movements against the police detonated or deepened social explosions. Many of the histories described are not typically thought of as antipolice movements, but purposefully framing them as such provides many rich lessons. In these historical movements, the police institutions became the focus of popular movements and in some cases were temporarily abolished. While my treatments of these massive events are relatively brief, I present them in order to reframe events and highlight themes relevant to the task of this book. In some instances, I interviewed participants in these struggles. From Russia in 1917 to Northern Ireland in the 1960s, South Africa in the 1980s, Mexico in 2006, and the Middle East and North Africa in 2011, I explore both the positive and negative lessons that can be gleaned from these powerful uprisings and revolutions.

Finally, in chapter five, "Revolutionary Abolitionism," I conclude by connecting the central arguments of the book and their implications. The cops, as a core component of the capitalist state tasked with reproducing and maintaining this unequal and oppressive order, will never be obsolete for the ruling class. Abolition will not be arrived at via an incremental path, and reforming away their core project within capitalism is not only impossible but will also be contested vociferously. In the struggle for abolition of the police, at a certain point, the movement will have to contend with the full force and violence of the capitalist state. This confrontation will have to draw on all the resources of a mobilized and organized society, including mass strikes, mutual aid, self-defense, and political education, as well as, importantly, uprising and revolution. Achieving the abolition of the police will require the revolutionary end of the current state machinery. To build a liberated world, our movements will need to imagine the end of policing as the end of capitalism and abolition as the revolutionary toppling of capitalism by socialist revolution carried out by a mass movement from below.

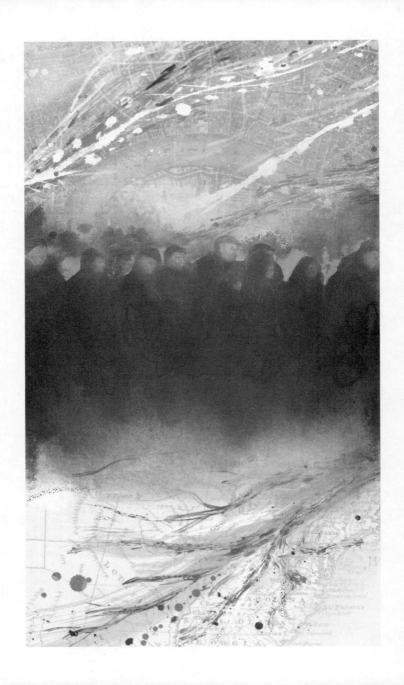

chapter 1
Origins of a Violent Order
Where Cops Come From

Nothing short of the most efficient police system will prevent strolling, vagrancy, theft, and the utter destruction of or serious injury of our industrial system.
—***Lynchburg Virginian***, editorial advocating
for racist Black Codes, 1865[1]

The people were justified in repelling such despotic and bloodthirsty power by any and every means at their disposal, because I believe that the institution of a police force is an infringement on the constitution and liberties possessed by our ancestors.
—**William Lovett**, British Chartist radical, 1838[2]

Burn the houses of them that have the most money.
—**John Hughson**, an organizer of the
1741 New York City insurrection[3]

The institution of the police is a modern invention, less than two hundred years old.[4] From today's flak-jacketed, assault-rifle-carrying, high-tech-surveillance-guided cops slowly cruising neighborhoods in squad cars and military-grade armored personnel vehicles to the blue-coated, top-hatted,

17

saber-and-baton-carrying *copper* walking the streets long ago, their basic function is the same. For those of us concerned with limiting and ending the day-to-day violence of the police, our task is to understand why they act as they do and their function in society. The social role of the police is historically determined and can be illuminated by looking at their violent origins. The police developed through a series of brutal experiments by the ruling class, testing the best means of securing their rule, reproducing, and maintaining the order of capitalism. Through successive iterations—from constable to colonial occupier, military gendarmerie, private security guard, and slave patrol—each form of policing served as the main tool of the capitalist class for securing their monopoly of violence. The enemy found its shape.

The Development of Capitalism

There is no origin story of the police without the story of the reorganization of human society by the birth, expansion, and dominance of the system of capitalism. While capitalism did not create inequality, it structured society such that new methods and tools were required to impose its uniquely unequal order— with threat of, and acts of, violence—in new ways. The police became one of the most important tools, specially adapted to fit the contours of this new social order.

All class societies of human history are distinguished by unequal access to the fruits of collective production. Whether king or pharaoh, huángdì or bey, shah or tlahtoāni, all class societies were marked by a class of individuals—often familial, in pre-capitalist societies—who controlled the surpluses and luxury produced by "regular" people. This rule was and is maintained by the capacity to use superior violence—in the form of armies—against those who oppose it. Various ideologies and mythologies were also built up over the raw force of arms, which aimed to make the unequal social arrangements appear natural and imbue the ruling class with special abilities or, in some cases, divine rights.

The rise of capitalism, a new economic system and social order that would eventually ensnare nearly every corner of the globe, transpired over roughly three hundred years, from the fourteenth century to the Industrial Revolution of 1750–1850.[5] Fueling its emergence were the world-shattering atrocities of colonialism, indigenous genocide, and chattel slavery that signaled what Marx called the "rosy dawn of capitalist production."[6]

It was in Europe that the rapacious appetite of capitalism emerged most sharply, and where both modern industrial capitalism and key developments and experiments in the invention of policing as we know it today were unleashed on the world.[7] To explore the social function of policing warrants a short detour through the origins of capitalism. The summary here is the barest of sketches, and, though undetailed and schematic, it provides the general context of the creation of the police. Europe in the feudal era was culturally and technologically backward in comparison with the great civilizations of China, India, Egypt, and Mesopotamia.[8] Much of the population of the continent lived a rural existence either as a small minority of warrior barons and religious elites who lorded over the land, or as part of the majority—serfs who worked the land and paid tribute with a percentage of their output to the lord or abbot "owners" of the land. Almost all things produced by society were for immediate consumption necessary for survival, or, in the case of the lords, for gratuitous luxury.[9] "The walls of the stomach of the feudal lord," to paraphrase Marx, was the "limitation of the exploitation of the serfs."[10]

Changes in technology, like improved and horse-drawn plows, advanced irrigation, fertilization, crop selection, and field rotation—some taken from the more advanced non-European civilizations—allowed for more efficient production of food.[11] Between 1000 and 1300 AD, the output of agricultural workers doubled.[12] This created a surplus above what could be immediately consumed and thus supported other social activity beyond production for immediate use.[13] Whoever controlled this surplus could exchange it for goods carried by traveling traders or made by artisans.[14] Over time, traveling traders became more substantial merchants, and markets, craftspeople, towns, and urban life grew, sprouting around castles and churches.[15] Towns were largely populated by tradesmen and people in skilled crafts guilds, and the percentage of people living in urban settings roughly doubled by 1300.[16] This urbanization and productive development temporarily stalled in the wake of the cataclysmic crisis of plague and famine that wiped out half of Europe's population, leaving whole villages abandoned. But it resumed apace and entered the period of the violence of expansive colonialism. Beginning in the 1500s, large rural landowners expanded their holdings in a massive wave of seizures, which displaced small tenant farmers who did not have access to enough land to meet their own subsistence and thus had to depend on a wage to survive. As of 1642—the start of the English Civil War—rural laborers made up half of England's population.[17]

This massive displacement caused individual farmers to be "suddenly dragged from their accustomed mode of life."[18] While some took up work on the countryside in order to survive, many comprised a mass of landless beggars and wanderers (known as vagabonds), "made strangers in the lands of their birth," who roamed the countryside, moving (or were moved) toward the cities to seek livelihood and subsistence.[19] In a process of staggering violence and terror, a series of laws were en-

Origins of a Violent Order

acted over the course of the sixteenth century, described by Marx as "bloody legislation against the expropriated," that carried out a campaign against those driven from their land. With the exception of licensed beggars who were labeled "indigent" and unable to work, anyone refusing waged work was considered a "vagrant" and liable to punishment by public flogging, disfigurement, branding, imprisonment, and, for a period of time beginning in 1547, literal enslavement.[20]

The displacement of small-scale agriculture drove these newly landless and destitute laborers into urban centers. Those who could not be absorbed into "productive" wage labor were condemned to a life of "vagrancy." The number of beggars flooding the streets of London provoked the clergy to pressure the king to open the first jail, or "house of correction," in 1553: Bridewell Prison.[21] The process of evicting peasant farmers from common lands and means of subsistence reached its apex through the Parliamentary Acts of Enclosure of 1760–1830, through which six million acres of land were expropriated by Parliament. This was, for Marx, one of the "circumstances of ruthless terrorism" that turned common lands into "modern private property" and "created for the urban industry the necessary supplies of free and rightless proletarians."[22]

The ruling class—in our case, the capitalist class that own all the means (tools, factories, raw materials) of producing goods in society—was quite explicit in its aims. A report created for the English Board of Agriculture in 1794 noted, "Once deprived of commons the laborers will work every day in the year, their children will be put to labor early."[23] This process gave birth to a new class: the *proletariat*, or workers compelled to sell their labor power on the market to capitalists for a wage in order to survive. The experience of this new working class was described by early radical, Jamaican-Scot abolitionist Robert Wedderburn: "I labor day and night with my hands to feed lazy and useless men, and they repay me with hunger and the sword. I sustain their life with the toil and sweat of my body, and they persecute my body with hardship until I am become a beggar. They live through me and I die through them."[24]

While our focus has been mostly on this process in England due to its position as the birthplace of modern industrial capitalism, other areas of Europe were undergoing variations on this process, including Italy, Germany, and France. In Paris, dispossessed former agricultural workers comprised a full one-third of the population.[25] In the Netherlands, the poor were rounded up in the first workhouses (*rasphuis*) as the vanguard of a system of forced labor that was to become the model for Europe.[26]

Relatedly, the "baleful projected shadow" of European colonization was spreading across the globe, leaving a wake of desolation behind the plunder.[27] In the three hundred years since the arrival of Columbus as an invader, ninety percent of the indigenous population of the so-called Americas had been killed, amounting to tens of millions of lives lost in a genocide and theft of the land from its indigenous inhabitants.[28] Similar catastrophe befell nearly the entire non-European world. Capitalism required colonialism to jump-start its engines, forming—as Guyanese Marxist Walter Rodney writes in *How Europe Underdeveloped Africa*—"an indispensable link in a chain of events which made possible the technological transformation of the base of European capitalism."[29] Capitalism repurposed colonialism, drawing upon its crude extraction of labor, land, and lives. Through these expanding bloody networks and infrastructures, capitalist laws of motion began operating on a global scale.[30]

Chattel slavery was the central institution: African people were kidnapped and enslaved, transported to the Caribbean and

Origins of a Violent Order   23

the Americas, dragged from their accustomed life, and forced into labor in chains. The massive camps of enslaved labor in the Americas were, according to Caribbean Marxist C. L. R. James, "More akin to later factories than the actual manufacturing as it existed in Europe."[31] James describes the enslaved Black labor working at huge sugar factories in the 1790s in what is now Haiti as being "closer to a modern proletariat than any group of workers in existence at the time," due to the size of the enslaved workforce and the scale of the industrial organization, as well as their understanding of the need for collective struggle.[32] The giant influx of bloody, stolen wealth generated by slavery and colonialism fueled the engine of new industrial production in the factory. Trinidadian historian Eric Williams points out that the profits obtained by the slave trade and production "provided one of the main streams of that accumulation of capital in England which financed the Industrial Revolution."[33] This is why Marx refers to chattel slavery as the "pedestal" that was "needed" for the development of the oppression of the European working class.[34] Indeed, the world's first corporation was the Dutch East India Company (Vereenigde Oostindische Compagnie), a colonial enterprise in the business of enslavement, which established a prototype for the capitalist corporate form.

While enslaved labor fueled the engines of nascent capitalist industry, the new European proletariat filled the factories to work the gears of the machine. Whether compelled through explicit state violence, vagrancy laws, and workhouses or the sheer need to survive, more and more people were forced to work under the same roof in factories, and the new working class concentrated in cities. The proportion of people living in towns in England increased from 9 percent in 1650 to 20 percent in 1800.[35] From 1750 to 1850, the number of cities in England with a population over 50,000 exploded, going from 2 to 29, and a majority of the overall population was urbanized.[36] Across the Atlantic, New York City more than tripled its population in thirty years, from 60,000 in 1800 to 200,000 by 1830.[37] The newly transformed urban landscape presented multiple challenges for the class of people who owned the wealth and the factories. The rich and powerful were now surrounded by large groups of potentially and actually restive workers forced to work long hours for poverty wages, both destitute and desperate.

The Smooth Operation of the Market: The Idea of the Police

The term "police" was not originally used as a descriptor of a force of uniformed agents in charge of law enforcement. Tracing the origin of the concept, and the term "police," sheds light on the need that was filled by its creation. The policing solution evolved as a component of ruling-class strategizing about how to organize a class society, and that purpose would later animate the institution of armed individuals that the police became.[38]

In its earliest uses, "police" was essentially a cognate of the word "policy." It enters English from the Old French *policie* and Late Latin *politia*, both of which referred to the civil administration and organization of the state.[39] Its root is the Ancient Greek *polis* (πόλις), meaning "city." "Police" was the term used by the new strata of civic administrators charged with ordering and regulating a society that was rapidly becoming more complex amid the changes in the economic and social order that would later emerge as modern capitalism. Especially in the states of France, England, Germany, and Russia, the emergence of more stratified apparatuses of society—the state in its protomodern form—created new theorizations of "the science of governing men"—as "police" was defined in 1770 by Paris police commissioner Jean-Charles Lemaire.[40]

The earliest institutional use of the name "police" can be traced to the 1667 Lieutenant-General of Police, established by French monarch Louis XIV, famous for consolidating the absolutist monarchy and proclaiming "L'État, c'est moi"—"I am the state."[41] The work of the Lieutenant-General of Police, as laid out in influential commissioner Nicolas de La Mare's multivolume work *Treatise on the Police,* devised regulations for the maintenance of roads, cleaning of sludge, other aspects of sanitation, lighting of the city, maintenance of maps, creation of a fire department, setting the price of bread, attending to the poor, the transport and storage of food and hay, the fixing of the price of foodstuffs, calibration of weights and scales, and some aspects of what today could be equated with management of petty crime.[42]

As we can see, the scope of regulation of order and governance was broad. The wide remit is further confirmed in the description that the Francophile Russian tsar Peter I wrote in the chapter on "Police Affairs" in his *Regulation of the Main Municipal Administration of 1724*:

> The police has its own special standing, namely: it facilitates rights and justice, begets good order and morality, gives everyone security from brigands, thieves, ravishers, deceivers and the like, drives out disorderly and useless modes of life, compels each to labor and to honest industry, makes a good inspector, a careful and kind servant, lays out towns and the streets in them, hinders inflation and delivers sufficiently in everything required for human life, guards against all illnesses that occur, brings about cleanliness on the streets and in houses, prohibits excess in domestic expenditures and all public vices,

cares for beggars, the poor, the sick, the crippled and other
needy, defends widows, orphans, and strangers according
to God's commandments, trains the young in sensible
cleanliness and honest knowledge; in short, over all these
the police is the soul of the citizenry in all good order and
the fundamental support of human security and comfort.[43]

The "goodness" of this order, of course, was determined by the
state and its rulers.

The first official usage of "police" in English was in Scotland with the 1714 creation of the Commissioners of Police, appointed by Queen Anne.[44] This was a body of nobles tasked with devising and carrying out regulations of order. Most of the regulations and laws developed as "police" in the decades following the institution's creation were of an economic type, such as ensuring the price of corn or grain, or rules around cleanliness and safety like the appropriate placement of fire-fighting devices in the cities.[45] Adam Smith—another Scot and a figure associated with the early theoretical development of capitalism—described the crucial concept of police in his 1762 *Lectures on Jurisprudence.* As critical police theorist Mark Neocleous points out, for Smith, the task of governance is described as "police" and covers all regulation needed to promote the "opulence" or prosperity of the state, including "three aspects (1) cleanliness, (2a) security against accidents such as fires, (2b) security attained through patrols and guards, and (3) cost of provisions and maintenance of the market."[46] While "security" is one component of its importance for Smith, Neocleus points out that "it is the smooth operation of the market—the cheapness and supply of commodities—that is the most important branch of the police."[47]

The importance of "police" as policy for governance had ob-

Origins of a Violent Order

vious ramifications for the structuring of a new republic in the United States.[48] The first law school in the US was the "Chair in Law and Police," created by Thomas Jefferson at William and Mary College, in the midst of the Revolutionary War.[49] The slave-owning Jefferson, thought of as the philosophical inspiration of the so-called founding fathers, saw the creation of the school as a training ground for administrators of the new independent state. "This single school," Jefferson wrote to James Madison in 1780, "by throwing from time to time new hands well principled, & well informed into the legislature, will be of infinite value."[50]

From the absolutist states to the early capitalist states, experiments in civil administration and the ordering of society were considered the activity of police. Here, we see how the daily functioning of the capitalist state is that of policing, which we will explore more in chapter three. But, as the need to administer order became more and more an administration of violence, an accompanying semantic shift also occurred—changing police as "public policy" to police as "armed patrol."

Precursors: Military Police, Constables, Night Watch, Thief-Takers

Before there were police forces as we understand them today, authorities sought to "police"—implement and maintain legal order—through different forms that were precursors of the modern institution. In feudal England, different districts (shires or counties) had a representative (the *shire reve,* or sheriff) appointed by the monarch to enforce the king's will in military, financial, and judicial matters.[51] The purely local management of towns by feudal lords was a challenge to royal authority and thus the sheriff system served in some ways as a counterbalance to, and to keep tabs on, the local lord of the area. When corruption and scandals degraded these positions, the legal and

Their End Is Our Beginning

administrative functions passed to a system of constables and courts of law. With local variations, this system was used widely, especially in England and in its colonies in America.

Constables were a small group of officials, representatives of the courts who served arrest warrants and other official legal papers. They were not a standing body of armed men, did not patrol the streets, and did not have any power to arrest people on their own volition unless they witnessed someone in the act of committing a crime, which almost never happened. In colonial New York, constables were even forbidden from executing warrants on Sundays, holidays, or against people traveling to or from "any publique fair or Markett."[52] The main method for catching perpetrators was what was called "hue and cry," whereby if an individual saw someone in the act of carrying out a crime, they would basically yell, "Stop thief!" and put responsibility on onlookers for detaining the suspect. The state generally relied on its subjects to produce security, a situation that the changing nature of society would profoundly upend as the cities filled with those who would war against the class system.[53]

In the urban setting of Paris, the equivalent position, *commissaire*, was at first purchased (as a venal office) and was similar to that of the constables in that commissaires were court officials who carried out warrants (*lettres de cachet*), kept record of complaints, and carried out street maintenance and cleaning of waste, and other such duties. To give a sense of scale, on the eve of the French Revolution of 1789 there was a total of only forty-eight commissaires in Paris, a city of almost 700,000.[54] Another unique capacity of the Parisian commissaires related to their origin in the autocratic state, namely that they also maintained a system of informers and spies (derogatively referred to as *mouches*, or flies, by those they snitched on) who surveilled political dissidents.[55]

Origins of a Violent Order

Additionally, most cities had some form of "night watch," a group of rotating volunteers who carried a lantern and a stick in an effort to minimize theft and arson (crimes against property), sounding the alarm only if they witnessed something suspect. In writings from this period, the most common complaints about watchmen had to do with their age (many were elderly) and the fact that many were habitually drunk.

France also had a succession of military policing systems, from the pre-revolution *maréchaussée* to the *gendarmerie* established in 1790. These were organized in a military manner, usually recruited from army veterans with military uniforms, were armed, and primarily patrolled the main roads in the countryside to protect shipments of goods, taxes, ammunition convoys, and the mail from bandits.[56] They also functioned to supervise troops on the march, prevent desertion, force conscription, and the like. An English aristocratic observer—Lord Blayney—gushed in 1794 that the gendarmerie "forms the most efficient military police in Europe, and is so well established, that not only the roads are safe, but the people are also kept in *complete political subjection*."[57] This gratuitous overstatement belies the wishes of aristocrats, while in reality the gendarmerie, like the night watch, were commonly thought of as "a crop of drunken, insubordinate, negligence [*sic*], sick, and aged," even by government officials.[58] While some of the military resemblances of the gendarmerie can be seen in the structure and trappings of the modern police, they remained an overtly military force (residing in barracks, for example) without the essential public quality—civilian, living among the community—of today's police; nor did they engage in twenty-four-hour urban patrol, a fundamental characteristic of modern police.[59]

Alongside these new experiments of the state in provision of class rule existed a host of private bodies to assist with the en-

30   **Their End Is Our Beginning**

forcement of their order. Much of the so-called solving of crime was handled by private "thief-takers," essentially bounty hunters, who would be paid, usually by businesses and the well-off, to track down, recover, and punish theft. In 1750, one experiment by court official and author Henry Fielding attempted to professionalize thief-taking with the creation of what some consider the first example of the professional police—the Bow Street Runners. Fielding acquired some government funding for the creation of an office of constables who had limited scope to try to solve reported crimes as well as to perform small scale foot-and-horse patrol around one section of London. Additionally, informal militia comprised largely of property owners took the form of the yeomanry or special constables in England, the *milice bourgeoise* in France, *hermandad* in Spain, even the later posse in the US. These "small armies of the well affected" played a role in patrols and could be called out to quell rebellion.[60] In the southern United States, this role emerged in one of the other key precursors to the police: the slave patrol.

Precursors: The Slave Patrol

In the US South, where the enslavement of people of African descent permeated every dimension of society, a different dynamic took shape. Instead of constables or night watches, another institution predated the modern police: the slave patrol, also called alarm men or searchers. The original system of the slave patrol is often attributed to colonial Barbados.

In the first decades of chattel slavery in the English colonies, there were few laws or legal restrictions on the behavior of enslaved people beyond, of course, the major fact of their bondage.[61] But as the system intensified, the enslaving class needed to create systems to control the inevitable attempts of the enslaved to flee or fight for their liberation. While the main perpetrator of ordering violence for the enslaved was the master and the labor camp overseer, the primary way that resistance and attempts at self-emancipation were repressed beyond the private boundaries of the labor camp was by ad hoc groupings of masters and overseers who would join up to hunt down those who fled. Eventually, this system, in a society structured by captive labor and captive lives, was deemed insufficient. In 1657, the Barbados legislature requested the governor take action due to grave concerns about "the great number of Negroes that are out in rebellion committing murders, robberies, and divers other mischiefs."[62] The private violence of the labor camp had to be translated to public violence for the whole society.[63] This was done through a series of legal slave codes enacted in Barbados, such as the 1661 *Act for Better Ordering and Governance of Negros*. These laws ensconced the racist order of slavery and established harsh punishment for violating them. They included severe restrictions on movement, curfews, a pass system, and more. Along with laying out various prescriptions for overseers and masters to keep their stolen lives under control, the act made it "lawful" for any individual to "apprehend" or even kill enslaved people found without a pass or unaccompanied by a white person.[64] The act also laid out a detailed set of payments and regulations around compensation—from the public funds of the national treasury—as to how much the slave owner would be refunded should someone whom they enslaved be killed. Last, the fear that enslaved Africans and poor and indentured whites were "prone to joyne together to revenge," in the words of one Barbadian slaver, was so strong that punishment—five years of slavery—was meted out for any white individual found to be an accomplice.[65] For our purposes, it is important to note that many of these legal codes were borrowed and adapted from the "bloody laws of vagabondage" developed over the previous century in England.[66] The violent construction of the European proletariat and the obscenity of African chattel slavery were tightly bound together. These borrowed legal codes and techniques of violence, infused with anti-Black racism, synthesized into an intense and effective horror and cruelty. The Barbados Slave Codes were the model for similar codes developed in Jamaica, Antigua, and—importantly—for the English colonies of North America, where, in South Carolina, Barbadian slave-owner colonists were a large proportion of the founders.

The new legal regulation of oppression was carried out largely by a militia—which included a small number of free Blacks—who ran a mounted patrol on Saturday nights, Sundays, and holidays, as well as at any gathering of enslaved people.[67] At those times, the enslaved were not under the direct discipline of work and the private overseer. However, the slave-owning ruling class required more experimentation. Laws regulating the enslaved, ordering society along racist lines, legally permitting and financially incentivizing collaboration by the general white population, were not enough. As Sally Hadden notes in her seminal work on slave patrols: "The continued reenactment of legislation might in fact suggest that slaves were able to flee or engage in other acts of resistance and that only a concerted effort could restrain them."[68] The militia were derided as ineffective due to the lack of investment of the lower class and non-slave-owning whites, as slave owner William Dickerson complained in a letter. The militia were an "ill established, ill armed, undisciplined, tattered rabble of poor whites," and "many of them have nothing to fight for, but the precarious possession of little plots of bad land on which they barely exist."[69] The system's flaw required the introduction of two thousand British troops to act almost exclusively as a control force of the enslaved. "These military measures," writes historian Hilary Beckles in his book *The First Black Slave Society*, "meant that the plantation was developed as a war zone."[70] It would remain so until emancipation.

Borrowing from the Barbadian example, English precedent, and experiments in the context of a new racist order, slave patrols came into existence in the southern US colonies in the first half of the eighteenth century. They were born from attempts to manage the giant influx of enslaved people in the public sphere, beyond the immediate lash of the overseer. As expressed in Virginia's 1672 law for apprehension and suppression of runaways, enslaved people had "lately beene and [were] now out in rebellion."[71] This concern was compounded by the specter of another great fear of the slave owners—solidarity between the enslaved and poor whites. The same Virginia law warned that if the apprehension and suppression of the enslaved resistance were not successful, "Dangerous consequences may arise to the country if other negroes, Indians, or [white] servants should happen to fly forth and joyne with them."[72]

Patrols were paid for by plantation owners and staffed by white vigilantes who supplied their own weapons. They largely straddled areas of the urban-rural divide and were initially informal and ad hoc in formation. In only a few of the early southern colonies were the patrols directly paid by the colonial administration.[73] But, as patrols became more and more established, they came loosely under the control of local militia or courts. Often but not exclusively operating at night, the armed and mounted slave patrols monitored the movement of the enslaved with dogs, harassed households and searched homes, and were entitled to use extreme violence of whippings, beatings, and even murder to impose the public discipline of chattel slavery.

The patrols were motivated by an attempt to prevent rebellion as well as the self-emancipation and escape of the "private property" of the masters. The movement of enslaved people was strictly regulated, especially after the implementation of the slave codes. As social scientist Ben Brucato points out in their history on the subject, however, regulation of movement was not absolute, as the slave pass system was designed "to ensure that slaves could travel to the market with commodities without taking any of them—or the profit derived from them—for themselves."[74] Violations included individuals' stealing themselves away—to use a term with cutting irony for individuals who did not "own" themselves—to see spouses, children, and relatives dispersed as a result of slavery's splintering of families, or in an attempt to meet the basic needs of communal social activity. Celebrations and religious practices were often seen as "dangerous" places where enslaved people could plot and plan resistance. It was these basic attempts to steal moments of time for autonomy and humanity, or what Saidiya Hartman calls "simple exercise of any claims of self," that the slave patrol terrorized with the lash, musket, and hound.[75]

In her history of slave patrols, Hadden notes that, throughout their development, patrols were plagued by staffing issues, which the slave-owning class attempted to solve through financial incentive or threat of punishment. From such problems it becomes clear that the design for the entire white public to police the enslaved population proved somewhat unreliable.[76] The legal attempt to turn "the entire white community" into a police force was not an easy task for the slave-owning class. Hadden quotes one North Carolina commander, who laments that, even one month after the Nat Turner rebellion, "There are many in this County who are quite refractory & scarcely can be brought in to do their service." "The Carolinians complained," Hadden writes,

Origins of a Violent Order 35

"that they did not own slaves, were uncertain whether they would be paid for patrolling, and therefore were unwilling to be patrollers."[77] One South Carolina regiment commander complained, in 1775, that "the slave patrols had 'stagnated' because working-class whites were lax in their participation and the gentry too often paid others to serve in their stead."[78] Hadden points out that it was not "poor whites" who predominantly made up the composition of the patrols, rather that property ownership was a prerequisite and that "middle-status groups . . . and some of the biggest land owners in the country" dominated the composition.[79]

While the primary function was clearly the surveillance and oppression of enslaved African Americans, the slave patrols also played an important role in "exerting social control over whites in the community."[80] As described by scholar Keri Leigh Merritt:

> The stain of racial slavery extended well beyond the master-slave relationship, making the maintenance of a stable, well-ordered society—in which poor whites and blacks were socially separated—imperative. Because masters were never able to achieve complete segregation between the two underclasses, the Deep South's slave owners were compelled to police the non-slaveholding population heavily, incarcerating lower-class white people for a variety of relationships with African Americans.[81]

The masters' fears of slave rebellion were bound up with intense anxiety about solidarity between the enslaved and poor whites—who, of course, had their own grievances with the system—in the South. There was substantial overlap between the worlds of poor whites in the South and enslaved Blacks through clandestine markets, social interaction, shared workplaces in urban environments, illicit interracial drinking spaces, and sexual relations. The latter was particularly challenging to slave owners, as Merritt describes, because it broke down the supposed iron wall of racial difference and "weaken[ed] the once heavily stratified southern hierarchy."[82] However, these concerns did not apply to the masters' own regimes of sexual violence and rape of enslaved Black women, which were an inexorable component of chattel slavery and thus legally permitted.[83] Merritt outlines how, in the later antebellum period, southern courts were peppered with hundreds of cases to "determine" an individual's race.[84]

Related, in many of the southern US states, the crime of murder warranted less of a sentence than white individuals' "stealing" slaves or free Black folks' assisting enslaved Blacks with flight or rebellion.[85] In a system based on the stolen, unfree labor of enslaved people, any perception of attempts to aid, abet, influence, or be influenced by enslaved people's struggles for freedom was a danger to the dominant order. It was under these pretexts that slave patrols would also surveil and raid the homes and semi-formal drinking spaces of poor whites.

Out of this concern, as in England, laws, especially those concerning vagrancy, were used as a primary tool for supervision and control of interaction between the enslaved Blacks and poor whites. Both groups, in the words of the abolitionist Frederick Douglass, were "plundered by the same plunderers."[86] Alongside the extralegal terroristic violence committed within the labor camps and by the slave patrols, a different legal system and accompanying jails were constructed primarily for the incarceration of poor whites. Narratives of ex-slaves—as Merritt observes—point this out repeatedly. In one such narrative, formerly enslaved Ruben Fox states: "There weren't no such things as jails for colored folks. There were jail all right enough, but only white folks were put in them."[87] Prison for enslaved people was "besides the point," as Ruth Wilson Gilmore bleakly remarks; "there was no purpose in locking up a tool with life in it."[88] The pairing of vagrancy laws, deployed for frequent imprisonment, with compulsory work can be considered the precedent and model for the Black Codes that were established after Emancipation. Prisons, a tool first constructed for poor whites, were in turn used to trap the formally emancipated African Americans into a racialized carceral order, and helped imbue the US prison system with a core of anti-Black racism.

The centrality of anti-Black racism in the US is a pillar on which systems of carceral violence continue to rely. As in the period described above, these systems also continued to plague non-Black people, albeit to quite different degrees. Far from springing "naturally" from the heads of working-class whites, anti-Black racism was imposed by systems of violence and imprisonment such as the slave patrols and early carceral infrastructure. It was "by a series of acts," writes historian Edmund Morgan about colonial Virginian legal codes, that the ruling class "deliberately did what it could to foster contempt of whites for blacks and Indians."[89] As scholar Barbara Fields points out: "A commonplace that few stop to examine holds that people are more readily oppressed when they are already perceived as inferior by nature. The reverse is more to the point. People are more readily perceived as inferior by nature when they are already seen as oppressed."[90] The modern police carry this heritage and serve this same function. "Police," Brucato writes, "wedded state power and race, such that internal security would be defined in racial terms, and that the internal enemy, as an object of state violence, would be racialized through the process of being defined and regulated."[91] This connection will be elaborated in later chapters, but now let us turn to

38   Their End Is Our Beginning

why these precursors of the modern police had to change to meet the challenges that tested their ability to maintain order. For this we must return to the riotous, unruly early city.

His Majesty King Mob: The Dangerous Class

During the early decades of capitalist development—first in England, then the United States—uprisings, rebellions, and strikes became commonplace. The participants were what elites would come to describe as "the dangerous class," which included white workers, immigrants, and enslaved and free Black people. At this point, the existing precursors to the police were attempts by the ruling class to organize and manage the urban environment. The emergence of the mob and the restive crowd posed a massive challenge to the urban order and thus required new solutions.

The hope and rebelliousness of the "dangerous class" grew with the promise of the American, French, and especially Haitian revolutions, which reverberated through the networks of the revolutionary Atlantic. Ruling classes found the spread of uprisings increasingly worrisome and unmanageable. Since the working class was largely employed in port cities, they were concentrated at nodal points of Atlantic trade, connected by news and word of mouth to these revolutionary developments even if they weren't personally able to participate.[92] The revolutionary waves created a profound problem for the capitalist class: How could they maintain control over the working masses in this context of revolt and compel them to dutifully submit to exploitation?

For about a week in June 1780, London was shaken by what some consider the most significant urban rebellion England has ever faced. Nominally instigated by progressive legislation to ease discrimination against Catholics, it detonated deep resentment against the wealthy and their fledgling carceral system. What be-

Origins of a Violent Order

came known as the Gordon Riots—in which Black radicals, including John Glover, Benjamin Bowsey, and Charlotte Gardiner, played leadership roles—saw, day after day, workers, armed with everything from rifles to frying pans, roaming the streets, openly plundering the homes of aristocrats, looting and destroying the homes of judges and magistrates, and attacking the properties of industrialists.[93] Newgate Prison—London's largest—and several other jails were burned to the ground, while workers freed hundreds of prisoners on a single night.[94] The offices of the Bow Street Runners, a police precursor, were raided and their records torched.[95] In what could be described as a near revolution, Parliament and the Bank of England almost fell to the uprising. Graffiti on the walls of the ruins of Newgate Prison proclaimed that the inmates had been released on the "authority of His Majesty King Mob." A nascent abolitionist sentiment of the participants can be heard in the later courtroom testimony of one of the liberators, who was asked by the judge about the "cause" of the riots. His reply: "There should not be a prison standing on the morrow in London."[96] Military encampments were built in parks, and, ultimately, it would take the army reoccupying the city to wrest control from King Mob, leaving four hundred to five hundred dead.[97]

The existing system of magistrates and constables completely failed to stem or slow the Gordon Riots. Subsequently, Parliament was unanimous that a new system of public order was needed to prevent any future insurrectionary occurrence that marked "every property" as target for appropriation by the unruly crowd.[98] While it is too simple to see the creation of the municipal police in London and elsewhere as a direct response to a single riotous act, events like the liberation of Newgate Prison instilled the ruling-class experiments to manage unruly workers with a new urgency and seriousness. In England and elsewhere, the new class of the free, enslaved, and dispossessed peoples not only resisted the new order but actively attacked it. It was directly because of the Gordon Riots that the first bill was introduced in Parliament for a "system of police" in 1785; although it failed to pass.[99] Prime Minister William Pitt argued that a solution was needed that was more efficient, cheaper, and would provoke less alarm than resorting to the army.[100]

Within the workplace—and the workhouse—employers devised all manner of disciplinary regimes to keep workers "in their place." Outside the factory gates, however, workers were beyond the immediate command and control of the bosses. Here, they could commiserate, air grievances, and—worst of all from the bosses' point of view—discuss ways to collectively fight back. This presented a volatile situation. At the time, the only real recourse that constables had for managing crowds was the reading of the Riot Act, a proclamation ordering dispersal that was read aloud to crowds deemed unruly or threatening to public order. Failure to comply exempted vigilantes and mobs from legal recourse when the crowd was then violently suppressed. However, this strategy proved less and less useful as the size of crowds increased with the dramatic growth of the urban proletariat. The size of the crowd could simply overwhelm the constable, as happened in 1792 in Edinburgh, during protests in solidarity with the French Revolution, where a sheriff sauntered up to the angry crowd, read the Riot Act, and was promptly run off by a hail of stones.[101]

Though the ruling class did its best to keep Black and white laborers divided, there were also instances where these two oppressed milieus converged and linked arms in struggle. Throughout the seventeenth and eighteenth centuries, multiracial rebellions—in 1676 in Virginia or in 1683 in Barbados, for example—were met with legal strictures that forbade trade, white people running away with Black enslaved persons, and many other interactions.[102] As Ben Brucato has written, the goal of such restrictions was "to encourage the growing division between white and Black worker."[103] In New York City, in 1712 and in 1741, attempts at insurrection and revolutionary arson were organized together by enslaved Africans, Irish immigrant dock workers, and poor whites, which almost burned the city to the ground.[104] Especially in the port cities, such cooperation made it "hard to police" these "dangerously insurrectionary connections," according to historian Ira Berlin.[105]

Overall, 70 percent of America's cities with a population over twenty thousand saw major disorder in the first half of the nineteenth century, and the threat of slave rebellion haunted the slavocracy in the South.[106] London experienced major riots almost every year of the second decade of the nineteenth century, and revolt was openly feared by those in power. Between 1825 and 1830, New York City saw riots once a month.[107] In Paris, food riots were commonplace in the latter half of the eighteenth century, but the commissaires were notably absent when they happened. One commissaire reported that, if he left his home, he would be "assailed and plundered by the crazed populace."[108] In 1775, the Flour Wars, riots of Gordon-level explosiveness, rocked Paris. Only one brave—or stupid—commissaire attempted to quell them, but he quickly found himself impotent to stop them and ended up being forced by the crowd to help disperse bread at the "price" set by the rioters.[109] Historian Eric Hobsbawm writes that these unruly expressions of crowds, looting, and machine-breaking were "a traditional and established part of the industrial conflict . . . in the early stages of the factory and mine" in what he calls "collective bargaining by riot."[110] This political situation was described by a conventional police historian, who bemoaned the fact that:

Their End Is Our Beginning

It was not difficult for political extremists to secure the following of a mob, incite them to rise, and lead them in a march upon Parliament. Mobs which marched on Parliament usually carried some grievances, real or imagined, which they hoped Parliament would redress. It was not unusual that mobs were unruly, destructive, and bore little regard for the well being of local residents and their property.[111]

This relative ease of resistance—even if it was not able to culminate in victory for the underclasses—stoked the fear and contempt of the ruling classes.

"We Must Break the Yoke": Insurrection in the Slavocracy

If we jump back to the American South, we can see how urbanization produced similar changes to the institution of the slave patrol. Urbanization moved and consolidated the free Black and enslaved populations into cities, a process described by historian Julius Scott as one of the "key demographic trends of the early national period."[112] In Charleston, for example, the number of free Black inhabitants more than tripled from 1790 to 1820.[113] This process was driven by rapid industrialization in the South that also had a tremendous impact upon the enslaved population. Although field work was still predominant, slave owners began leasing out individuals for work, meaning enslaved Blacks worked more and more in the textile mills, iron works, mines, tobacco factories, hemp factories, and tanneries of the cities.[114] Free and enslaved Black artisans and "hired out" workers all took part in a sort of quasi-proletarianization.[115] The process would be a factor in the doubling of the industrial output of the South by the mid-nineteenth century. But the urbanization of the South also brought increasing fears of revolt and required changes in the apparatus of repression.

Revolts of the enslaved—from the Stono rebellion to the German Coast uprising to Gabriel Prosser's rebellion to Nat Turner's revolt—struck fear into the hearts of the slave-owning ruling class, and, as resistance from below became ever more difficult to manage, the slavocracy opted for more professionalized and reliable ways of containing it. There was great anxiety about the events in Jamaica, where, in 1739, fugitive maroon communities in the mountains united and fought a guerilla war with the British to a standstill, winning the maroons limited autonomy.[116] But few things haunted the slave owners more than the example set by the Haitian Revolution, which began in 1791 and culminated in the liberation of the island's Black population, giving enslaved people in the United States more confidence in rebellions. In 1796, a number of Black citizens of Charleston were executed for a large-scale plot to burn the city to the ground; they were described as having "intended to make a St. Domingo business of it" (St. Domingo was the name used for Haiti at the time).[117] Fears sparked by the success of the Haitian Revolution provoked ports from Charleston to Boston to ban, and in some places deport, Black people originating from the Caribbean.[118] Social controls like curfews and restrictions on movement targeted Black folks—free as well as enslaved. But these were difficult to enforce with ad hoc bands of vigilantes.

While the enslaver class relied upon the cities, they also strove to keep the social space of the labor camp and the city separate, fearing that field workers would be "ruined" by exposure to the cosmopolitan interconnections and propensity to revolt of the free Black and proletarianized enslaved workers of the city.[119] The hiring-out system expanded the already existing networks of communication and connection between the rural and the urban. Moreover, the various legal restrictions proved unable to completely regulate city workers, to the point where "neither owners nor municipal officials could effectively monitor the enslaved bricklayers, carpenters, painters, and other craft workers who traveled freely around the city and surrounding countryside."[120] It was from these craft workers that many of the ranks and leaders of major attempted revolts emerged, such as Gabriel Prosser (a blacksmith) or Denmark Vesey (a carpenter).[121]

The white ruling class in Charleston, a city that was 60 percent Black in 1820, acted on its anxieties with a more intensive and professionalized watch system than other contemporary cities in the form of the City Watch and Guard. This was especially the case on Sundays, market days when movement and interaction were freer among both the enslaved and free Black majority population. It was on these days that—similar to Barbados—day patrols of musket-armed and blue-uniformed squads would "observe and suppress indecent or riotous behavior" at the markets.[122] In the time before the invention of the modern police, it is no coincidence that Charleston, as David Whitehouse points out, was the most heavily policed major city in the US and also "the only one where a majority of the people were enslaved."[123]

Then, in 1822, a planned insurrection in Charleston was uncovered that confirmed the worst fears of the white slave-owning class. The conspiracy consisted of an extensive network in both the city and labor camps, with a plan to assassinate key officials, loot weapons depots, kill as many whites as possible, set fire to the city, and either escape on boats to Haiti (where revolt leader Denmark Vesey reportedly had contacts) or establish an armed outpost of freedom. Although the plan was aborted before attempted, and thirty-five people were hanged in response, the

Origins of a Violent Order

planned insurrection reflected the explosive potential of Black rebellion and the challenges of the city.

In 1822, in direct response to the thwarting of the planned slave insurrection of Denmark Vesey and his comrades, a daytime patrol was created. By 1856, this patrol had become fully incorporated into a modern uniformed police force.[124] The escalation in repression required the creation of a new organization with more permanent and centralized authority than the slave patrols. A Charlestonian slave owner in 1845 described the change in a perversely matter-of-fact way:

> [In the rural setting] the mere occasional riding about and general supervision of a patrol may be sufficient. But, some more energetic and scrutinizing system is absolutely necessary in cities, where from the very denseness of population and closely contiguous settlements there must be need of closer and more careful circumspection.[125]

While it is somewhat simplistic to see the slave patrol as simply turning into the modern police via linear progression, there is an unbroken blue line in the history of the US South from the experiments of the slave patrol to the formation of the modern police, as the private violence of the labor camp was moved into the public city.

Two years before the Denmark Vesey conspiracy, on August 16, 1819, in Manchester, England's industrial center, one hundred thousand workers marched in organized columns onto St. Peter's Field as part of a demonstration for suffrage and for the lowering of food prices. This was the culmination of a years-long process of organizing and politicization in which the working class progressed from hunger marches to strikes, to a General Union

46   **Their End Is Our Beginning**

expressly forbidden by law, to political organizations fighting for radical democracy.[126] The same year witnessed illegal unions parading in the streets, while state attempts to arrest the reformers proved inadequate when juries refused to find them guilty. Here, arrayed on St. Peter's Field, "King Mob" now appeared as a disciplined army. The volunteer yeomanry militia was sent in first to disperse the protests and arrest one of the leaders, Henry Hunt. The yeomanry was comprised of volunteers drawn from bosses and shop owners—the equivalent of the "cities business mafia"—and thus its members were recognizably from the same class responsible for abuses, hoarding of grain, and driving up of prices: the very target of the workers' anger.[127] Workers fought to stop the raid and the arrest of Hunt, carrying out a "de-arrest," to use contemporary parlance. In response, the waiting English military charged the crowd and committed what came to be known as the Peterloo Massacre, in which eleven were killed and four hundred injured. This act of brutal repression had the opposite effect to quelling the protests. Several nights of rioting and unrest in Manchester and surrounding towns followed. A military occupation was required to quell the resistance.[128]

This bloody event created scores of working-class martyrs and provoked an uproar and radicalization. Some sections of the movement began amassing arms in defense, training for military action, and spreading calls for "revenge for Peterloo."[129] The radical wing of the workers' movement began agitating for an insurrection against the government to occur in November 1819. "Reform cannot be achieved without bloodshed," one radical publication proclaimed.[130] Although the more conservative leadership called off the armed rising, the political mood can be seen in the report of a police informant who attended a delegate meeting representing 12,500 workers. The spy stated that workers had begun arming themselves to prepare and that there was "much regret on the part of many" that the insurrection had been called off. One speaker railed, "If we had met all over England on that day the business would have been done before now."[131] An 1820 editorial in the *London Times* lamented, "Radicalism is every day most alarmingly and portentously increasing; and will, we predict more and more, till, without change, . . . end is certain."[132] A relatively new urban ruling class was frightened and still determining how to control the emergence of the powerful new working class.

Experimental Violence: The Police Fix

For the ruling classes, this problem was ultimately solved via the modern police force. Of course, organized repression and violence have been used by the ruling class for as long as there have been class divisions, but modern policing is a very specific kind of repressive institution with a number of historically unique features. Some histories simplify the process of emergence and present it as proceeding from either London or the slave patrols directly to the modern police. A closer reading of history reveals that modern cops came about as the preferred tool through a process of ruling-class experimentation, rooted in different repressive precursors and different institutional inertias, but nonetheless a conscientious process of mutual borrowing and sharing experiences.

Taken together, the threats of strikes, rebellions, riots, and slave insurrections required a shift toward the creation of a new mechanism of social control, a repressive force capable of controlling crowds, ruling the public spaces of streets and squares, and clamping down on collective action. Before this shift, there had been attempts at implementing police-like agencies but they were rejected on the grounds that they were an unneeded expenditure and an unjustified limitation on freedom. As late as 1818,

Their End Is Our Beginning

in Great Britain, the Parliamentary Committee criticized a plan for a central police authority as making "every servant a spy on the house of his master and all classes of society spies on each other."[133] Even conservatives of the time, such as Scottish economist David Robinson, criticized the institution of the police in ways that today sound left-wing, writing in 1831:

> The police officer is really a soldier in disguise, in some respects he is a more dangerous character than the soldier. What difference does it make in the eye of the constitution whether his coat be a blue or a red one; or whether he be armed with a staff or a firelock? He is as much the mercenary and slave of the Executive, as the soldier; and the latter is always in readiness to assist him, if the firelock or bayonet be necessary. Certain of his duties are of the most detestable description, one is, he is to make him self a general spy.[134]

It should be noted that even conservative criticisms of this new force were in some ways more honest about its function as "mercenary of the executive" than commentary by liberals today.

Riots, rebellion, and resistance were not new to capitalism, but the limitations of military solutions to quell them became apparent, prompting some rethinking of repressive systems. Peasant wars, revolts of the enslaved, and other rural rebellions were simpler to manage, as they were usually formed by clusters of individuals located away from centers of power, in the fields and forests. Those terrains are more conducive to common practices of warfare: close the gates, raise the drawbridge, send out the troops, crush the rebellion. Agricultural production, especially in the noncapitalist context, is less centralized. A hypothetical peasant army

Origins of a Violent Order

could burn some fields and it would have less immediate economic impact than, say, the destruction or occupation of a factory, or the immobilization of a transportation point required for distribution, like major roads, ports, or docks. In cities, despite walls and fences built around dwellings and between neighborhoods, the sheer proximity of the rich living near workers and the poor provoked much concern. Sir George Nicholls, the principal architect of the repressive New Poor Law (one of the first omnibus legal moves to criminalize poverty in England), regarded the poor as "potential Jacobins, . . . ready to prey on the property of their richer neighbours."[135] Physical proximity meant the threat to the rich of resistance and rebellion could happen—as H. G. Wells would write of the period—"within an easy walk of his front door."[136]

In the words of legal scholar Sidney Harring, what was required was "a full time, permanent force capable of continuously asserting the power of the capitalist state up and down every street in every city."[137] Assembled piecemeal through a process of trial and error, the constables and the night watch (as well as the slave patrols in the South) were eventually fused into a new professional standing body of armed individuals with both public funding and legitimacy. Its main job, then as now, had two components:

1. to regularly patrol working-class neighborhoods and, through the threat of armed force, keep the lower orders in their place and protect the property interests of the rich. In the US, this included special control over Black people (both enslaved and free) as an essential component.
2. to manage large crowds by making sure that when people tried to protest, strike, or organize they would be met with overwhelming force.

50   **Their End Is Our Beginning**

These two components—regular patrol and crowd control—continue to be the main functions of policing to this day.[138] I will return to this in the next chapter.

The modern police force was modeled explicitly on techniques of colonization and occupation. In addition to the slave patrols, the other roots of the policing family tree can be traced back to what is typically considered the first modern police force, the London Metropolitan Police, created in 1829 by then home secretary and prime minister-to-be, Robert Peel.[139] Peel developed his ideas for the new institution through serving the British government in maintaining colonial control of Ireland. Peel found that uniformed soldiers of the British Army were good at fighting wars but were not equipped to maintain order, as they often further inflamed Irish resistance by firing on crowds, were expensive to maintain, and imposed a visual of occupying troops that was difficult for the colonized to stomach. On the floor of Parliament, Peel argued that an expansion of magistrates and constables was needed in areas of occupied Ireland that "might unhappily become the scene of disturbance."[140] An "effective police" was needed, without "having recourse on every occasion the cumbrous, though powerful instrument, of a standing army."[141] Peel also emphasized that this new force would be cheaper than an army. Notably, Peel gave the project a racialized character as well, as he thought that the Irish had a "natural predilection for outrage and a lawless life."[142] By 1822, Peel's efforts had led to the creation of the Royal Irish Constabulary as a more effective body for colonial domination. The task was to try to create a foreign military occupation that didn't look *too much* like a foreign military occupation. Soon, the ideas Peel developed while managing colonization would inform the invention of the new London Metropolitan Police in 1829.

In England, Peterloo's open and violent repression had created martyrs and inflamed the situation. Additionally, in the wake of Peterloo, the radical wing of the workers' movement argued for simultaneous rebellions across geographical areas, exposing limitations of military deployments that were generally able to respond only to one area at a time. Furthermore, in addition to the expense and logistical drawbacks to the use of the military, an oft-stated concern held that police duties were "bad for military discipline and morale."[143] Drawing on a practice widely used in British colonial bodies, the constabulary and the new police sought as much as possible to draw their personnel from the ranks of those being policed as a means of deflecting the perception of an "outsider" presence and foreign occupation. As elsewhere, the preventative strategies for occupying colonized peoples were repurposed for the task of domestic repression.

Above all, capitalist employers desired a powerless, obedient labor force that would regularly submit to exploitation. In *Capital*, Marx describes how the ruling class "used the police to accelerate the accumulation of capital by increasing the degree of exploitation of labor."[144] The degree of exploitation in this case was increased through the general ordering and discipline of working-class life, then later by driving down wages, mandating speed-ups, and the like. Both active and passive resistance of the "dangerous classes" had to be neutralized and the rebellious populations rendered obedient, orderly wage workers. The goal of such efforts—to extract as much wealth from workers as possible—was not merely greed but a structural imperative driven by competition on the capitalist market.[145]

This brings out a key contradiction at the heart of capitalism. In order to most efficiently extract the maximum profit from the labor of workers, it was necessary to assemble them all in the

Their End Is Our Beginning

same space, into massive factories. But, by assembling them all in one place and forcing them to cooperate on the job, employers also increased the capacity for collective working-class struggle against exploitation and tyranny. A key function of the modern police force was, simply put, to manage this contradiction on behalf of the owning class.

While nowadays the ubiquity of the police has been normalized, the arrival of top-hatted, blue jacketed, truncheon-wielding goons on September 29, 1829, was reviled by the working class. Less than two months after the appearance of the Metropolitan Police, demonstrators marched on the British Parliament against this experiment in violence. Bills posted around the city announced the mobilization, proclaiming: "Liberty or death! Britons!! And Honest Men!!! The time has at last arrived. All London meets on Tuesday. . . . These damned Police are now going to be armed. Englishmen will you put up with this?"[146] A few years later, after the new force was deployed at a demonstration that derided them as "raw lobsters" and "blue devils," a police constable was killed trying to break up a riot. Public hostility to the police was such that the jury found a verdict of justifiable homicide.[147] In 1850, the town of Aberystwyth, Wales, was put to a test to determine if police were to be added. Public discussion on the need for this new body included determining if the town could quell "crime" on its own. In this trial period, the town had no disorder and opponents of the police declared victory:

> The Inhabitants of Aberystwyth do not require the surveillance of a couple of Bludgeon-men to keep them from becoming Pickpockets and Thieves. . . . As far as Aberystwyth is concerned, the Truncheons and hired Spies may henceforth be consigned to oblivion in the commissioners

yard along with rusty old Iron, rotten Timber, and broken Pipes, as perfectly useless relics of bygone days.[148]

There was street fighting in Birmingham against the new police, and a public assembly of citizens declared them "a bullying and unconstitutional force."[149] Friedrich Engels noted, in his survey of working-class Manchester, "It is ridiculous to assert that the English working-man fears the police, when every week in Manchester policemen are beaten, and last year an attempt was made to storm a station-house."[150] At the time of their formation, large parts of the public saw with crystal clarity that the police were an occupying force of class enemies, spies, and bludgeon-men.

From Precursors to Full-Blown Police Forces

In the first few years of the new force, the Metropolitan Police handled London riots without military intervention.[151] Then, by the 1830s and '40s, the perception that the new police had suppressed the first mass working-class political party, the Chartist movement—using "less than lethal violence"—confirmed for the ruling class the usefulness of this new organization and led to its adoption across England.[152] Foreign observers also began to express interest in the civilian, preventative body.[153]

However, the creation of the London Metropolitan Police was not the sole origin point for the creation of the modern police globally. Rather, it represented the crystallization of a period of ruling-class experimentation in repression and control that gathered threads from bloody laws of vagabondage to slave patrols, private security guards, various forms of militia, colonial occupation, and military policing. All were attempts to violently order the new world of capital and the specific challenges it presented for the ruling class, largely centered in the urban environment.

54 **Their End Is Our Beginning**

With that caveat, it is true that Peel's police model did become a reference point that was copied and adapted to local characteristics in many locales. These adaptations often coalesced with the more French-influenced style of military policing of the gendarmerie, described earlier, which was also a reference point for places like Germany, Russia, and the French colonies.

While the French military-style model was influential for the creation of the English system, the success of the British police model led the French, in 1854, under Louis Napoleon (Napoleon III), to attempt to reproduce the London Metropolitan Police in Paris with the creation and expansion of the *sergents de ville*, whose main function was the implementation of civilian beat patrols.[154] These changes were related to attempts to close the revolutionary chapter in France and were connected to the physical renovation of Paris, such as widening the streets, which made the creation of barricades—a characteristic symbol and tactic of the revolutionary period—more difficult.[155]

The British colonial system of the Royal Irish Constabulary (RIC) was exported throughout the British Empire's many tendrils of colonial control and served as the model for police systems in the colonized nations. RIC officers were sent to Jamaica to help institute the system there. After Ireland won independence from England for the majority of its land in 1921, large sections of the disbanded RIC and the notorious Black and Tans were redeployed to Palestine, where 96 percent of the new Palestine Police's first recruits were ex-RIC.[156] The racist and violent attitude of the Palestine Police to its new target was clearly expressed by Commandant Angus McNeil, who said: "I should try to spread terror in the land ... you would only have to be really brutal and bloodthirsty for about a month and [the Arabs] would be eating out of your hand."[157]

Origins of a Violent Order

In the Sindh province of what was then India (contemporary Pakistan), the Irish model was introduced and imposed by British colonialism in 1843 by governor Charles Napier.[158] By 1861, the system had been systematized and made uniform across the colonized territory in direct response to the great revolt of 1857, the Sepoy Mutiny of Indian soldiers against the colonial government. In addition to concerns about cost, the loyalty of the soldiers tasked with suppressing riots and rebellions was now suspect, and there was a need to keep the potentially rebellious soldiers under tighter discipline.[159] The result was the creation of the Indian Imperial Police.

In Egypt, during the colonial takeover by the British in 1882, the colonists saw the control and reorganization of the police as the first, most important component of securing their foreign rule—"more important than that of the army."[160] The police were established as the most "loyal and dependable parallel force" to both secure public order and counterbalance mutiny in the army.[161]

Brazil, along with the US, was one of the world's most extensive slave states. A similar colonial-era setup of civilian night watch (*guarda*), judicial constable (*quadrilheiro*), and slave patrol (*capitão do mato*) ran into limitations in its capacity to institute capitalist order, prevent resistance, and respond to political crisis.[162] For almost ninety years, beginning in 1809, a host of different experiments were implemented: military policing (*Guarda Real*), national guards, voluntary militia of the propertied (municipal guard), and the urban guard—an explicit "imitation of the acclaimed police of the city of London."[163] The latter was disbanded roughly twenty years later, after the abolition of slavery and the consolidation of full authority by the state led to a more French-style gendarmerie structure to discipline and order public behavior.[164]

In Japan, the institution of capitalist industrialization took place through the events of the Meiji Restoration, in which a new capitalist bureaucratic state was developed. The new capitalist class was committed to the need for Western-style police, so, in 1872, Superintendent General Kawaji Toshiyoshi toured Europe to investigate systems of policing. The English model of civilian patrol, along with the more military-type centralization of the French, was used in the creation of the Japanese system in 1874.[165]

These are only a few examples, but almost all the current police organizations formed under the domination of European colonization derive from the colonial institutions imposed by the European states. That basic form endured through the anticolonial independence struggles, even if reforms were passed that removed some of the trappings of colonialism and adjusted its composition; the colonial police smoothly became the postcolonial police.

Back in the US, settler colonialism also contributed to the formation of modern policing. Historian Roxanne Dunbar-Ortiz has described the colonization laws of a newly independent Mexico in the first decades of the nineteenth century, which allowed forty thousand US Americans to move into the territory, nearly all of them slavers intending to expand their labor camps.[166] In 1823, one of the prominent slaver-colonists, Stephen F. Austin formed a privately funded militia called the Texas Rangers in order to "extinguish Native presence in Texas" and to serve as a slave patrol.[167] The fear of the liberatory struggle of Haiti haunted him. "I sometimes shudder . . .," Austin wrote, to "think that a large part of America will be Santo Domingoized."[168] Then, in 1829, Mexico abolished slavery, threatening the foul profits of the slaver-colonists like Austin. The slaver-colonists went to war against Mexico to preserve slavery,

Origins of a Violent Order

creating an independent Texan state before it was incorporated into the US. One of the first acts of the newly independent slave state was to formally institutionalize the Texas Rangers. Dunbar-Ortiz writes that the rangers were then "tasked with destroying Indigenous towns, elimination of Native nations in Texas, pursuing ethnic cleansing and suppressing protest from Tejanos, former Mexican citizens." The rangers also functioned as a slave patrol, especially guarding the border against enslaved people escaping to Mexico, and as a paramilitary force assisting in the US war of conquest against Mexico in 1846.[169] Historian Kelly Lytle Hernández describes how "raw physical violence was the Rangers's principle strategy" and their notorious aptitude for brutality earned them the nickname Texas Devils.[170] The Texas Rangers, a combination settler militia and slave patrol, were seamlessly incorporated into the state police body and into the early US Border Patrol and still exist today.[171]

In the US territories as a whole, the first major modern police force was established in Boston in 1838. Growing out of the context created by colonial expansion, enslavement, and industrialization, the newly minted Boston Police were crafted, to quote policy makers of the time, to "imitate, as far as it may be, the system of London."[172] New York City followed, with the creation of the Day and Night Police in 1844. It, too, was modeled on London's system.[173] New York City's mayor went to England, writes nineteenth-century New York cop Arthur Casey in his memoir, and "was much impressed by what he saw of the London police," so he brought back a "single copper star-shaped badge."[174]

The story of the creation of the police in Chicago exemplifies many of the above trends. In historian Sam Mitrani's history of the institution, he describes how mid-nineteenth-cen-

58   **Their End Is Our Beginning**

tury Chicago witnessed an explosion of immigration, driven by industrialization. The chaotic city continued to sprawl, with a population composed primarily of immigrant workers. Immigration from 1851 to 1854 more than tripled that of the entire preceding decade.[175] Most workers lived almost entirely outside any direct contact with the state or control of their day-to-day lives. In 1852, the Chicago population was about forty thousand people and only had a fourteen-person, part-time watch.[176] As was common elsewhere around the country, private security was hired by employers to protect and guard certain business interests. But, due to expense, private security—such as the Pinkertons—could not be funded directly by business to patrol the entire city. The ruling class, while keen to throw money at private security, much preferred that the forces of repression be socialized, for the reason of cost and the ideological function of their appearing "public." In 1853, using New York and London as models, a practically insignificant department of full-time paid constables with power to arrest was created in Chicago.[177] Strikes that year provoked the leading employers of the city to assemble and circulate a petition that the police stop the strikes: "A number of persons have this day been traversing our streets for the avowed purpose of preventing those who did not fall in with their peculiar views from prosecuting their daily labor." Railroad-worker strikes later in the year required the state militia to quell the rebellion. Then, in 1855, the Chicago Beer Riots proved to be the decisive event for the creation of a modern police force.

Fueled by nativist anti-immigrant politics, new Chicago mayor Levi Boone made moves to restrict liquor licenses in 1855. Pubs were an important social space for an immigrant population cramped into tiny and squalid living quarters, and

Origins of a Violent Order

they would also often offer free food, cash checks, and provide loans.[178] Additionally, the clash over drinking expressed broader trends about the bosses' struggle to control a new class of wage workers, including how much time they had to work, how much time belonged to the workers, and how they spent their time.[179] Alcohol was seen as the cause of disorder, creating unproductive, unreliable workers. As one steel factory owner articulated the sentiment: "Today's drinker and debaucher is tomorrow's striker for higher wages."[180]

A protest by tavern owners at City Hall against Mayor Boone's new restrictions saw sixty arrested. In response, a large armed demonstration of German and Irish immigrants marched on City Hall to free the tavern owners. The city raised its drawbridges over the Chicago River to slow down the approaching mob, allowing the city's tiny body of constables time to deputize 150 individuals on the spot. When the bridges were lowered, the two sides charged, and a melée ensued. Boone declared martial law and called in the National Guard and other armed forces.[181]

Two days after the Beer Riot, the city's leading businessmen held a "Law and Order" public meeting to push for an actual police force.[182] The meeting created a committee to work with the city government on this task, and a week later the city council passed the modernizing reforms that created the Chicago Police Department. As Mitrani states: "The modern Chicago police force was born in the aftermath of a riot that the existing force had been unable to put down without substantial assistance."[183]

While not every creation of the police—in the US or elsewhere in the world—was directly preceded by riots, this general trend, and the knowledge of its occurring elsewhere, drove city after city to follow a similar pattern of fusing the nightwatch and constables in a uniformed, professional body, organized on

60 Their End Is Our Beginning

a military basis, and with street patrols as a primary activity. At long last, the modern police were born.

Conclusion: "I Believe We Are Strong Enough to Suppress Any Uprising"[184]

In the almost two hundred years since the emergence of the modern police, countless developments have occurred to professionalize, centralize, and sharpen this tool of violence. From the time of the baton-wielding "bobbie" in a crisp blue uniform to the super-soldier body-armored paramilitary of the contemporary SWAT-style cop, much has changed. However, an examination of the origins of the institution shows that its central function remains largely unchanged, albeit sometimes obscured by other layers and activities added to its remit. Moreover, the manner in which they operate—asserting power up and down every street and public space around the world—is intimately related to their core purpose.

Modern police came onto the scene with the birth of capitalism. Indeed, in many ways they functioned as the midwives of capitalism as a social system, hands bloodied by the task. Through force and violence, capitalism reorganized the peoples of the world in new relations of production. As working people organized in workplaces and in cities, new challenges were created for a ruling class hellbent on preserving its wealth and maintaining the order of the system necessary to accumulate more.

To respond to these challenges, the ruling class internationally experimented with different forms of repressive apparatuses. By the first half of the nineteenth century, many threads were woven into the cloth of the modern police: ruling-class vigilantism, draconian legal codes and civil administration, militia, private security, bounty hunters, sheriffs, constables, security guards and various iterations of the watch, military

Origins of a Violent Order

gendarmerie, slave patrols, and the colonial constabulary. The creation of policing as an institution was not a linear process—especially in the case of the US, it was not imposed by a single, central authority. Rather, it was a historical process that the capitalist class underwent internationally. It was a history, of course, of class struggle. As a result, now, in every country in the world, there exist bodies of armed individuals that, while marked by important and notable local variations and differences, are almost identical in the social role they play. It has become a ruling-class consensus internationally that the police are their best tool to maintain domestic order.

While the early institution of the cops exhibited characteristics of an experimental nature—for example, their uneven, unprofessional, sometimes rag-tag organization—this changed in the course of subsequent historical developments. The "capitalist class," Sidney Harring writes, "seized the opportunity to transform the late nineteenth and early-twentieth century departments into very effective participants in the class struggle on the side of the capitalists."[185] The core purpose of the police was to provide a mechanism by which the power of the ruling class could be brought to bear on the lives and habits of individual members of urban society: an instrument of the capitalist state, a uniformed, salaried force, public in funding and bearing, whose primary responsibility is to patrol and wield the monopoly of legitimate violence. This function of the police from then to now remains unchanged, and any movement to tackle the violent institution has to come squarely to terms with its origin, role, and function on behalf of the capitalist state and its rulers.

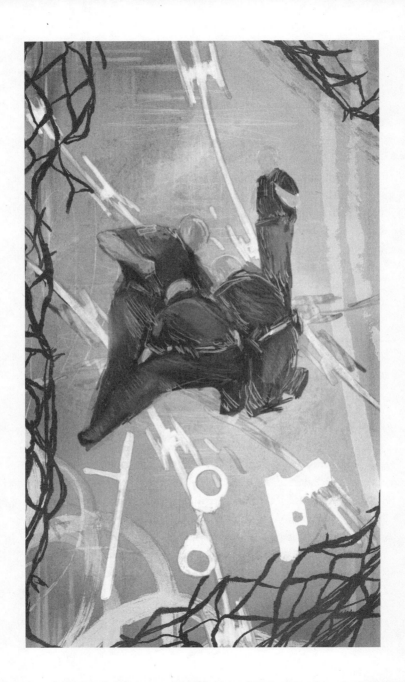

chapter 2
"Bullies in Blue Suits"
What Cops Do

*There is more law in the end of the policeman's nightstick
than in a decision of the Supreme Court.*
—Officer Alexander Williams[1]

*You just slammed my head into the ground.
Do you not even care about that?*
—Sandra Bland[2]

At one o'clock in the morning of March 13, 2020, non-uniformed Louisville cops raided the home of Breonna Taylor—a twenty-six-year-old Black EMT—using a "no-knock" warrant that allowed them to enter without warning or permission. Enacting a legalized home invasion in the dark of night, police smashed down the door with a battering ram, entered with guns drawn, and fired a hail of thirty-two bullets. They killed Breonna Taylor and wounded her boyfriend.

The rationale for the warrant legalizing the night attack on Taylor's private residence was that she knew an alleged drug dealer named Jamarcus Glover. Glover, however, had already been arrested ten miles away, hours before the raid. Yet, under the auspices of fighting the crime of "drug dealing," the Louisville cops saw association as complicity; then, with egregious force and paramilitary tactics, they racially profiled and murdered a working-class Black woman.[3] This is what cops do.

The Sackler family is one of the richest families in America, with a combined net worth of thirteen billion dollars. Much of their wealth comes from their family business, Purdue Pharma, which develops and sells narcotics such as OxyContin. Their multibillion-dollar trade in opioids—realized through falsified research, corruption, and an entire infrastructure of duplicitous marketing and promotion—unleashed an epidemic that has spread beyond prescription pills.[4] The opioid crisis has directly killed hundreds of thousands since 1999, with an estimated 145 Americans dying a day in 2017, and a total of eighty thousand dying in 2021, per the Centers for Disease Control and Prevention.[5] In most states, overdose surpassed car accidents as cause of death, and cities like Canton, Ohio, ran out of space in morgues for bodies, forcing them to call on federal assistance for refrigerated trucks usually utilized for natural disasters.[6]

The deadly consequences of the Sackler family's drug-dealing reach far beyond anything done by alleged dealers like Jamarcus Glover. While it appears that some civil cases have mandated that the Sacklers pay restitution for their drug peddling,[7] it seems unlikely that any criminal charges are forthcoming. Unsurprisingly as well, the amount they have to pay is proportionally small for them, leaving multiple billions still in their pockets. And what cops *did not* do is break into the home of one of the Sacklers' many mansions and execute random individuals who may have associated with them.

These juxtaposed stories demonstrate the class-based aspects of "crime" and the enforcement carried out by the cops.

The previous chapter laid out how the function of the police since their origin has been to serve as a violent tool held by the ruling class to secure capitalist order. It is not the commonly held belief that policing serves such a purpose, and it is certainly not the narrative presented by the cops themselves or the politicians of both major political parties in the United States.

Instead, the official justification for the existence of the police is a series of myths repeated loudly in polite society about "fighting crime," which also provides the rationale for their exorbitant budget. The concepts of crime, fighting it, and preventing it serve as both the ideological *raison d'être* for the police and the operative pretense for their violence. At the same time, crime exists as a distinct social problem, fear of which is real, but which is also often stoked and distorted by politicians and mass media, sometimes into the realm of bleak fantasy. The myth-making around crime has seeped so pervasively into public discourse that it is impossible to understand what cops actually do without addressing these myths head on. Central here is the very notion of crime. As will become evident in this chapter, the historical construction of crime was not motivated by any benevolent intent on behalf of cops or the state but, instead, is bound up with social control. Furthermore, cops are uniquely ineffective at dealing with the actual social phenomenon of crime. For the majority of working people, therefore, what cops do is socially useless. In reality, the role of police as they exist involves—to quote historian Micol Seigel—"The translation of state violence into human form."[8]

"At War Against the Enemies of Society": Enforcers of Order

Despite the persistence of the claim that the function of the police is to fight crime, from the earliest days of the institution, eradicating crime had basically nothing to do with their design. A historical review of the development of the police in the US since their creation will demonstrate that the development and expansion of policing has been in response to challenges to the stability of the system rather than concerns about crime as a social concern.

In Boston, for example, crime went down between 1820 and 1830, the decade before the creation of their police department, and, in the city marshal's report of 1824, crime was not even mentioned.[9] Boston mayor Josiah Quincy wrote, in 1822:

> Poverty, vice and crime, in the degree to which they are witnessed in our day, are, in fact some measure the necessary consequences of the social state. Just in proportions the higher and happier parts of the machine of society are elevated and enlarged, these parts, which are, by necessity or accident, beneath and below, became sunken and depressed.[10]

This position was common. A *pro*-law-and-order lawyer argued, in 1828, to the committee that established the London Police: "I think the increase of crime in the Metropolis has been rather over stated."[11] In Chicago in 1855, the city council's Committee on Police, which established the police department, argued for the new police to be given broad powers that included "matters not criminal" because the public order of the city was to be maintained even when no obvious criminal activity was present.[12]

The majority of arrests by regular patrols in the early years of policing involved activities like existing in public in places deemed out of bounds by the ruling class ("vagrancy" in legalese) and drinking while not rich. The approach was a global trend of the early nineteenth-century police institution. For example, 64 percent of all arrests in Chicago in the first decades of policing were for drunk and disorderly conduct; 90 percent of arrests in Rio de Janeiro were for public order offenses like drunk and disorderly conduct, curfew violations, and vagrancy; and the same for roughly 50 percent of arrests in working-class Manchester, England, to pick three large cities with a geographical spread.[13]

This trend persists with stark clarity throughout the history of the police in the United States. Every major development and expansion of the US police came about not to better serve the public but in response to challenges to the ability of the state to manage its order. Not all these expansions were intended to increase purely repressive capacities, and many were seen as efforts to fine-tune the weapon of class rule and repair the legitimacy of the institution. Nonetheless, all significant changes in the institution served to increase the cops' capacity for violence and the scope of their operations.

The first major expansion occurred with the "professionalization" of the police that took place in the years prior to World War II. The model for the first state police—the Pennsylvania State Constabulary—came about as a direct response by president Theodore Roosevelt to the 1902 Anthracite Coal Strike in eastern Pennsylvania. When the private police of the coal bosses attempted to smash the strike, workers fought back. In response to open street battles, the National Guard was called in, leading Roosevelt to express concern about "the certainty of riots that could develop into social war."[14] He intervened and founded a commission to "find a solution," concluding that "peace and order . . . should be maintained at any cost, but should be maintained by regularly appointed and responsible officers . . . at the expense of the public."[15] Governor Samuel Pennypacker created the constabulary—modeled on the United States' Philippines Constabulary—as a result of this fear of "social war," and it went on to

Their End Is Our Beginning

become the model for the majority of the new state police established thereafter.[16] As David Correia documents in his history of the strike, this solution was lobbied for by the coal bosses—as one mine president wrote, the constabulary "affords more protection to our industry . . . .and as we know has saved us money."[17] Along with its cheapness to the bosses, it afforded legitimacy for violence. Industrialist L. C. Smith remarked on the benefit that "the enemy"—that is, regular people—sees that the constabulary arrests, shoots, and kills strikers "as a legalized officer of the law" as opposed to on behalf of the coal magnates.[18] John C. Groome, the wealthy banker and wine merchant hired to organize the new state police, spent three weeks in occupied Ireland studying the "organization and practical workings" of the Royal Irish Constabulary to draw lessons from colonial occupation for the new police.[19] Eighty percent of the recruits to the new force were soldiers steeled in US wars for colonial dominance of the Philippines, Cuba, and China—people like August Vollmer, who would later become an important police "reformer."[20]

In the early twentieth century, the police's role as semi-decentralized strike breaker and riot squad became systematized and militarized largely due to efforts by so-called reformers like Vollmer. Vollmer is considered the "father of modern policing" and credited with many of the techniques of the modern police, like mobile units on horseback or car, the lie detector, and what is called "pin-mapping"—using data to map "hot spots" of crime. He created the first ever police training school, in Berkeley, in 1908. Vollmer described the role of the police as "conducting a war against the enemies of society" and claimed that, without the police, "civilization now existing on this hemisphere would perish."[21] For Vollmer, war was no mere metaphor, as he had learned and developed most of his techniques while in the mil-

"Bullies in Blue Suits"

itary enforcing US colonial rule over the Philippines during the Philippine-American War.[22] Those military operations involved campaigns like that of US General Jacob H. Smith, who told his troops, in no uncertain terms: "I want no prisoners. I wish you to kill and burn. The more you kill and burn, the better it will please me."[23] Pin-mapping, as historian Julian Go has pointed out, was used by the US military to track Filipino freedom fighters in order to carry out brutal seek-and-kill attacks, like those in the province of Samar that killed 15,000 Filipinos.[24] Along with Vollmer, pioneers in policing such as Francis Vinton Greene, of the New York City police department, were schooled in the act of colonial domination in the Philippines and Cuba before they implemented these new techniques across the US.[25]

The process of police expansion and "professionalization" stretched into the postwar period. In Chicago, so-called professionalization was enacted by O. W. Wilson—a Vollmer protégé—who served as police superintendent from 1960 to 1967. Historian Simon Balto, in his book *Occupied Territory*, notes that despite declining rates of serious crime when Wilson took over the department, he implemented a new system of "aggressive preventative patrol" designed to provide "constant surveillance of every corner of the city."[26] Wilson's focus on making arrests in areas of "selective enforcement," Balto emphasizes, "systematically turned previous police repression of the black community into formal police department policy."[27] Arrests of Black Chicagoans under Wilson increased by 65 percent, capturing fifty thousand Black people in less than a decade, with the blanket "disorderly conduct" charge as the primary justification.[28] Wilson also made changes in the system of gathering crime statistics, shifting from the prior norm of counting *executed* crimes to counting *attempted* crime (a more

Their End Is Our Beginning

subjective assessment). This change in bookkeeping manufactured a 90 percent increase in crime in a single year, summoning a phantom crime wave.[29] Vollmer's work around aggressive preventative control, often drawing on supposed "data-driven" models, presaged the later practices of "stop-and-frisk," "broken windows," and "zero tolerance" policing that are familiar to today's activists. Then as now, the rapid intensification of policing methods proved ineffective even by their own metrics, and in Wilson's final years in office violent crime *rose* by 40 percent.[30]

The next series of shifts in policing approaches coincided with the explosion of mass incarceration and developed through several waves of bipartisan legislation and policy. The War on Crime agenda, initiated during the Lyndon B. Johnson presidency, subsequently morphed into the War on Drugs under Reagan, which was expanded, in turn, under Bill Clinton's 1994 federal crime bill. Under the veneer of modernizing the police force and integrating local police with federal institutions, the construction of the modern police state and its carceral apparatus has had profound and violent ramifications, especially, but not exclusively, for Black Americans.

The predecessor of the War on Crime agenda was the 1965 Law Enforcement Assistance Act (LEAA), enacted in the wake of the summer of the first urban rebellions that would continue to sweep US cities in the following years. One of these rebellions occurred in Harlem in response to the 1964 killing of fifteen-year old James Powell. After chasing off a white assailant, Powell was shot down in the street by a cop. As Mariame Kaba recounts in *Resisting Police Violence in Harlem*, one of Powell's friends yelled out to the cop, "Why did you shoot him?" The cop pointed at his badge and said, "This is why."[31] Six nights of riots, street fights with police, and militant demonstrations subsequently rocked

"Bullies in Blue Suits"

Harlem. Four more rebellions would erupt in response to local outrages, reflecting the simmering rage of Harlem in the 1960s.

The rebellions were fueled both by the heightened aspirations and radicalization of the decades-long Civil Rights movement as well as the frustrations with the limitations of the reforms achieved. "Voting rights," activist Charles Koen remarked, "could not be eaten or turned into shelter."[32] With a supermajority of Democrats in the House, the same legislative session that passed the landmark Voting Rights Act, ending formal disenfranchisement of Black voters, also passed the LEAA. The police legislation would—per carceral scholar Marie Gottschalk—"legitimate a major role for federal government in crime policy," paving the way for escalation of policing in terms of funding and weaponry, and would justify increases in police capacity on the national level to reduce instability and disruption.[33] Both sets of legislation came just weeks before the Watts Rebellion in Los Angeles, which Martin Luther King Jr. described as "the beginning of a stirring of those people in our society who have been passed by."[34] LA police chief William Parker invoked the language of counterinsurgency, describing Watts as like "fighting the Viet Cong." One of Parker's commanders, Daryl Gates—who would go on to become chief—claimed that the "streets of America had become foreign territory."[35] As historian Elizabeth Hinton documents in her essential history of the rebellions, Watts set off a series of events that "did not represent a wave of criminality, but a sustained insurgency," while the views of cops like Parker and Gates show that they feared its revolutionary potential.[36] Hinton catalogs 1,829 rebellions that occurred from the summer of 1967 through 1970.

The 1967 Detroit Rebellion halted automobile production in the city for three days, disrupting the American economy to a greater extent than previous risings.[37] Michigan governor

George Romney appealed for federal troops, worrying that the rebellion would soon evolve into "an organized state of insurrection."[38] "It suddenly seemed as if the whole country had come unglued," one White House official wrote to the president as both Detroit and Newark rose up.[39] The year 1968 marked a high point in the wave of rebellions, as rage and flame exploded on America's streets in response to the assassination of Dr. King and were met with harsh repression. Chicago's mayor Richard J. Daley, one of the Democratic Party's most powerful national figures, issued a "shoot-to-kill" order on participants in the rebellion.[40] The Black rebellions that challenged the US domestically occurred in an international context that included the Tet Offensive in Vietnam, which dealt a blow against US imperialism, and an uprising in Prague against the Stalinist regime in the USSR, the other major global power. In France, in May 1968, students and workers revolted, carrying out what was then the largest general strike in history. From Mexico City to Senegal, the specter of global revolt haunted ruling classes the world over. In the US, where movements against police violence often served as detonators of larger movements, Black rebellion represented the vanguard of the 1960s social movements. As scholar-activist Keeanga-Yamahtta Taylor argues:

> Not only was the Black movement a threat to the racial status quo, but it also acted as a catalyst for many other mobilizations against oppression. From the antiwar movement to the struggle for women's liberation, the Black movement was a conduit for questioning American democracy and capitalism. Its generative power provided a focal point for the counteroffensive that was to come.[41]

"Bullies in Blue Suits"

Thus, the prime target of the "law-and-order" rhetoric and practice that came crashing down in this context was the Black rebellion. The pattern was further reinforced by President Johnson's 1968 Omnibus Crime Control and Safe Streets Act. Despite the findings of the federal government's own Kerner Commission, which identified structural racism as a "cause" of the rebellions and prescribed massive investment in welfare and social programs, none of these policies were pursued by the Johnson administration.[42] Instead, the Safe Streets Act inaugurated a tremendous investment—$25 billion in today's dollars—in expanding police infrastructure, hiring, and equipment. The Safe Streets Act integrated local and state police apparatuses more strongly with the federal government and expanded various modernization and professionalization practices. Urban areas were the focus of surveillance and control, as these were the hotbeds of the "crime" motivating the state intervention: rebellion and insurrection against racism, economic inequality, and state violence.

Ruth Wilson Gilmore described the social earthquakes of this period internationally, while "here at home, there were also the beginnings of a revolution."[43] Accordingly, the expansion of policing and the rise of mass incarceration amount to what "we might call counterrevolution," in Gilmore's terms. In the context of this crisis, the ruling class and their state moved to make crime the "all-purpose explanation for the struggles and disorder that were going on."[44] The result was that the state decided to "put everyone in prison for part of or all of their lives for doing things that we didn't used to put people in prison for."[45] Indeed, right before the dawn of mass incarceration, the carceral population in the US was at its postwar low, and, in the preceding period, crime was "stagnant and then declining" across "all categories of crime."[46] "The systemic imprisonment of young Black men," writes Hinton in her work on the rebellions, "effectively removed from cities a significant portion of the young people" on the vanguard of the rebellions.[47] Since the Civil War, Black Americans had always been disproportionately incarcerated, but, at this point, they—along with Latinx people—approached a majority population in prisons. The history of this period demonstrates starkly how the expansion of police is precipitated by challenges to the stability of the system. The serialization of policing, jails, and crime did not arise in response to rising crime; rather, as Gilmore pithily states: "Crime went up, crime came down, we cracked down."[48] To obscure these realities and justify the existence of the police, a series of myths about cops and crime are often presented.

Myth 1: The concept of crime relates to acts harmful to society.

The principal definition of crime is an act that violates a legal code, permitting or proscribing possible police action and punishment. However, the purpose of this legal and conceptual construction is hardly related to the securing of universal rights or the benevolent improvement of all of society, and is rather a component of the order of class rule. In a society built around exploitation of one class by another, "crime" is not a neutral legal concept; it has a class function, manifest both in what behaviors are considered to be a crime and also in its selective enforcement.

The most violent and socially harmful acts in the history of the US have been carried out by the government and wealthy corporations, even if those acts aren't formally considered crimes per legal statute. Chattel slavery's brutal kidnapping and theft of life and body, the stealing of land and associated genocide of Indigenous peoples, the concentration camps that interned Japanese Americans in the 1940s—all of these were legal. Officially legal atrocities in the annals of US history span from the bombing of

"Bullies in Blue Suits" 75

civilian cities in Japan with atomic weaponry to the carpet bombing of Cambodia, to the more recent devastation of Iraq and Afghanistan. In each of these premeditated mass murders, the planners and directors of death sat protected in boardrooms while cops were brutalizing the people protesting their wicked acts.

The actions of states and corporations that are primarily responsible for the rapidly spiraling crisis of global burning and climate catastrophe—an existential threat to our ecosystem—are not often considered as criminal in the legal sense. Like the Sacklers, willful perpetrators of corporate actions with massive antisocial consequences usually face *at best* civil cases and financial settlements. This contradiction was obvious in the major labor strikes of the late nineteenth and twentieth centuries. Police came out to beat and murder the striking workers organizing around low pay and physically unsafe working conditions, but they kicked in no wood-paneled doors to corporate executive offices to pummel a Carnegie, Pullman, or a Rockefeller with a baton.

Friedrich Engels uses the term "social murder" to describe such large-scale antisocial behaviors in his work *The Condition of the Working Class in England.* He explains that when an individual acts to commit bodily harm causing death, the legal term *murder* is ascribed, but when the conditions of society (shaped by powerful corporations) cause early death to individuals, then:

> Its deed is murder just as surely as the deed of the single individual; disguised, malicious murder, murder against which none can defend himself, which does not seem what it is, because no man sees the murderer, because the death of the victim seems a natural one, since the offense is more one of omission than of commission. But murder it remains.[49]

Their End Is Our Beginning

The same reality is captured well by abolitionist scholar Ruth Wilson Gilmore's oft-quoted definition of racism, namely as "the state-sanctioned or extralegal production and exploitation of group-differentiated vulnerability to premature death."[50] By extension, one could say that racism is the legalized production of social murder.

However, while corporations are given free rein to pollute and poison, vandalism and littering are heavily policed. Activities carried out for survival, like shoplifting, informal economies and street trade, sex work, and the like are deemed crimes while, at the same time, the grotesque inequality that severely limits the options for people seeking survival is not considered criminal. The racialized character of "crime" drives home the disparity. The War on Drugs has been primarily waged against Black America despite nearly equal rates of drug use among white folks.[51] Consider, too, how rowdy celebrations at sporting events by crowds of white men are received with a "boys will be boys" attitude, whereas the people of Baltimore, Ferguson, Minneapolis, and elsewhere are slandered as "rioters" when they take to the streets to protest police murder and abuse.

As a further example, in the past few years corporate media, locally and nationally, have decried retail theft and looting as a social ill at "crisis levels."[52] The actual amount of loss from organized retail theft was estimated by the National Retail Federation at $2.1 billion in 2020 nationwide.[53] Compare that with the fact that these same corporations carry out an estimated $15 billion a year in wage theft *from their own employees*.[54] Yet, major cities like Chicago have large departments with dozens of cops roving major shopping districts for the "crisis" of retail theft, while Chicago devotes just five bureaucrats in the Office of Labor Standards—housed within another office—to handle wage theft.[55] Once again, it is clear that the legal order is constructed for the protection of private property and regulation of a well-ordered market, while the daily exploitation of working people and theft of their labor in the extraction of profit is the basic building block for the running of capitalist society.

If "crime" is strictly defined as breaking the law, then we must always remember that the laws we have are the product of class society, and the legal system is designed to serve those at the top. To draw again on Engels' *The Condition of the Working Class in England*:

> Certainly the law is sacred to the bourgeois, for it is of his own making, put through with his approval and for his protection and benefit. He knows that even if a particular law may injure him as an individual, still the complex of legislation as a whole protects his interests. . . . He holds it to be holy and that the policeman's club (which is really his own club) holds a power for him that is wonderfully reassuring. But for the worker it certainly does not. The worker knows only too well and from too long experience that the law is a rod that the bourgeois holds over his head.[56]

In its definition and enforcement, the ideology of "crime" serves as reassurance for the rich and a club for the exploited and oppressed. To put it more starkly, in the words of Marxist legal theorist Evgeny Pashukanis: "Criminal justice in the bourgeois state is organized class terror, which differs only in degree from the so-called emergency measures taken in civil war."[57]

Of course, in the US, crime has been deeply racialized or, to paraphrase Naomi Murakawa, the problem of racism in society has been criminalized.[58] After the destruction of chattel slavery, the myth of Black criminality was used to justify the construction of various apparatuses of repression to maintain control and restrict the freedom dreams of Black Americans.[59] Maintaining a systemic racist apparatus of social control was in the interest of the ruling class because, due to its particular history, racist oppression underpins the entire class order of the United States.[60] The racist connection of criminality with Black people has been remarkably resilient and consistently applied to every expansion of policing.[61] It serves both as a justification of the occupation of Black communities by trigger-happy cops and as an explanation for the poverty and inequality that affect Black folks in particular in this burning house of America. Crime, then, as it is officially conceived, has little to do with acts harmful to society.

Myth 2: Crime prevention is designed to eliminate crime.

From Robert Peel to the present, "crime prevention" is championed by cops and their backers as the reason society needs the police.[62] This "preventative" component of policing is a core component distinguishing the police as a socially justified institution. In some ways, this championing is pure cynicism, which is obvious if you plumb the comments and ideology of the most pro-police propagandists who spew all manner of racist "political demonology." However, if (per the above) the category of crime is disconnected from what is harmful to society, it is reasonable to ask, what is actually being "prevented"? A closer examination of preventative police practices reveals more strategies to implement their core function: the social organizing of working people and the oppressed.

The notion of preventative policing can be attributed to Patrick Colquhoun, considered the leading police theorist of the eighteenth and nineteenth centuries. Colquhoun was the Scottish agent of the association of slave traders and labor camp own-

"Bullies in Blue Suits" 79

ers in the Caribbean colonies, and he especially focused on their shipping trade and the docks on London's Thames River.[63] In the 1790s, roughly a third of all of London's adult labor force was employed on the docks, and roughly a quarter of the trade came from America—driven by the stolen labor of the enslaved.[64] Colquhoun's concern was how to organize and maximize profit in an industry greatly expanded because of slavery. As Peter Linebaugh points out in his work *The London Hanged*, that meant converting this new workforce into waged labor and minimizing or eliminating what had been the traditional method of compensation for workers—the "customary wage" or perquisites, which consisted of a small amount of the goods they moved, for personal use or resale. Transitioning to a system of waged labor—which was more efficient and maximized profits for the slaver merchants—required a degree of supervision and enforcement more robust than the security guards employed by the dock owners. Colquhoun published a work—*A Treatise on the Police of the Metropolis*—and, in 1798, successfully achieved state subsidies for the private Thames River Police. Fully marrying the economic and the legal, the Thames River Police were responsible not only for surveillance and repression but also for accounting, setting rates of compensation, and paying the workers' wages.[65]

"Police in this Country may be considered as a new Science, in the PREVENTION and DETECTION of CRIMES," wrote Colquhoun.[66] However, the focus of this new science was not the betterment of regular people victimized by illegal behavior but, as both Linebaugh and Mark Neocleous note, (1) the enforcement of wage labor, and, related, (2) the prevention of those able to work from refusing to work—which Colquhoun characterized as immoral and depraved. Perhaps more honest than the charlatan advocates of modern trickle-down theory,

Colquhoun saw poverty as "necessary and indispensable" for profit. Having an impoverished class forced into cheap wage labor is—he writes—"the source of wealth, since without labor there would be no riches, no refinement, no comfort, and no benefit to those who may be possessed of wealth."[67] A laboring poor was required for capitalism, but such a "general army of Delinquents" needed to be *disciplined*.[68] This new preventive science was, as Neocleous astutely puts it, "explicitly designed to end the appropriation of any means of subsistence other than the wage."[69] What was actually "prevented" by policing was alternative means of survival outside the formal market, a remit that can be traced all the way up to contemporary policing's focus on unregulated drug trade, sex work, and other informal economies. While these activities might not explicitly be considered resistance to the system, Robin D. G. Kelley, in his social history of the "underclass," describes how "opposition to wage labor" and "participation in the illicit economy can potentially lead to a more direct challenge to the sanctity of "naturalness" of private property as well as enable workers to resist industrial discipline."[70] Crime "prevention" is primarily about disciplining people to rely solely on the market for survival. Ruth Wilson Gilmore makes the connection to earlier eras of capitalist discipline when she describes today's policing and organized abandonment as "not unlike the enclosures of England, Scotland, and Ireland, and the people cast adrift have fewer and fewer options for what they do, or can do; and the forces of organized violence contour those options into particular pathways: do this or you will be arrested."[71] Participation in the labor market is enforced by criminalizing other modes of survival. "The battle to create a disciplined proletariat was fought," writes political scientist David McNally, "as a campaign against anything that provided laborers with an element of independence from the labor market."[72]

The theories of "preventative policing" that informed institutions like the Thames River Police were neatly transposed onto a public police force as it was expanded and retooled to deal with the rebellious crowd, as discussed in chapter one. Again, we can see that the police function is not purely to "protect private property"—a function that simple security guards could perform—but to impose, through violence or threat of violence, the social order and social relations of capitalism.[73] Their point was not to fix the impoverished conditions in which working people lived and that produced so-called crime—indeed, these were seen as not just inevitable but as a *desirable necessity* for the creation of profit. For Colquhoun, the goal was to manage poverty and other social ills *just enough* so that working people kept working. It is thus no surprise that, just three months after their creation, a mob attempted to burn down the office of the Thames River Police with the police inside.

Myth 3: Police solve crime.

The perception of the detective as the typical or even archetypal cop is commonplace, as evidenced by the protagonists in best-selling mystery novels and a barrage of police propaganda shows making up roughly 20 percent of all television programming.[74] In light of the frequent mythologization, it may be surprising to discover that the role of the detective, the quintessential "crimesolver," didn't actually exist in some American police departments for the first fifty to seventy-five years of their existence.[75] When we examine actual police practice throughout history and today, it becomes clear that the first tool of the cop is not the magnifying glass or the fingerprint kit but the nightstick, the truncheon, a weapon to force compliance and discipline crowds.

The distribution of personnel is telling in this regard. Almost 70 percent of all cops nationally are patrol officers, and only 15 percent work in "investigations."[76] On average, the percent of police budgets allocated to patrol is four times that of the second-highest category.[77] The goal of constant patrolling is to present a physical reminder to the population—especially the working-class Black population, whose liberation movement, as Taylor described, has been a catalyst for radical change generally—of the persistent standing threat by the state to inflict violence and discipline anyone who challenges the legitimacy of the existing order. It is this *threat* that is the special tool of the police.

Sociologist Egon Bittner, whose work is widely taught and considered definitional in police education, clearly states that "the police role is far better understood by saying that their ability to arrest offenders is incidental to their authority to use force."[78] "The capacity to use coercive force," he writes, "lends thematic unity to all police activity in the same sense in which, let us say, the capacity to cure illness lends unity to everything that is ordinarily done in the field of medical practice."[79] All police practice and authority is rooted in this threat of force. Whether it be their blinking lights instructing you to pull over, the barked command to "move along" or "stop right there," or the timbre of that specific sharp bang on your door, what often coerces obedience is the knowledge of the firearm they carry. Cops act as "situational despots," in the words of sociologist Stuart Schrader, able to respond with lethal violence, for the most part at their complete discretion.[80]

But does this threat of force mean they can't solve crimes? From their origin two hundred years ago to the present, the main way that police catch those who commit crimes is by someone who has seen the crime telling the police what happened.[81]

Solving crimes in this way does not require a large body of swaggering armed guards. One older study found that the majority of cops make one felony arrest per year and spend less than 2 percent of their time responding to crimes in progress.[82] One study found that US police could be estimated to encounter a street robbery only once in fourteen years.[83] According to national data compiled by the FBI, police charge someone they apprehend with a crime—called the "clearance rate"—less than half the time.[84] But, as Shima Baughman's review of fifty years of crime data points out, the figures in this area are not adjusted for crimes not reported, or for the chance of acquittal, as being charged with a crime does not necessarily indicate guilt (as anyone should know).[85] Baughman's adjustment found that cops "solve" serious crimes only 2 percent of the time. And, of course, this also does not account for wrongful convictions, which occur approximately 6 percent of the time, per the Innocence Project.[86] Rather than "solving" crime, most of the time cops are on patrol, suspiciously scrutinizing those who've done nothing wrong.[87] "If a worker stands still he is seen to be resting or idling," socialist Audrey Farrell points out. "If a policeman stands doing nothing he is seen to be carrying out the mystical and dangerous task of catching criminals and making society safer."[88]

Of the roughly ten million police arrests in the US annually, 80 percent of them continue to be for minor drug and "quality of life" offenses like disorderly conduct, public urination, vagrancy, unlicensed street vending, and the like.[89] Policing these small offenses aggressively is a common practice in what is called "broken windows" or "order maintenance" policing. But these practices, as this book has established, are not deviations from the preventative patrol that comprises the main remit of policing but, rather, fit squarely within the standard mission of policing since its creation. Broken Windows Theory, zero tolerance, stop-and-frisk, and the variety of related strategies are merely intensifications of this common practice, with an emphasis on arrest, and arrest numbers specifically, driving police activity.[90]

The so-called Broken Windows Theory, coined by George Kelling (a police chief) and James Q. Wilson, blamed "culture" for poverty and "naturalized" criminal behavior in a framework informed by racist eugenicists like Charles Murray and Herbert Spencer.[91] Wilson worked alongside conservative political scientist Edward Banfield as a consultant on various presidential task forces under Nixon, advocating the racist pathologization of crime and advocating for social programs to be cut.[92]

Kelling and Wilson's theory comes from their short, nine-page 1982 article published in a cultural magazine with scant empirical research. Broken Windows is less a theory with any rigor than an ideological position that was deployed as the justification for ramping up police presence and aggression in the late 1980s and 1990s. As many have pointed out, broken windows policing does little more than further criminalize the poor and marginalized, and reproduce and reify racism.[93] Instead of identifying the crime and then looking for the perpetrator to solve it, this police practice is akin to identifying a community of people determined to be perpetrators and then looking for the crime. Often associated with 1990s New York City, the draconian policy was crudely summarized by police chief William Bratton: "If you peed in the street you were going to jail."[94] After three years of implementation, the NYPD were making more arrests than offenses reported, and racial profiling had become an explicit practice.[95] Despite these practices being ruled unconstitutional in 2013, they have continued.[96] Similar policing practices, albeit less well-known, were instituted around the country. In Chicago,

"Bullies in Blue Suits" 85

under the umbrella of a 1992 loitering ordinance billed as an anti-gang measure, police could, astonishingly, arrest any group of three or more people standing together "with no apparent purpose." As a result, forty-two thousand people were arrested over a two-year period.[97] As in New York, these practices continue: recent investigative reporting found that, despite a 2015 legal settlement with the ACLU to reduce what cops term "investigative stops," Chicago police made an staggering 4.5 million stops in the subsequent six-year period.[98] That's the equivalent of every Chicago resident getting stopped twice, although, of course, a grossly disproportionate number of stops occurred in Chicago's largely Black and brown neighborhoods. The version of the tactic deployed in Washington DC during the same time period involved "jump out" squads, the theory of which was described succinctly by one DC cop: "If we pull everyone over they will eventually learn that we aren't playing games anymore."[99] These practices of patrol, surveillance, and harassment have nothing to do with solving crime.

Myth 4: More police prevent crime.

In addition to cops largely failing to stop or solve acts deemed illegal, the presence of more police is not effective at preventing crimes from happening in the first place. There is no correlation between the per capita size of a police force and reduction of crime rate. Indeed, it is often the case that the places with higher per capita police forces have higher rates of crime. Chicago's troubling murder rate in recent years is but one glaring example.

The empirical data reflects this, although such data comes with an important caveat that official crime statistics should be regarded with a high degree of suspicion. As outlined at the beginning of this chapter, the definition of crime itself is a ruling-class political construction. Additionally, the data on crime comes from the cops themselves, a highly biased source with a long history of cooking the books to further their political agenda.[100] The problem is compounded by the fact that police monopolize the raw data, which inhibits "researchers from fact-checking police-department analyses and claims about crime," as sociologist Richard Vargas points out.[101] Finally, crime studies often come from institutions like University of Chicago's Crime Lab, an institution with a mutually beneficial economic relationship with police departments that thus operates, essentially, as "a research arm for the police."[102]

However, even with these caveats, their own data does not support police effectiveness at crime prevention. In a 2008 review of thirty-six studies on police and crime rates, researchers found that there was "little evidence that more police reduce crime."[103] Similarly, a 2013 systematic review of sixty-two studies over forty-two years confirmed that the impact on crime by number of police is "small, and not statistically significant."[104] One 2007 study that is hardly critical of the police found, "discouragingly," that the $8 billion spent federally on local departments and the hiring of a hundred thousand cops over a five-year period did "little to reduce crime."[105] Finally, a significant 2006 study by two of the preeminent specialists on the topic reviewed twenty years of police practice and concluded, "There is one thing that is a myth: [that] the police have a substantial, broad, and independent impact on the nation's crime rate."[106]

There have been attempts to refute this body of research, such as the article "Police Force Size and Civilian Race," a co-author of which, Morgan Williams, conveniently made the rounds of popular media in the wake of spreading calls to defund the police in 2020.[107] The authors argue that, in roughly 50 percent of cities studied, each increase of 10 cops decreases homicides by 1. However, the study has severe limitations and can hardly be considered conclusive. First, the authors find that, in large Black cities, the decrease in homicides did not occur, and they also find that, overall, an increase in the number of police increases the number of "order maintenance" arrests, with disproportionate negative effects on Black populations. Even one of the co-authors of the study admits, "Crime goes up and down for a million reasons that are completely independent of the police."[108] Increasing police per capita, then, cannot be said to correlate significantly to reductions in homicide rates, and when the known drawbacks to increasing police numbers—admitted by the study's authors—include racially disproportionate police stops, arrest, imprisonment, and brutality, there is no comparison with the more effective, longer-term, noncarceral means of increasing public safety. A hard connection between the police and prevention of crime is a dangerous myth.

This myth often evokes the example of New York City under police commissioner William Bratton and mayor Rudolph Giuliani—once seen by liberals as "America's Mayor" before his slide into sniveling Trump collaborator. From 1994 to 2001, Giuliani and Bratton implemented a zero-tolerance, Broken Windows policing approach, paired with the use of the high-tech CompStat system—the computerized version of Vollmer's pin-mapping strategy for colonial counterinsurgency. During this period, crime rates decreased, and this phenomenon has been linked by some to the changes in the department. This false correlation—which I will explore more below—has been repeated giddily in the popular press and scholarly journals so frequently that it is sometimes considered conventional wisdom. Since the 1990s, hundreds of police departments have adopted various versions of CompStat algorithmic pin-mapping.[109] According to Jordan Camp and Christina Heatherton, the echo

Their End Is Our Beginning

chamber championing the "success" of the NYC experience has made Broken Windows policing the go-to, exported "urban strategy enabling the gentrification of cities—a class project that has displaced the urban multiracial working class worldwide."[110]

But it didn't work, even in New York. Sociologist Loïc Wacquant compellingly demolishes the correlation between Broken Windows and the NYC crime drop in his book *Punishing the Poor*. Wacquant points out, first, that reported criminal violence had begun to drop precipitously three years before Giuliani took office (even though media coverage of crime had increased). Secondly, the drop in crime levels during that time period was a national phenomenon, which also occurred in cities that did not deploy the same strategy of Broken Windows policing. Last, the uniqueness of the Giuliani turn is suspect, as the previous mayor attempted a similar policy, nine years before Giuliani, that corresponded to a sharp increase in violence and homicide.[111] Wacquant and others conclude that the trends in the crime rate in NYC operated "independent of the activity of the police."[112] Overall, the notion that more police presence prevents crime, even in aggressive applications like New York's Broken Windows policy and use of stop-and-frisk, is not rooted in fact.

When combined with the massive increase in contact between cops and civilians and racist stereotypes attached to criminality, the policing of "quality of life" offenses raises the question: "Whose life is it, anyway, that we're talking about?"[113] The sharp increase in police abuse, brutality, racial profiling, and the sheer number of lives broken by imprisonment show the real cost of the Broken Windows approach. The high-profile tragedies that occurred in New York in the late '90s, such as the police murder of Amadou Diallo, who was shot nineteen times in a hail of forty-one bullets, or the police rape of Abner Louima with a broomstick in

"Bullies in Blue Suits" 89

a precinct house, should be evidence enough against Giuliani and Bratton's strategy. But it is the quality of *Black* lives that the system disregards, along with those of other poor, working-class, and oppressed people. Sadly, this brutality is often seen as merely an overreach of police activity as opposed to its logical conclusion.

Myth 5: In the absence of police there would be chaos.

Police, the story goes, are in the end the only thing holding civilization back from the brink. In the words of then-president Bill Clinton, cops are "sentinels of liberty," who are "nothing less than our buffer from chaos."[114] If we didn't have our brave policemen and women, we are told, all the evils of society lurking beneath the surface would erupt into anarchy, producing scenes of angry lawless mobs as depicted in Hollywood movies. However, on several occasions, this "thin blue line of defense" ceased to be operational, and the results were quite different from what the Clintons of the world predicted.

In 2014 and 2015, the NYPD conducted a "slowdown" in response to Mayor Bill de Blasio's criticism (however limp) of the police killing of Eric Garner. During this overreaction, cops stopped carrying out "unnecessary arrests" for a short period of time. The fact that the NYPD admitted to "unnecessary arrests" is damning enough. Moreover, according to a study in the journal *Nature*, the rates of minor drug arrests and quality-of-life offenses during this time plummeted, yet, somehow, New York City did not descend into a spiral of chaos. Most interesting, researchers found that the reporting of major crimes (felony robbery, murder, and assault) fell by half during the time of the slowdown. To be clear, the metric measured not the number of major crimes investigated or reported by police, but rather the decreased number of complaints received by the police.[115]

90   **Their End Is Our Beginning**

Similar events occurred in Chicago in early 2019, when Chicago police carried out a similar slowdown, protesting the conviction of one of their own for the murder of seventeen-year-old Laquan McDonald. For several weeks, after threatening that Chicago residents would "pay the price" for a department cowed by the bright light of accountability, police purposely reduced the use of stop-and-frisk street stops. Obviously, the number of minor offenses coming from street stops diminished, and, as in New York, the number of violent crime incidents also dropped.[116]

Actual police work stoppages are fairly rare, though one of the longer police strikes in the postwar era was in Finland, in 1976, which lasted 17 days. Reports indicated that the national strike caused a slight but "not significant" increase in crime. However, despite the absence of police from the streets across the country for over two weeks, official state reports on the events are clear that "order was generally maintained" and the police strike "did not contribute to a radical breakdown in public order."[117] Chaos and anarchy did not reign.

Some more limited experiments seem to reflect this same trend. In December 2020, police withdrew for five days from an area of several blocks deemed a so-called crime "hotspot" in the Brownsville neighborhood of Brooklyn.[118] Concurrent with the withdrawal, crisis intervention and violence interrupter groups came in to engage in conflict management, and an influx of agencies set up tents to provide information on access to community resources. Over five days, there was only one 911 call—made on accident. While limited and politically complicated, as it was carried out in concert between neighborhood NGOs and the NYPD, this episode serves as yet another antidote to pro-police myth-making.

Another exceptional example may at first appear to be counterevidence to the argument, but, ultimately, it further debunks

"Bullies in Blue Suits" 91

the thin blue line myth. In Brazil, a number of police strikes from the late 2010s into the 2020s were violent and chaotic. In the Ceará police strike of 2020, over two hundred people were killed during the thirteen-day strike. However, many of the rioters were the police themselves.[119] The police strike was unpopular and politically motivated, targeting the state government of the leftist Workers Party (PT). It also occurred in the context of ongoing gang conflict between the police and the First Capital Command (PCC) cartel. In Ceará, the cops donned masks and balaclavas and took over the streets, intimidated stores to close, and murdered a state senator who was leading a protest against the police.[120] The cops' purposeful incitement of violence was described as "armed blackmail" by one of Brazil's largest newspapers.[121] As the events of Ceará indicate, it is not the absence of cops that opens the floodgates for violence and murder but the cops themselves, who stoke and carry out the violence.

From these examples we should not draw the conclusion that if police were to magically disappear tomorrow—independent of profound changes on the level of society—social problems such as crime would similarly, automatically vanish. In a world still bearing the scars of the past and wounds of the present system of racist capitalism, it would be naïve to think that addressing deep-rooted social problems would be so simple. But, examples like these do reveal the falsity in the mythologies of cops as valiant, sacrificing defenders of order. From the evidence we have, it is simply not the case that without police society and civilization would automatically descend into chaos and collapse. In chapter four, we will return to this and look at some other examples in which, amid social struggle and contexts of radical mass self-activity, the police have been forced to disappear.

Myth 6: Cops keep us safe.

While mythologies around "crime" are certainly central to obfuscating the real role of the police for a majority of people, cops are also tasked with responding to a number of other social problems and intervening in emergency situations under the pretense of providing safety. Across the country, violent police institutions are ostensibly the lead governmental agencies dealing with homelessness, mental illness, school discipline, youth unemployment, drug abuse, and domestic violence. This situation represents the warped funding priorities of the state and a total absence of reasoned consideration on appropriately dealing with social problems, resulting in absurdities like thousands of asylum seekers being housed in police stations in Chicago or using cops as substitute teachers in Oklahoma.

Some may argue that some hypothetical situations are so dangerous or so violent that policing is the only solution: a mental health crisis, a fight, an escalating incident of domestic violence, or, most dramatic, a school shooting. Isn't it necessary, the argument goes, to have someone who can intervene with force to keep people safe in circumstances such as these?

First, cops have an extensive record of overreacting and making situations worse, up to the point of killing those involved. This is often the case when responding to mental health crises. When the family of Stephon Watts, a Black fifteen-year-old on the autism spectrum, called 911 during a mental health crisis in 2012, the Calumet City police arrived and murdered him. Despite Watts's calming down and his parents calling back to cancel the call, and despite the police knowing Stephon's issues after having had ten prior calls the same year, they came anyway and shot him twice, killing him in front of his parents.[122] From Eleanor Bumpurs in 1984 to Quintonio LeGrier in 2015, stories like these are disturbingly common. Indeed, according to a study conducted by the Treatment Advocacy Center, those who suffer from untreated mental illness are sixteen times more likely to be murdered by a cop.[123] Data collected by the *Washington Post* found that one in four people killed by the cops were people with mental illness.[124] Despite ableist panic about the risk to the general populace of violence by "deranged" individuals, the reality is that people with mental health issues are at much greater risk of being victims of violence, and the police pose a particular danger for them specifically.

Thankfully, partially buoyed by political shifts and successful organizing as a result of the 2020 rebellions, alternative institutions to the police have been created in cities across the country to respond to instances of mental health emergencies. These efforts rely on trained individuals, social workers, EMTs, and sometimes peer workers, though, unfortunately, many still include or work with the police as a part of their intervention. However, the success of nonpolice models like the Crisis Assistance Helping Out On The Streets (CAHOOTS) program in Eugene, Oregon, is a positive move forward. Programs like CAHOOTS serve as an example that removing police from teams responding to mental health calls has not only yielded better and safer support for individuals in crisis but also avoided a spate of dangerous situations. Social worker Lindsey Bailey has pointed out that, of the twenty-four thousand calls that CAHOOTS receives annually, less than 1 percent have required police back-up to manage the situation.[125] Denver's Support Team Assisted Response (STAR) program, in its first fifteen months of operation, handled thousands of calls with no resulting arrests, and areas where STAR was operating experienced a 34 percent decrease in the crime rate.[126]

Programs like these are good examples, but they are also only the tip of the iceberg. Abolitionists like Mariame Kaba and Andrea Ritchie have written about how even nonpolice "intervention" around mental health crises can resemble what they term "soft policing," only scratching the surface of the more fundamental issues that undergird mental health.[127] Many mental health crises do not occur in a void but as the product of social conditions—lack of housing, food, or other needs that can compound stress and appear to be, or manifest as, a mental disturbance. Everyday stressors can cause many people to act abnormally, even individuals with more of their needs met. As Kaba and Ritchie argue, "Not every police function requires 'Something Else' . . . Many situations (e.g. homelessness, mental health, 'loitering,' shoplifting) require no 'alternative' beyond ensuring that everyone's needs are met. Others require a multitude of responses and systems built around meeting individual and collective needs."[128]

Another kind of situation that police are often tasked with managing is domestic and gender-based violence and sexual assault. A *New York Times* review of publicly available 911 information found that police spend 7 percent of their time responding to domestic violence calls, two to seven times more than the amount of time they spend on other "violent crime."[129] The very real prevalence of misogynistic brutality is deployed as another "reason" police are needed, while, at the same time, the one-size-fits-all use of police as interveners gets in the way of funding and the development of more intensive, appropriate, safe, and effective solutions. Per the CDC, homicide is one of the the leading cause of death for Black women aged fifteen to thirty-four, and a vast majority of these tragedies occur in the context of domestic or intimate partner violence.[130] However, police-based responses in-

"Bullies in Blue Suits" 95

volving armed officers showing up to "save" a "battered woman" is far from effective, and in many cases it actually makes the situation worse. As INCITE!, a national network of feminists of color, has pointed out, since 1973, rates of domestic violence victimization have remained fairly constant even while increased focus on punishment and tough-on-crime carceral solutions have dramatically expanded prison populations.[131]

Barely trained cops are not equipped to effectively intervene in or deescalate such a pervasive, entrenched, intimate, and emotionally fraught situation as abuse and intimate partner violence, and to use police in that way is to display pure negligence toward survivors and those who have been killed. Often, when the police are called it is because there are no other accessible resources, and those involved want an immediate end to the violence but not necessarily punishment. In many cases, the decision to involve the cops is an act of desperation and not desire. A comprehensive study by the ACLU found that 88 percent of survivors said that police did not believe them or take them seriously.[132] It is for this reason that less than half of domestic violence survivors call the police in the first place.[133] For survivors of sexual violence committed by a stranger, the numbers are roughly the same. Even fewer survivors of sexual violence committed by someone known to the survivor choose to call the cops—and these situations account for 80 percent of cases.[134] Studies like these document that survivors do not call the police because of both the ineffectiveness of their intervention and the fact the police are the police—armed agents of a vast repressive apparatus of harm that brings other risks. The list of why people might hesitate to call the police out of legitimate fears is lengthy: immigration status, past legal involvement, lack of control in the process, concern for the abuser's legal or immigration or economic status, or concern over the state taking custody of children, to name a few. Many studies show that arresting the abuser often only increases violence.[135] One could argue that police response is more of a deterrent on survivors' seeking help than a deterrent to the violence itself. Resources for developing alternatives remain scarce; instead, more gasoline in the form of cops is thrown on the fire.

Police often behave more harshly to criminalize survivors who act in self-defense than the abusers themselves. Important organizing networks like Survived & Punished work to bring light and justice to cases like that of Marissa Alexander, who was sentenced to twenty years in prison for firing a warning shot into the ceiling above her attacking husband, and Cyntoia Brown Long, who received a life sentence for killing her forty-year-old assaulter when she was sixteen. Brown Long and Alexander have both been freed due to successful organizing. There are many more who have not.[136]

Grimmer still is the irony that the people supposedly keeping survivors—mostly women—safe are often abusers themselves. Several studies have shown that domestic violence occurs in 28 to 40 percent of police households, three to four times higher than the national rate.[137] Studies also indicate that because most of these data are based on self-reporting by abusive cops themselves, they are likely vastly underreported. Moreover, a *New York Times* investigation found that police were less likely to face disciplinary action for domestic violence than for almost any other kind of misconduct.[138] Cops are disciplined more for smoking a joint than for beating their partner. We are left with a situation in which literally thousands of abusive cops are walking around as the first responders to instances of domestic abuse.

"Bullies in Blue Suits" 97

Sexual misconduct is equally rife. According to lawyer and abolitionist Derecka Purnell, sexual misconduct is the second most frequent kind of police violence complaint, with one complaint every five days, nationally.[139] As Purnell writes, "Since 2005, more than five thousand cops have been arrested for sexual violence, misconduct, and child pornography possession . . . and only 400 lost their badge."[140] The routine and repeated nature of sexual violence cases—like San Diego cop Anthony Arevalos, Oklahoma City's Daniel Holtzclaw (both of whom had dozens of victims), or the multiple Chicago officers under investigation for sexual violence committed against underage asylum seekers housed in the city's police stations—show that police sexual violence is, to quote one wide-reaching study, a "subcultural norm."[141] Far from preventing sexual and gender-based violence, the police promote it.

Their interventions are regularly violent themselves. As this chapter was being written, a twenty-seven-year-old Black woman named Niani Finlayson in Los Angeles County frantically called 911, asking for the police, because she and her daughter were being assaulted by an ex-boyfriend who was refusing to leave her home. Police arrived and entered the residence. Within three seconds of entering (take a moment from reading to count to three) the cops shot Finlayson four times, murdering her in front of her nine-year-old daughter. It was revealed later that Ty Shelton—the cop who shot down the victim—had murdered another Black person two years previous while responding to another domestic violence call.[142] Finlayson was yet another senseless, preventable, unfortunately commonplace death due to the state's use of a violent repressive force to attend to social problems.

In this context, INCITE!'s arguments against criminalization ring truer than ever:

Their End Is Our Beginning

Law enforcement approaches to violence against women may deter some acts of violence in the short term. However, as an overall strategy for ending violence, criminalization has not worked. In fact, the overall impact of mandatory arrest laws for domestic violence have led to decreases in the number of battered women who kill their partners in self-defense, but they have not led to a decrease in the number of batterers who kill their partners. Thus, the law protects batterers more than it protects survivors.[143]

Abolitionists like Mariame Kaba and others with long experience in this work have also pointed out that the criminalization of domestic violence can exacerbate the existing economic and environmental stressors that are often a "causal factor in gender-based violence."[144] People who have been criminalized, unemployed, or underemployed are more likely to engage in abusive violence. Similar to the teams developed for mental health crises, alternative, nonpolice crisis intervention methods with trained professionals specializing in both crisis de-escalation and domestic violence, connected with robust support systems, could provide clear alternatives with the right resources. However, even alternatives like these focus extensively on the individual abuser and occur only after the fact. A more holistic approach to ameliorate the conditions that foster the cycle of trauma and abuse is needed. Additionally, the focus on criminalization not only fails to do justice by survivors but also offers no real path to change for those who perpetrate this kind of violence, many of whom are not beyond recovery.[145] Locking everyone up is not the solution. Emphasis on the necessity of police intervention often functions as a stand-in for greater systemic social change and inhibits substantial movement to real, deeper solutions.

The epidemic of mass shootings, especially the horrific school shootings that continue to plague the US, are also cited (out of understandable fear) as justifications for reliance on the police. The year 2023 ended with the most mass shootings on record, with thirty-eight incidents in which four or more people, excluding the shooter, were killed.[146] Even though 68 percent of these shootings occurred in private homes, the public nature of many of these events added another chilling layer to life in this country—especially when the incidents occur in schools and against children. People feel unsafe at the harrowing prospect of rogue individuals wielding assault rifles and weapons designed for war in places like schools, houses of worship, bowling alleys, or supermarkets. It can be hard to imagine a solution other than to have a similarly armed group of individuals swoop in to stop the attacker.

But even in these situations, police don't keep us safe. In 2022, the country reeled from the mass murder of twenty-one elementary schoolchildren and teachers in Uvalde, Texas. The assailant, armed with an AR-15, was undeterred from entering by the school's assigned cop. Uvalde police established a perimeter and waited for one hour and fourteen minutes while the children inside were massacred. While the police cowered outside, the survivors inside hid, smeared themselves in their classmates' blood pretending to be dead, and called 911 over and over. As minutes ticked by, parents of the children drove miles to arrive at the school and, in the face of police inaction, heroically attempted to enter the school to rescue their children. The cops violently stopped them from doing so, tackling them to the ground, handcuffing some, and even using pepper spray. And then the police waited some more. Eventually, a Border Patrol tactical unit arrived and killed the shooter.[147]

The blatant mishandling of the situation provoked even liberal media like the *New York Times* to criticize the cops. Subsequently, the Texas Department of Public Safety was forced to admit they made the "wrong decision"—a rare moment in which the police admitted fault. But, while the tragedy of Uvalde is one of the more egregious examples of the uselessness of cops in preventing massacres, it is not an exception.

Prior to Uvalde, during the high-profile 2018 school shooting in Parkland, Florida, the school cop, Scot Peterson, huddled right outside the building while seventeen people were killed. A 2019 study in the *Journal of the American Medical Association* found that "armed guards were not associated with significant reduction in rates of injuries" and even that "the rate of deaths was 2.83 times *greater* in schools with an armed guard present."[148] There are incredibly few, rare cases of police stopping a school shooting, in the act, with no casualties.[149] In an analysis of two decades of data, one study asked the question, "Who stops the bad guy with a gun?"[150] It found that, in a majority of "active shooter incidents," the incident ended before police arrived, with the shooter leaving, committing suicide, or being subdued by a bystander. Police stopped the attacker less than a third of the time. Adam Lankford, a professor who has studied mass shootings for more than a decade, is quoted in the study: "It's direct, indisputable, empirical evidence that this kind of common claim that 'the only thing that stops a bad guy with the gun is a good guy with the gun' is wrong."[151]

Despite this, calls for police and SWAT units to have "more" training or better equipment to act "more quickly" and rush in the next time ring out from liberal media outlets after events like Uvalde. But it boggles the mind to consider what more training and equipment are even possible. As Akela Lacy pointed out in

"Bullies in Blue Suits"

The Intercept, 40 percent of the Uvalde city budget goes to policing.[152] On top of that, their school cops are further funded via the federal Community Oriented Policing Services program, and the department received a half-million dollar grant the year of the shooting for more equipment under the pretense of the War on Drugs. Two months prior to the shooting, the Uvalde cops did active shooter trainings, and, leading up to the incident, the Uvalde SWAT team bragged on social media about touring local schools.[153]

It should also be noted that police who "rush in quicker" in general frequently escalate situations and kill more people. "Swift action" is what resulted in the murder of Breonna Taylor; the killing of Tarika Wilson—who was holding her son—by a SWAT team in Lima, Ohio; the killing of seven-year-old Aiyana Jones in Detroit; the killing of Dexter Reed, mentioned in the introduction; and many others. Per the ACLU, roughly 124 SWAT paramilitary raids occur *per day* in the US and disproportionately affect Black Americans, who make up 40 percent of those raided.[154]

It is beyond the scope of this book to discuss the deep-rooted and complicated factors from which the terrible and specifically US phenomenon of mass shootings arises. But, for our purposes, even the few cases mentioned here, which would seem to represent classic cases for armed force to be met with armed force, fail to live up to the argument.

The police—however trained and armed—do not function preventatively at all in these instances and perhaps even contribute to their likelihood. Even with most of our schools, airports, train stations, and workplaces looking more and more like prisons, shootings have only increased. A myopic policy focus that prioritizes the police response as most critical severely impairs our ability to address the root causes of the violence. These root causes range from the boomerang effect of US imperialism domestically—or the way in which the "warfare state models behavior for the polity," in the words of Ruth Wilson Gilmore—to the impact of the massive domestic arms industry (also related to US imperialism), or what Jeff Sparrow, in his classic essay on this topic, identifies as the "profound social derangement" of neoliberal decay and imperial aggression.[155] Addressing these problems means taking on state-sanctioned militarism and the profound inequality and lack of resources that create situations of alienation, desperation, and trauma.

While it may be true that, in some instances, the intervention of an armed unit may mean that twenty rather than forty people are killed, one must pause to ask if that is a calculus we must accept. Given these options, we have to admit that the policing "solutions" are still a complete failure. The misconception of the need for the "good guy with a gun" is used to continually re-legitimize the police and reinforce the necessity of omnipresent militarized cops everywhere. Yet the shootings continue. Since the 1999 Columbine shooting, the police "fix" for mass shootings—especially in schools—has been the *only* solution carried out, and it has failed miserably.

Abolition is a presence, as Gilmore reminds us, and that means efforts to abolish the police are not simply oriented toward getting rid of the police, though that would be a necessary start. Parallel to removing police from the equation, we must create something new in their place that can better deal with social problems and bring about real safety.

"Lookin' at the world like, 'Where do we go?'": What do we say about crime?[156]

While police are clearly a terrible solution to social problems and keeping us safe, it remains true that most people feel the only option available to them in these situations—mental health crisis, domestic violence, and the like—is to call the police. This is largely because government budget cuts have gutted services that could support and articulate a clinically appropriate community intervention plan to respond to social problems. Without these, only the police remain. More services can be developed, and some do exist that are better attuned to the root causes, that offer alternatives better equipped to provide safety. But, in a society that prioritizes wealth extraction over human life, they are not a priority. Importantly, the reason such alternatives do not exist on a large scale is not due to a lack of imagination by the trained professionals who work in these fields but to our lack of power and resources to make them a reality. This is a political choice by the state, its managers, its politicians, and the ruling-class backers and sycophants who proclaim their ideology.

Regardless of what could be possible, in our current situation it must be acknowledged that many working-class people and people of color see crime and community violence as a worrying concern. A majority of Americans believe that the crime rate has been going up, despite crime rates having steadily fallen in the past fifty years.[157] In the last half century, property crimes have dropped by 45.4 percent, while the violent crime rate has remained relatively stagnant and then declined over most categories. According to FBI and Bureau of Justice Statistics figures since 1993, violent crime has fallen 50 to 74 percent.[158]

Still, concerns for the safety of oneself and one's family and neighbors are real and often based in the lived experiences of certain communities. Most crime occurs within demographic categories—that is, most victims of crime are the same ethnicity as the perpetrators. Since crime itself is often born of conditions of capitalist inequality, poverty, and deprivation, and inequality in the US is still disproportionately racialized, that means there is a warranted feeling of unsafety among many Black Americans. A contradiction emerges from such feelings, wherein some Black Americans can feel simultaneously over-policed and under-policed. Some of these dynamics were apparent in Chicago's 2023 mayoral election, which was dominated by the question of crime. While 84 percent of Black Chicagoans reported feeling unsafe, and many supported calls for more policing to provide what was perceived as some kind of immediate relief, at the same time 85 percent of Black Chicagoans saw "relations with the police" as "negative" and the cops as "untrustworthy."[159] Residents—especially Black and brown Chicagoans—saw alleviation of crime as better served by jobs programs, mental health programs, and more services to address "root causes."[160] Yet, while the idea of police abolition took a giant leap into the mainstream as a result of the 2020 rebellion, it still provokes uncertainty. That apprehension is understandable if, for example, one lives in a community reeling from gun violence, and immediate-term solutions are desperately sought. But, just as in the cases of mental health crises and domestic violence, the real problem is that the only recourse available to people is to call the cops, who end up exacerbating these problems.

Throwing cops at social problems like crime, mental health issues, and even gun violence fails to produce any long-term positive changes that could truly address these issues. Cops do not provide safety in any real meaningful way.

Conclusion: Force Doctrine—Compelling Compliance of an Unwilling Subject[161]

If police don't keep us safe and do not solve, stop, or prevent crime, then what do they do? The cops are designed primarily to enforce state power and demonstrate the monopoly of legitimate

"Bullies in Blue Suits" 105

violence on the street. Cops patrol, equipped to respond and repress resistance of the urban crowd, to enforce the market order, and are organized around anti-Black racism. Therefore, it is no surprise that what they do is patrol, harass, stop, frisk, question, carry out petty traffic stops, issue obnoxious tickets and citations, abuse, brutalize, torture, and fill the prisons of this country. What police do is destroy communities. Even when they are deployed as a last-ditch effort by the capitalist state to manage social problems that emerge from the capitalist system, their doctrine of force informs their daily practice. What they do is kill.

Getting killed by the police is one of the leading causes of death for young Black men, according to a National Academy of Sciences study.[162] At one in a thousand, "That's better odds of being killed by police than you have of winning a lot of scratch-off lottery games," writes study author Frank Edwards. While anti-Black racism is central to police practice—thus, victims are disproportionately African American—roughly 45 percent of those killed by police are white. Even with the massive racial disparity around prison, as Keeanga-Yamahtta Taylor notes, "The rate at which white people in the United States are incarcerated is still higher than the incarceration rate of almost every country in the world."[163] While racism organizes and determines the main target, state violence is expressed broadly.

It is not some anonymous "bad guy" that poses a danger to our collective safety but the police themselves. More than three-quarters of all homicides are committed by someone the victim knows. But, of all killings by strangers in the US, more than a third are carried out by police.[164] This means that if you're killed by someone you don't know, there's a one in three chance that the killer will be a cop. In spite of the hype in our cultural imaginary, the threat of the random person in a darkened alley or the specter of being stalked by a serial killer are both statistical anomalies. Cops, in contrast, are demonstrably a profound social problem.

Nor are police necessarily brave individuals who take great personal risk to keep the world safe. According to the US Department of Labor, being a cop is only the fourteenth most dangerous job for which there is data. If we measure danger in terms of the rate of death or injury on the job, jobs such as fisherman, farmer, garbage collector, and taxi driver are far more dangerous than being a cop.[165]

In 2023—the deadliest year for cop violence in the past decade—70 percent of fatal police shootings occurred when cops were responding to a suspected nonviolent crime, traffic stop, or no crime whatsoever.[166] In the vast majority of cases, the situations in which Black and brown people are killed by police are tragically innocuous. Alton Sterling was selling CDs. Philando Castile was pulled over for a traffic stop. Tyre Nichols was pulled over for a traffic stop. Dexter Reed was pulled over for a traffic stop. Walter Scott had a broken brake light. Freddie Gray "made eye contact" with a cop. That was all that was needed for a death sentence. Sandra Bland was driving; Eric Garner was selling cigarettes; Tamir Rice and Rekia Boyd were hanging out in parks; Michael Brown was walking in the street; and Stephon Clark was in his own backyard. George Floyd was purchasing food. Breonna Taylor was sleeping in her home. Rayshard Brooks was napping in his car. Elijah McClain was dancing while walking home.

These are not examples of situations in which the police *had* to intervene. Before they turned up, there was little (if any) danger. Prior to the police arriving, there was no wrong done to a member of the community that had to be righted. Virtually all these killings were the result of the "routine stops" determined by racial profiling, focused on suspicion of drug possession or distribution and so-called "quality-of-life" offenses. We don't need alternative methods for the cops to use in these circumstances: We just need them to stop. But the problems do not end there. Even when intervening in situations that are unsafe, cops often make them worse. Any safety they provide is the exception, not the norm, and comes at tremendous social cost. As violence workers and discretionary despots, police bring violence everywhere they go. It is what cops do. Their very presence is the problem. Their abolition is the solution.

chapter 3
The Police State and Its Functionaries

Police were our government.
—W. E. B. Du Bois[1]

Representatives of a power which estranges them from society, they have to be given prestige by means of special decrees, which invest them with a peculiar sanctity and inviolability. The lowest police officer of the civilized state has more "authority" than all the organs of gentile society put together.
—Friedrich Engels[2]

For the vast majority of people in the United States, the sphere of politics is almost completely divorced from daily life. Many feel, rightly, that we do not live in a democracy. The state is felt to be out of reach or estranged from society. While some of us have the right to vote in federal and local electoral races, we do so in an atomized form, via secret ballot and in most cases disconnected from actual collective decision-making. Of course, even these elections are largely rigged via a matrix of voter suppression measures that include gerrymandering; severe restrictions on political representation by the enforced two-party system; outright voter disenfranchisement excluding 4.6 million people, or one out of every nineteen African Americans; and an electoral college

109

created during the era of slavery, the machinations of which have resulted in two of the last four presidents being elected without the majority of votes.[3] In a system in which the candidate who spent the most money wins congressional elections 93 percent of the time, and in which the predominance of funding comes from wealthy individual donors and corporate PACs, the horizon of choice is established by the rich and powerful well before some of us have the opportunity to check a box or not.[4]

Then, even if we vote someone into office, ordinary people have no real power over elected officials' activity. On the federal level, there is no way to exert control by recalling someone. The common rejoinder to this point invokes the notion of "holding politicians accountable" after their election. But, at even a basic level of democracy, you shouldn't need to pressure someone to do the thing that you voted for them to do. There is, after all, an army of roughly twelve thousand *official* congressional lobbyists—twenty-two for every one member of the US Congress—and many more unofficial lobbyists that plays a similar role on a much grander scale. The premise that we must lobby someone to do what they have ostensibly been put in office to do accepts that the role of the people is to be subjects, at most exerting soft pressure on government officials rather than democratically controlling the direction of society.

In the United States, the two political cartels that substitute for "parties" do not allow people to actually "join" or collectively participate in a way that would organize individual political preferences to exert them on a collective scale. In the words of political scientist Arthur Lipow, membership in these parties means, on a practical level, "that individuals register their party preference with an agency of the state or are habitual voters for one or another party."[5] Or, as Maurice Duverger, a pioneer in the study

The Police State and Its Functionaries

of electoral systems, puts it bluntly, membership in one of these US parties "has no meaning."[6]

Confirming what millions of people know from daily experience, one prominent 2014 empirical study of over twenty years of policy concluded, "Average citizens have little or no independent influence" on governmental policy, and the US should no longer be considered an actual democracy.[7]

The vast majority of the state, including the repressive apparatuses of the army, police, and much of the carceral system, is not elected, and ordinary people have next to no control over them.[8] The majority of elections are for the legislature, which handles only the general case of laws and not the specifics of what the state actually does, enforces, or advocates on the international stage.[9] Last, but most important, at the place where most of us spend the majority of our waking time—at work—we are not existing in even a formal democracy. Even though the vast majority are compelled to sell their labor to survive, we have no control over the priorities, pacing, or conditions of our work, though perhaps if you are lucky enough to have a fighting union, you can negotiate the terms of your exploitation to a greater or lesser degree.

In a society in which most people are given very little meaningful choice over the operation of the state that governs them, democracy is in reality a farce. That is, unless you are a member of the ruling class. In class societies, states serve a very crucial and defined function: imposing the rule of one class over another. The modern capitalist state, as described in a famous line from *The Communist Manifesto*, is "but a committee for managing the common affairs of the whole bourgeoisie." But what are those common affairs? Primarily, these include ensuring the smooth functioning of capital accumulation for the capitalist class of any given country. At the core of this capacity for managing capitalist order is

Their End Is Our Beginning

a "special body of armed men," to use an oft-quoted phrase of Russian revolutionary V. I. Lenin.[10] Two elements constitute the operating principles of the capitalist state in general: the "management of capitalist interests" and the monopoly on overwhelming violence (or the threat thereof). Cops serve centrally in both of these components. "To try to discuss police," writes critical police theorist Mark Neocleous, "without discussing state power is like discussing the 'economy' without mentioning capital."[11] The police are the state at its core and states are police projects.

This chapter will examine the relationship between capitalism and capitalist states and the centrality of police to that relationship. An important part of this connection is racism, a project of the capitalist state that infuses the police mission. Finally, the institutional role of police within these structures shape their class position, which is important to understand for social movements organizing working-class people. Far from allies of any left-wing movement, "the police are," as the Russian revolutionary Leon Trotsky put it, "fierce, implacable, hated and hating foes. To win them over is out of the question."[12] Ultimately, capitalist states are the key obstacle to abolition; consequently, the police are class enemies to our movements.

States in Capitalism

What makes a state capitalist? It is not simply that the individuals at its helm are capitalists themselves (though many are). States are not blank vessels for resource distribution and society-wide coordination that "serve the purpose of securing society as a whole's ability to organize its affairs."[13] The class nature of states is structurally fashioned by the role that states play in capitalism, conditioning their behavior "for class ends, with class consequences."[14]

The capitalist class exerts *massive* influence over the state—

The Police State and Its Functionaries

the electoral system runs on their campaign contributions, policy is affected by lobbying that only the wealthy can afford, and state officials are often pulled directly from the pool of CEOs of major Wall Street firms or other owners of different kinds of capital. Because of this, it can be tempting to view the state as a simple tool or instrument that is directed by a cohort of billionaires sitting around a table in a darkened room wearing top hats and twirling their mustaches. However, although Marx and Engels referred to the state as "but a committee for managing the common affairs of the whole bourgeoisie," the state is not a mere instrument wielded by a unified ruling class.

Such an "instrumentalist" theory—as pointed out by radical sociologist Fred Block—misses two key features of the state.[15] First, even though the state does serve as a tool for class rule, it must appear as if it doesn't to remain stable. Overt dictatorships and despotism are often politically brittle due to their lack of access—real or illusory—for working people to participate and invest in the legitimacy of state power. The fact that the modern capitalist state appears as a "neutral" intermediary between social groups and classes serves an important function. In most capitalist states political power has some degree of institutional separation from the "private sphere" of exploitation at the workplace. So, the state takes on the form of a "public" and "impersonal" power, standing above classes defined in production.[16]

Second, and more important, the general interests of capital are not always shared or known by the individual capitalists themselves. Capitalists *as a class* are not class conscious. Jeff Bezos, for example, is guided by his own best interest in making the most profit from his slice of the economic pie, and this creates blinders rooted in his interests, limiting his ability to know or advocate for the best interest of the system as a whole, even if he wanted to.

On the market, capitalists are in *competition* with each other, each compelled to realize values and obtain profits at the expense of the others in order to survive and grow. Competition between them proceeds simultaneously alongside the strong solidarity they have with each other when their collective interests are threatened by the working class. It is why Marx and Engels referred to them as a "hostile band of brothers."[17] That contradictory relationship—both collaboration and competition—is dramatically sharper in the case of imperialism, or competition between capitalists of different states. These dynamics will be discussed later in this chapter.

Because of the competitive and crisis-prone nature of capitalism, sometimes the state may have to act against the private interest of this or that capitalist, with policies such as price controls or restrictions on exports, or to ensure social reproduction (for instance, making sure that there is a supply of workers able to carry out work), or even to quell class conflict by making concessions to workers (as in the case of the New Deal, which was implemented largely out of fear of insurrection).[18] The separate roles of the private capitalist and the managers of the state apparatus has led, in many capitalist societies, to a division of labor between the two, where state managers are primarily concerned with maintaining and reproducing the social and economic order against even the protestations of some capitalists.[19]

To the extent that the capitalist class does become consciously a class with some kind of coherent collective interest, it is often through the process of being organized in the state. The ruling class pursues capitalist interests with the aid of idea-generating para-state institutions like parties, think tanks, and NGOs; nonstate institutions like universities or elite media also contribute.[20] These institutions often address state actors whom they hope might do something with their ideas. In the US con-

The Police State and Its Functionaries

text, the two major parties each have a share in the US state. For policy-forming purposes, they're integrated with the capitalist class directly through lobbying, social connections, and financial flows. The two parties are thus amalgamators of sectional interests, horse-traders among those interests, and practical reconcilers of internal conflicts for the class. As parties go, the two US parties are not strongly differentiated by their policies, but the parties (or party factions, like the neo-cons of the 1990s and 2000s) are available to become *vehicles* for policy alternatives when the ruling class needs such alternatives.

The bipartisan expansion of police power fits here. While there are slightly varying sectional interests that distinguish the shifting policy priorities of the two major parties, the continuity and expansion of police power and violence is a shared project related to the power of the capitalist state itself. The unwavering commitment becomes clear from the historical shifts outlined in the previous chapter, from the crime bills under Clinton in the 1990s to the militarization of the police under the auspices of the War on Terror organized under G. W. Bush and Obama, to Trumpian reaction and Biden's backlash "fund the police" programs. While there are small differences, the general direction is unified when it comes to the repressive core of the state.

As such, the state is the organized *means* by which an interest is formulated and pursued on behalf of the capitalist class as a whole, including the arbitration of conflicts within the class. In other words, the state is the way that members of the ruling class gain collective *agency* as a class. "The special characteristics of capitalism put a premium on finding political leaders," writes American socialist Hal Draper in his work on the state, "who can take, and stick to, an overall and farsighted view of the interests and needs of the system as a whole, rather than the shortsighted, close-up blurred vision characteristic of the busy profit seeker."[21]

State managers play a central role in enacting this ruling-class agency. Yet, they may also develop their own special interests related to their role in the state, differentiated from the immediate needs of profit-making. A structural analysis highlights two key reasons *why* the state necessarily functions to serve capitalists' overall interests.[22] First, states rely on tax revenue and borrowing to pay for their functioning and functionaries. Both of these depend on a growing economy, profitability, and a business climate that promotes investment.[23] In a capitalist society, the level of economic activity, and therefore the health of the economy on capitalist terms as well as potential tax revenue, is determined by the degree to which capitalists choose to invest, expand, hire, or start new ventures. Without the accumulation of profit by a national business class, tax revenue is harder to come by and the potential for borrowing from private capitalist financial institutions is at risk. State managers know this and, to a greater or lesser degree, are *conscious* of their mandate to foster an investment-friendly business climate for the expanded reproduction of national capital: national bank chairs, treasury secretaries, career undersecretaries of all sorts, and many elected officials quickly come to know what their job is, and they know that they can be replaced by others who will fulfill the same role if they fail.

That role for the state becomes even more pronounced during inevitable periods of economic crisis. When capitalism is in a bust cycle, the job of state managers is to work to restart the capitalist economic engine and facilitate capitalist investment on which the economy and state legitimacy depend.[24] In almost all circumstances, therefore, the state has to make pro-business decisions—which often carry with them austerity for the working class. No direct stimulus will *make* capitalists invest. Even with

The Police State and Its Functionaries 117

the most extreme measures, such as the quantitative easing that moves interest rates into the negative and effectively pays capitalists to borrow, the state remains dependent upon the subjective decisions of those who own capital to invest or not.

Given this dependence, states are further disciplined to serve the interests of capital via the threat of capital flight, always a potential weapon in the hands of a dissatisfied capitalist class. This continual threat haunts attempts at reform or nationalization of the economy because owners of capital can literally take their money and assets and leave the country. The economic shockwaves caused by capital flight can be paralyzing for any social democratic reform project.[25] None of this, however, should diminish the fact that capitalism requires the state system. Whereas capital and money are immensely mobile, commodities have physical form—they need chains of social production. These chains are then anchored in the fact that production "has the most territorial requirements of all: fixed capital, land, a readily available workforce, etc."[26] Capitalism requires a system of states to ensure the conditions of accumulation wherever it may flee, and, at a certain point, the sunk costs of investment are far too high to pack up and move complex production processes.

The second structural feature of states in capitalism pertains to the relationship between them. What makes a state capitalist, writes Marxist scholar Colin Barker, is not just national relations between particular states and their domestic capitalist (or working) classes but their enmeshment in a "system of inter-related states, whose external relations with each other [are] essential to their definition and their form."[27] The chaotic competition of capitalism scales out beyond national borders into the realm of relations among different states. Capitalists of different states interrelate and interact through trade, commerce, and international supply lines as well as through competition for markets, natural resources, and geopolitical position. On this international stage, states function outwardly to create a favorable business climate and jockey for position for their national capitalist class. They are not accountable to any laws or world government. They are ruthlessly competitive because if they want to maintain their power, they must increase GDP, expand their militaries, and control resources at the expense of other states. Capitalist competition dictates the logic of inter-state competition, and states continually define themselves against and in relation with each other. Shifts in the development of one state act upon and are mutually affected by the other parts of the world system.[28]

Thus, the defining feature of the modern state is its *multiplicity*, the competition among many states. The system of capitalism does not just create "the state" but a system of multiple states. "There will be many capitalist states," wrote Neil Davidson, "as long as there are many capitals . . . The trajectory of geoeconomic competition ultimately ends in geopolitical rivalry."[29] And with geopolitical rivalry come the forces of imperialism, armed forces, and war that lurk behind the tentative bonds of diplomacy. As in capitalist competition on the market, competition among states is the starting point for understanding the exploitative relations of each state with its domestic subjects and the carceral forms it takes on, including its borders, prisons and, most essential, its police. *Military* competition between states has domestic ramifications, compelling the revolutionization of the means of destruction or violence, which states in turn deploy against domestic populations and social movements. As a matter of course, the technology created for foreign wars will, at some point, come back to be used on domestic populations. "There is no clear dividing line," writes Palestinian human rights attorney Noura Erakat

The Police State and Its Functionaries

of the boomerang effect of the colonial genocide in Palestine and infinite wars abroad fueling repression and authoritarianism in the US, "between imperial geography and the metropole."[30]

Harsha Walia summarizes the role of states in capitalism perhaps best:

> The state creates the conditions for capital investment; protects private property; implements tax rates; subsidizes banks and corporations; regulates the flow and flexibility of surplus populations, including through borders and prison; and authorizes an entire legal regime sanctioning the violence of dispossession, extraction and commodification of land and labor. The state, therefore, enshrines capitalist relations.[31]

The decisions of states and their managers are driven by the need to secure a positive business climate for capital investment. State managers pursue this project outwardly, on behalf of their national capitalist class against other states, and inwardly, against challenges or disruptions by their own subjects.[32] It is policing, as Neocleous' important work on the subject puts it, that "is the most direct way in which the power of the state manifests itself to its subjects."[33]

What States Do for Capitalism

Capitalism needs states because it is a market-based system. On a basic level, markets are mechanisms for independent producers to exchange goods in order to reciprocally meet needs. However, those exchanges require certain established rules to be reliable. Because "neither of the two people exchanging in the market can regulate the exchange relation unilaterally," a "third party" is required, "who personifies the reciprocal guarantees which the owners of commodities mutually agree to as proprietors" and can regulate the market transaction.[34] States fulfill this role as guarantors of market "contracts," ultimately ensuring compliance with market "rules" by threat of force.

The reason market rules have to be constantly policed within capitalism is because markets are not actually set up to meet people's needs. We live in societies in which our needs for survival and reproduction are met (though they are often unmet) not by intentional or democratic plans but rather as a byproduct of competition for profit on the market. People who own the means to make bread (have the factory, flour, and so on) produce the loaves and then try to sell them at a price determined by what can make a profit and still actually be sold. In the figurative and sometimes literal market, commodities necessary for survival are bought and sold. But, most people—the working class—do not already own products to exchange, so they are forced to lease out their labor for money in order to buy the means of sustenance or other goods on the market.

Buying and using labor power from dispossessed workers is the way that capitalists add value and generate profits, so they have an interest in keeping workers from being able to sustain themselves outside of the market, as discussed at multiple points in this book. In other words, for these existing property relations to work, they have to systematically exclude individuals from the objects of their need. In order for bread to be *sold* on the market to people who need it, the people who need it have to be denied access to it and prevented from just taking it rather than paying for it. The motive to steal, rob, trespass, and the like is continually recreated through the pressure of material need. "Commodity-producing society is always potentially a thief-producing

The Police State and Its Functionaries 121

society," writes Barker.[35] The need to defend private property, market legitimacy, and keep workers dependent on selling their labor in order to survive gave rise to the need for some sort of protection agencies with means of violence. "The most developed form of such protective agencies are states," and police fulfill this core function of states within capitalism.[36]

For states, creating and maintaining "market order" requires an organization of violent force. Many contemporary states have more layers of bureaucracy and complexity than earlier iterations and, starting in the (exceptional) postwar period, for a time took on select welfare functions.[37] But even though states have taken on more pervasive roles and institutional layers since their earlier forms, the centrality of the capitalist state's repressive, policing function remains unchanged. From raw numbers alone, the state can clearly be characterized as a special body of armed men.

The special bodies of armed men can be loosely divided between those who use force directed beyond the geographical borders of the state—the military—and those whose target is the domestic population within the geographical borders—the police. While this is a bit of a simplification, as the two components often overlap and interact in important ways, the distinction is useful on a general level. While the former—the standing army—is a feature of the earliest, pre-capitalist states, the police are an institution that developed along with, and as a constitutive part of, the capitalist state. Police, and the entire carceral apparatus of which they are a crucial part, create and recreate capitalist order through immense violence.

Today, two million people in the United States are locked behind bars, constituting the largest number of incarcerated people in the world—both in absolute numbers and in proportion to national population. Over a thousand people are murdered by the police every year, with many thousands more brutalized. At a rate of three people per day, 2024 saw the most people killed by police in a year, breaking the record-breaking number from 2023, which broke the record from 2022.[38] And, of course, the carceral violence this country imposes is racialized to its core, with anti-Black racism as a central operating and targeting mechanism. Concentration camps along the borders lock up over forty thousand people annually, fleeing circumstances in their countries often related to American political and economic meddling, dividing families and facilitating endemic cases of sexual assault. Any notion of personal privacy is obsolete, as the National Security Agency can access almost all our data, and the growing interconnection between Big Tech and the state only secures this stranglehold.[39] The police state acts beyond the border. As of April 2024, the US military is currently operating in 41 percent of the world's countries, maintains military bases in eighty countries, and stations combat troops in fourteen.[40] In 2024, the US directly bombed at least four countries by planes and drones, as well as provided military support and coordination for the Israeli genocide in Gaza. On top of this, the US wages crippling economic war via sanctions on approximately twenty more.[41]

The centrality of this violence to the state apparatus is demonstrated concretely through the numbers, both in personnel and in funds. Federal and local budgets—much of which come from workers' tax dollars—still devote huge amounts of cash to "armed men." On the federal level, over half of all discretionary spending goes to the Department of Defense, while over $80 billion is spent annually on prisons across the country. On the local level, most major municipal budgets devoted one-third to police, for $80 billion nationally spent per year.[42] Together, this puts the total for police and prisons at $160 billion per year—the largest

The Police State and Its Functionaries

expense after the military in the federal budget, and double the amount spent federally on health.[43]

Relative personnel sizes further illustrate what this really means for the state. The Department of Labor, for example, has 17,000 employees, while the Department of Education has 4,000 employees. The nonmilitary federal workforce is 2 million, and 700,000 (35 percent) of those are civilians working for the Department of Defense.[44] Comparatively, military personnel in the Department of Defense—the largest employer in the world—comprise another 2.5 million people.[45] There are also 35,400 employed by the Federal Bureau of Prisons; 60,000 members of the Border Patrol (federal cops); and 91,000 in the FBI, CIA, and NSA (also federal cops).[46] Excluding civilian contractors, that makes 75 percent of total federal employees members of a body of armed men. It is estimated that over one million municipal cops are roving the nation's streets.[47] In pretty much every city, the police constitute roughly 30 percent of all city employees and in most cases those numbers dwarf all other city departments. In Chicago, roughly 40 percent of the city's employees are cops. In St. Louis, the number is 50 percent.

Even while its repressive violence is sometimes less visible in more stable capitalist democracies, the threat of violence remains credible and effective as a means of ensuring capitalist order and continued capitalist growth. The state, in the words of Marx, is a "national war engine of capital against labor."[48]

Racism Is a Project of the Capitalist State

Maintaining conditions for capital investment and a positive business climate require an orderly society, socially and politically structured according to the needs of the market as much as possible. Accordingly, the state is responsible for managing not just business, trade, and taxation policy, but also the often chaotic conditions arising from crisis-level inequality in the population.

Racism—anti-Black racism especially but not exclusively—figures centrally in how society is ordered by the activity of states and their policing bodies. Here it is helpful to define our terms. The term "racism" is often used to mean discriminatory attitudes and stereotypes. Sometimes the analysis goes deeper, recognizing how racism operates on the level of institutions, such as discriminatory housing policies and banking practices creating stark racial wealth gaps that last for generations. Both the ideological and institutional aspects are important manifestations of racism, but they do not identify the root causes of racism in capitalist society. To borrow from the work of Jamaican-British Marxist Stuart Hall, on a structural level, racism "works to reproduce the class relations of the whole society in a specific form on an extended scale; and we have been noting the way race, as a structural feature of each sector in this complex process of social reproduction, serves to 're-produce' that working class in a racially stratified and internally antagonistic form."[49] Racism, Hall writes, is "a key constituent in this reproduction of class relations . . . which provides the material and social base on which 'racism' as ideology flourishes."

To see how racism is key to the state project of creating a favorable capitalist business climate, it is useful to consider the shifts in US cities under neoliberalism as manufacturing centers were shuttered and were transformed into locations for finance, corporate headquarters, real estate, and the related gentrification and new urbanism.[50] This required—to quote David McNally—a "sanitizing mission" to "present cities as spaces for investment." It was a project fundamentally "concerned with segregating and hiding the poor and with criminalizing the non-conforming."[51] The job of "sanitizing" and "segregating,"

The Police State and Its Functionaries

of course, falls to the police, the racist advance guard of gentrification who patrol areas targeted for investment as a means of ensuring property values continue to appreciate. City politicians and police chiefs are quite explicit with this in the common claims to "clean up" parts of the city. As a result, "quality of life" arrests skyrocket in areas targeted for real estate investment.[52] It is a highly racialized process from the start, including the intentional depression or economic organized abandonment of Black and brown communities in the major metropoles as a means of increasing the margin of gain on investment.

The result is more racist murder, like the killing of Breonna Taylor, described in the previous chapter. According to lawyers for Taylor's family, part of what motivated police targeting her involved attempts to evict residents residing in the path of a planned neighborhood renewal project. Indeed, the home of the man with whom Taylor's presumed association sealed her death warrant was purchased by the city for $1 after his arrest.[53]

The organized abandonment of working-class Black neighborhoods is enacted through the economic violence of budget cuts, political disenfranchisement, lack of investment resulting in job scarcity, and entrenched workplace and housing discrimination. Managing the symptoms of these decisions by the powerful create conditions of insecurity that discourage investment and drive down property values. State managers don't want to fix the problem, and they utilize the police to control the immiserated conditions just enough to prevent disruption to the larger system. When there is real money to be made by capitalist-driven investment facilitated by state infrastructure and the interest of finance and real estate, this occurs with little say in how and what investment occurs by the people living in those communities. Then the cops, as advance guard for gentrification, mobilize to get capital

Their End Is Our Beginning

flowing. Community attitudes toward and concerns about crime are a distant second in the state's priorities after the need to create a positive business climate.

Lastly, capitalism is a system that depends on compelling most people to sell their labor on the market to survive, but it also necessitates a large number of unemployed people as part of its basic operation. This "reserve army of labor," as Marx called it, includes both unemployed and underemployed populations that can be tapped by capitalist firms when the need arises, and it thus serves as a disciplinary mechanism to keep employed workers in line and wages low. If employment is not automatic, you can be fired and replaced by an unemployed person who needs your job and would perhaps work for lower wages. At the same time, capitalist production cannot function in a situation in which nonparticipation in the labor market is the norm, so any existence outside of formal employment is systematically discouraged. Marxist writer Sean Larson, in his treatment of this question, describes how this contradiction is maintained:

> To resolve this dilemma, capitalist societies have historically relied upon ascriptive categories (race, gender, nationality) to justify the relegation of entire segments of the dispossessed populations to a status of reserve for the labor market, subsisting outside of the formal employment relation in various informal economies. In this way, the expectation of participation in the labor market is enforced, while non-participation is only made available in severely restricted or criminalized ways.[54]

For the sake of capitalist profits in general, life outside of employment is designed to be extremely unstable. To survive in

The Police State and Its Functionaries 127

this precarious state, many people have few options but to engage in street economies or informal and illegal business. Criminalized jobs like "hustling," sex work, or the informal drug trade are a few examples.[55] The demands of living in the urban conditions of organized abandonment "require an economy utterly different from what most of America can imagine," writes Sudhir Alladi Venkatesh in his fascinating sociological work on Chicago neighborhoods.[56] While the size of the informal economy is difficult to estimate, some put it at 17 percent of all workers, whose income, if taxed, would amount to $93 billion in tax revenue.[57] In the US, due to the ongoing legacies of slavery, Jim Crow, mass incarceration, and other forms of racism, Black and brown folks are over-represented among the unemployed and have also been used to signify this category in racist political campaigns.[58] In these days of the near absence of any social welfare, regulation of this surplus population is left to the police and serves as a partial driver of the tidal wave of mass incarceration locking people up in prisons. "Capitalism requires inequality and racism enshrines it," Ruth Wilson Gilmore writes, and thus "criminalization and mass incarceration are class war."[59]

Consequently, the racism enshrining capitalist inequality is a "state and state-backed project of domination and violence."[60] The reproduction of racism is needed to maintain and provisionally explain or justify systematic inequality, control and manage a surplus population, and regulate and differentiate a stratified labor market. As Larson describes:

> For socialists, the "structures" of what we call "structural racism" have to be understood as the structures of the capitalist state. These structures have historical origins, develop within historically and socially concrete

circumstances, and result from a series of decisions made by real people. But they are structures nonetheless, and are subject to the imperatives of capitalism.[61]

Through these structures—to quote Gilmore again—"the state's management of racial categories is analogous to the management of highways and ports or telecommunication; racist ideological and material practices are infrastructure."[62] A central cog in this carceral infrastructure of the capitalist state upholding and reproducing racism is the police.

"The PDs Are the Enemies": The Social Class of the Cops[63]

As discussed, the institution of the police is a component of the state, shaped in design and practice for the maintenance of capitalist and racist order. That social role binds their interests to that of the state in a unique way while amputating any possibility of finding solidarity outside the interest of the state and its ruling class. For anyone attempting to overturn a class-based system, this relationship is why the police cannot be considered as "working class" or potential allies in struggle. The question of police and class has strategic ramifications for our movements: Can they be swayed to take our side? Could the police be changed "from the inside" by well-meaning individuals? Should we seek to organize and include them in our movements? The answer is a stark, simple, definitive *no*.

It is true that a majority of cops come from working-class backgrounds. The police job itself certainly involves working for a wage, the broadest definition of what could be considered "working class." And certain conditions of the job—long hours and overtime, medical benefits, pensions, and more—all carry semblances of working-class concerns. Police even have pro-

The Police State and Its Functionaries 129

fessional associations that some call unions. At the same time, cops do not generate surplus value, in that they do not directly generate profit for any private capitalist or even the state. Even the fees from fines and ticketing that many police departments disproportionately extort from working-class people of color do not cover the massive expenditure of city budgets required by the police.[64] But workers like public school teachers and other professions connected with the social reproduction of new workers also do not generate profit, yet they are usually considered part of the working class. So, are cops workers after all?

Not exactly. To understand the class positioning of the police, it is helpful to draw on the work of E. P. Thompson and Ellen Meiksins Wood, who describe class not as a structural location or a "thing" but as a social relationship. It is not, Thompson writes, "this or that part of the machine, but *the way the machine works* once it is set in motion . . . the movement itself, the heat, the thundering noise."[65] This framework is important for understanding not just the material conditions in which an individual lives but how the relationship to their conditions and to others shape how they behave "in class ways."[66] Thompson describes how class formation came about as the working class "came to feel an identity of interests as between themselves, and as against their rulers and employers."[67] This relationship is shaped by conflict with the capitalist class and the state. The capitalist division of society into the rough categories of those who own and those who don't fosters a shared interest among those who don't own *against* this unequal dichotomy, even if that underlying interest is masked.

Some people are not capitalists and don't own businesses, corporations, or natural resources, but their interests nevertheless diverge from the interests of the working class more broadly. This stratum still has to work for a wage (often higher) to survive, *but* the nature of their relationship to workers is conflictual, since the interests of this stratum are tied to state managers and employers. High-level managers and supervisors are one example of this; while they may not own the business or means of production, the entirety of their job is to manage and discipline workers. They may be won to the struggle against capital as individuals, but importantly *as a class* their interests are aligned with the bosses. There is much written in Marxism about this middle stratum, but one of the commonalities is that they are unable to collectively assert an independent political position in the struggle between classes because of the way their social relationship to workers and capital warps their interests. Members of this middle stratum are sometimes pulled by the working-class movement and sometimes swayed by other forces. This is why socialists—from Marx to Trotsky—have described how this middle stratum is especially susceptible to fascism.[68]

Cops are an example of this middle stratum and an extreme one at that. Unlike others in this layer, their social relationship and function is solely as a repressive apparatus of the state *against* the working class. Their interests—not as individuals, but as a social stratum—are never genuinely aligned with working-class interests. "The fundamental question is this," writes Robin D. G. Kelley, "How does their relationship to racial capitalism and the state shape their relationship to other workers?"[69] Police are an extreme example because they are even more solidly antagonistic against workers than are managers, supervisors, and small shopkeepers. Cops can be considered, in effect, a uniquely repressive, hyperdisciplinary managerial class.[70]

While managers tell workers what to do and have the power to hire and fire based on the boss's desire, the police dominate workers with the attitude of an occupier. The cop tells workers

The Police State and Its Functionaries 131

what to do and has the power to shoot and kill if opposed—or even per whim or common cowardice. Indeed, police training is saturated with quasi-fascistic "law and order" ideology that encourages cops to identify with their role as disciplinarian, enforcer, and keeper of the status quo. One example of this is the existence of national "killer cop" contests, reported on by David Correia, who described the multiple events of police from around the country competing in fun-filled shooting events like a "head-shot only" game. "Police win," Correia writes, "if they can kill everyone."[71]

In a racist society, enforcing the status quo means keeping a boot on the necks of people of color. Indeed, many police are trained to see themselves as legitimately occupying the roles of judge, jury, and executioner when they interact with Black people. As Trotsky put it, "Such training does not fail to leave its effects."[72] Cops' material ties to the state therefore foster a deep psychological interest in protecting, enlarging, and defending their repressive, racist vocation. This is a powerful social relation and one that places their interests apart from that of working-class people, who have no such material dependence upon repression of other workers. No other group of "public workers" so actively advocates against any oversight *from* the public in their use of violence *against* the public. James Baldwin describes this well when he writes: "The police are the hired enemies of this population. . . . [they are] quite stunningly ignorant; and since they know they are hated, they are always afraid. One cannot possibly arrive at a more sure-fire formula for cruelty."[73]

The behavior of police "unions" or associations such as the Fraternal Order of Police (FOP) and the Patrolmen's Benevolent Association (PBA) reflects this point about collective interests quite dramatically. Such associations often advocate for

Their End Is Our Beginning

job security, protection, and material resources for cops, and it would be easy to confuse this advocacy with standard workplace demands advocated by the labor movement. But what are "job security" and "protection" for cops? In practice, it means defending police who brutalize and kill, while removing any kind of public accountability or oversight. More resources for cops means more military-grade weapons for them to use while terrorizing and surveilling Black, brown, and working-class communities. Indeed, police associations are quite explicit about this. In the FAQ of the Border Police Union, they describe the need for a union as follows:

> It was not unusual in the past for Border Patrol management to "throw an agent to the wolves" to appease special interest groups . . . [who] regularly make unsubstantiated allegations of civil rights abuses against agents in an attempt to slander and defame the US Border Patrol. This places a very heavy burden on management and administration officials who, at times, forfeit their personal integrity.[74]

This is the official and primary reason given for this union's existence—to help cops carry out the migrant worker expulsion machine's dictates against the protests of any of its critics. Cops are class enemies by their own self-definition.

This is the reason why, after every police murder of innocent Black folks, the FOP representative is first up not only to defend the killer cop but also to slander the victim, often in grotesquely racist terms. Commonplace are statements like the Chicago FOP head's response to the 2021 shooting of thirteen-year-old Adam Toledo in Chicago, in which he called the murder of a child "100 percent justified" and the officer "heroic." It is also the reason po-

The Police State and Its Functionaries

lice union contracts with cities invariably include various protections for officers who face allegations of abuse as well as hurdles for the public to file complaints.[75] Moreover, the separate interests of the police are the reason police associations around the country have been such solid supporters of figures like Trump, and why the "Blue Lives Matter" flag has become a fixture of the Nazi and white supremacist movement.[76] At least those extremists are honest when they admit that pro-cop means anti-Black.

One section of the left—influenced by figures like Adolph Reed—argues that while "police unions are wrong on the matter of police violence, through protracted work [police associations] might be moved to a more just position."[77] Such advocates are forced to admit that "there is good evidence to support" the conclusion that the police are "permanently reactionary."[78] The overwhelming evidence on police unions show them to be reactionary, racist, unaccountable, implicated in cover-ups, co-mingling with far right groups, and documented as having a long history with the Ku Klux Klan, with scant support to the contrary.[79] Indeed no other group of public "workers" is *designed* to do violence against the public. Therefore, as Dan Berger writes in a critique of this very position, "Being 'wrong on the matter of police violence' is a disqualifying disposition."[80]

The culture of silence and solidarity within police ranks ensures that there is no criticism from within. This "police culture" is generated and perpetuated by the institution of policing and its relationship to the state. There may be a minute handful of individual cops who have spoken up against police abuses at great personal risk, but juxtaposed with resistance in the military, there is no comparison.[81] Unlike in the military, where during every major war there is mass resistance—defections during the American Civil War, the soldier mutiny ending World War I, GI refusals to fight and "fragging" or killing of officers during the war in Vietnam, Iraq Veterans Against the War during Iraq, to name a few—there is no analogous historical or contemporary example of resistance movements among police at any level beyond that of isolated, rare cases.

An analogy that Darren Seals, a neighbor of Mike Brown, told me at Brown's funeral in Ferguson, Missouri, captures the political consequences. He said: "It's like you've got a bucket with a thousand poisonous snakes, and there are four or five good snakes. I'm not reaching my hand in and taking a risk with those five good snakes with those thousand in there. That's the police."[82]

Not only is there historically next to no organized resistance to the excesses of policing within the ranks, but when cops do rebel it is usually on the side of the state or far-right coups directed at state officials. This was seen in Bolivia in 2019, when Bolivian police made international headlines by "joining" anti-government protests.[83] It quickly became apparent that what was happening was not the police joining a mass movement but entering the fray as shock troops for a coup, carried out by pro-US capitalist and explicitly fascist forces, that deposed the democratically elected leftist president, Evo Morales.[84] Less than a week after the police "joined" the protest, they were carrying out a pogrom against mostly Indigenous activists in order to cement the reactionary coup against Morales.

The takeaway was most clearly expressed by Russian revolutionary Leon Trotsky, who said, "The worker who becomes a policeman in the service of the capitalist state is a bourgeois cop, not a worker."[85] Police should never be seen as allies of a working-class movement, and our position toward the institution should not be cooperation or compromise but antagonism. Cops

The Police State and Its Functionaries 135

should be seen as a separate social class with opposing interests, conditioned by the police's relationship with the state.

Black Cop: "You can't play both sides of the fence."[86]

Similar to the way that the relationship of cops to the state situates how they behave in "class ways" in antagonism toward workers, even Black cops can carry out the state project of racism. Just as many cops come from working-class backgrounds, it's true that many come from oppressed groups as well. While the demographics of policing skew whiter, with the percentage of white officers exceeding the percentage of the US white population, the relative diversity of the police is notable.[87] Nationwide, 12 percent of police are Black, the same percentage that Black folks comprise in the general population.[88] The NYPD is 53 percent nonwhite, with 15 percent of the force Black, in comparison with 20 percent of the city's population. The Los Angeles Police Department also has similar parity, with 10 percent of officers Black in a city that is 11 percent African American. In Chicago, a city that is 29 percent Black, 21 percent of its cops are Black, the same demographic percentage as the city's teachers. Of the top ten largest departments in the country, only two of them are majority white.[89]

Thankfully, the notion that having more Black cops is the key to fixing the institution has less prominence these days. In the recent past, even sections of the Black radical left argued for it as a component of the notion of Black community control. The prominent Black Power figure, SNCC leader, and Black Panther Kwame Ture (Stokely Carmichael) argued in 1967 that "a black sheriff can end police brutality."[90] The Panthers themselves shifted from their early focus on ending police brutality through armed self-defense (point seven of their famous ten-point program) to advocating that police be made up of people "from the community" and calling for "progressive police leadership" paired with community control.[91] This shift presaged the party's "shift to the middle" under Bobby Seale's 1973 Oakland mayoral campaign, which moderated their radical politics to the point of eventually entering the Democratic Party.[92] While this position has waned to some extent on the left, liberals still adhere to the idea that a more diverse policing body will cure the terminal disease of its violence and racism rather than admit that these features are part of its normal functioning.[93]

Starting in the early 1970s, police departments became more diverse, especially in the major cities. As of 2022, of the top fifty departments in the country, twenty-six were headed by Black chiefs.[94] Yet, the violence of the police has only become more militarized and lethal.

It also should be pointed out that there is nothing new about the notion of having the composition of police bodies drawn from the communities they police. This tactic, often termed *community policing*, is—to quote police historian Matthew Guariglia's work on racial policing in postwar NYC—"as old as policing itself."[95] It was part of the ruling-class motivation, from as far back as colonial policing bodies like the Royal Irish Constabulary, to improve the optics and legitimacy of the occupying force and also because it was believed that embedding within the community would increase the ease of police intelligence gathering. Increased demographic "representation" in police forces does not reduce the violence; it only serves to legitimize it.

It's important to keep the big picture in view here: policing is about enforcing a racist, radically unequal status quo. Because of this, the social role of police aligns Black cops against the interests of the Black population. Studies actually find that Black cops are as likely as white cops to commit abuse and murder.[96] Black police

The Police State and Its Functionaries

chiefs have presided over departments (Chicago, Baltimore, Dallas, and others) with egregious records of murder and racism.[97] A Black police chief, mayor, and National Guard Major General all suppressed the 2015 Baltimore uprising, which arose in response to the murder of Freddie Gray. The effect of this social role is precisely expressed by Black deputy police chief Malik Aziz, who said:

> I can no more separate my black skin from the color of this uniform that I don every day for so many years. This is what we have to understand even as black officers. Black people will shout to us, "Black lives matter." You know what our response is to the black people who shout to my black self that black lives matter? Is yes, they do, and it's starting with me. What's your response to that? My life has to matter, too.[98]

To officers like Aziz, the real criticisms of police violence are swept under the rug of crude racial representation. The fact that cops like Aziz cannot separate his oppressed identity from his oppressor occupation reflects the contradiction of the Black cop. The community says, "Stop killing us," and the Black cop says "What about me?"

One more illustration of this dynamic that has an air of tragedy is the story of Alex Kueng. Kueng witnessed the police abuse of a sibling and decided to be a cop, as he thought it the best way to change a broken system and told his mother he wanted to change it from the inside.[99] According to his mother, he thought improved diversity of the police would fix the institution and repair the relationship between the police and the Black community. Then, on May 25, 2020, Kueng held down George Floyd to the pavement while Derek Chauvin murdered him.

The solution to police brutality is not greater diversity of the police ranks. Being a cop, no matter who you are, is to take part in an occupation whose role is the violent and racist service of the state.

Familial Tension between Police and the State

The general belligerence of the police sometimes creates the impression that they are rogue actors or even a body that functions politically with interests autonomous from those of the ruling class. However, their existence as a socially cohesive, reactionary block is not at odds with the state but is rather a consequence of the role they play in enforcing the fundamental role of states within capitalism. Despite disagreements and feuds around strategic perspectives, while tension between police and different levels of governments exists, overall, the family is unified in the interests of capital.

In 2014, New York City mayor Bill de Blasio had a prominent conflict with the city's police association—the Patrolmen's Benevolent Association—and its cartoonishly super-villain-esque president, Patrick Lynch (who, among other things, blamed Eric Garner for his own choking death and dubbed the officer who killed him an "Eagle Scout"). A series of simmering issues came to a head after the killing of two NYPD cops. At their funeral, the uniformed officers standing at attention turned their backs on the mayor when he gave the eulogy.

Starting in 2018, Chicago mayor Lori Lightfoot and FOP president John Catanzara (a wannabe-Trumpian figure) sparred publicly around a number of events, including the city's mandate, in the fall of 2021, for city workers to receive the Covid vaccine. At the height of the conflict, Lightfoot disciplined officers without pay for refusing the vaccine and accused Catanzara

The Police State and Its Functionaries 139

of working to "induce an insurrection."[100] In 2023, Catanzara feuded with then mayoral candidate Brandon Johnson, threatening ominously that if Johnson won the mayorship there would be "blood in the streets."

Public battles like these with politicians often involve bullying by top cops and especially by their "unions." Their ever-escalating demands—almost always granted—for a greater and greater share of city budgets have been characterized by some as "extorting" democratically elected politicians.[101] The frighteningly commonplace overlap of police personnel with far-right and white supremacist organizations like the Oath Keepers, the Proud Boys, and the KKK adds to this. A widely reported 2022 article documented an "epidemic of white supremacists in police departments" and identified hundreds of scandals in over forty states related to this activity.[102] In 2006, even the FBI warned about the Nazi creep in cop ranks.[103] At least thirty off-duty cops participated in the debacle of January 6, 2021, fifteen of whom were charged as a result of the breaking and entering of the Capitol.

While the far-right overlap is a real danger, the conflicts between police headquarters and city halls can be overstated. After the dramatic gesture at the funeral in NYC, Lynch stated that it was de Blasio's "words, not his policies" that bothered them.[104] Lightfoot's entire short tenure as Chicago mayor was characterized by tough-on-crime policies, delivering what was then the largest police budget in that city's history, flipping on a campaign promise and building a new $95 million cop academy, and spending over a quarter of a billion dollars of federal Covid relief money on the police. In his first year in office, her successor, Brandon Johnson, offered CPD the largest raise it had received since the 1990s. In the end, while strategic questions of how to establish the best business climate or the acceptable amount of repression can create dramatic familial tension, the overall interests of the police and the state are aligned in the pursuit and maintenance of market order. This familial tension can also occur within different sections and levels of the state, and the process of determining the best action for business interests can provoke sharp disagreements and internecine conflict. The issues at stake range from fights about segregation in the 1960s to fights between Republican governors and Democratic mayors around asylum seekers today. But, in the end, what they are about is the best way to maintain capitalist stability and the highest rate of profit.

Such tensions arise as a consequence of the core police mission itself. Trained and conditioned as the attack dogs of states defending capitalist interests, a rabid and bellicose attitude has to be encouraged, to a greater or lesser extent. There are scarce alternatives, if the goal is to establish a body of people drawn from the ranks of workers and the oppressed, whose principal mission is to threaten and use violent force against their own. And, the sizable number of hardened racists notwithstanding, a large number of people become police with the goal of accessing a well-paying public job or because they buy into ideology about the benevolent role of police in society. But, to some extent due to the intensity of the pro-cop propaganda in the media and popular culture, police are socialized to develop a uniquely entitled psychology in which they frequently see themselves as victims, despite in reality being the biggest bullies on the block. The emergence of the "Blue Lives Matter" phenomenon, as a kneejerk response to the simple assertion that Black people are people, speaks to this clearly.

The police behave in ways sometimes at odds with local government, but, outside of situations of exceptional crisis, they should not be seen as a rogue threat, independent from a class-neutral state. Undoubtedly, any fascist movement in this

The Police State and Its Functionaries 141

country will find the police and their associations strongly represented.[105] However, to borrow the words of Stuart Hall on the overuse of "fascism," overstating the independent threat of the police to the state "cover[s] up, conveniently, everything which it is most important to keep in view."[106] What is important to keep in view is that the state itself necessarily acts on behalf of the ruling capitalist class, against the interests of working people. It is the state that funnels public tax dollars into corporate subsidies and war profiteers; it is the state building concentration camps for migrants on the southern border; it is the state that is expanding oil production amid a world on fire. Cops are its key agents and the main functionaries that allow states to operate in this way.

To fulfill their designated social role for the state, police are trained as ruthless attack dogs. To pursue the metaphor, sometimes an attack dog, trained in aggression, will bark or snap at its master even though the master still holds the leash. This dynamic mirrors that between the police and the state. The intensity and cruelty of police violence is not an aberration or a challenge to the state; rather, it is precisely how states maintain their power.

A Conclusion and a Segue

The set of institutions and personnel that comprise states in capitalism are the organized *means* by which the capitalist class formulates and pursues its interests in securing a market order conducive to the free flow and accumulation of capital. The behavior, policies, and general projects of states are shaped by the global competition at the heart of realizing value under capitalism. The world of capitalism, writes Colin Barker:

> is characterized not by the superimposition of "a state"
> but rather a condition of political anarchy. Only anarchy

142 Their End Is Our Beginning

> is not here linked with a condition of statelessness, but by a condition of having many states. . . . States stand in hierarchical and despotic relation to those they rule, while between their many units is anarchy. The rivalry between states, and the formal equality between them that is involved in their mutual recognition, is matched by their exploitative relations with their subjects.[107]

In states' relationship between each other and their relationship to their subjects, "all their practice and authority is rooted in the threat" and ability to use force, as Bittner pointedly remarks in reference to the police.

Understanding the police, especially with the aim to combat them, requires an understanding of capitalist states. The state's relative separation from, and placement of itself above, society is a function of the need for a special institution to generalize the interest of the capitalist system and act to further and reproduce it.[108] The violent role that cops take on in service of this end puts the police in conflict with the vast majority of the population, working-class people, and the oppressed, especially. This relation of hostility shapes their "class ways" as being in antagonism *as a class* against us: their material interest situates them as class enemies. As racism in the US is a core element in the reproduction of capitalist relations, the police have a special role in the reproduction of and reification of racism. Entrenching and expanding racism is a violent process enacted through the patrol of the occupier, the locks on the cages, the callousness of the courts, and, most blatantly, through the firing of the gun. Because it is so vital to the fundamental purpose of policing, the racism of the institution can even act through demographically diverse police forces, revealing the peculiar power of anti-Black racism in this ruinous country. Although police may have friction with local state officials, these are better understood as familial tensions rather than true conflicts of interest. It is the state that sets the agenda according to its own structural needs, and the police that allow it to do so. Every capitalist state is a police state.

These features of the relationship of the police and state have ramifications for our political aims about how we seek to organize. States are, at their core, "special bodies of armed men," and the most important special body for a state in relation to its own population is the police. The police, as an institution, are unreformable, and we cannot expect to shift the institution in any positive direction. No appeals should be made for them to change themselves or come to our side. Our appeal, our demand, is for them to be defunded, disarmed, disbanded, smashed, abolished.

chapter 4

An Ever-Raging Fire
International Revolt and Resistance

The police ran; what a moment of liberation.
—**Ibrahim**, Egyptian labor activist
and organizer of January 25, 2011[1]

Abolition of the police, the army and the bureaucracy.
—**Lenin**, on the tasks of the revolution, April 7, 1917[2]

I n June 2010, a young man in his twenties, from a lower middle-class neighborhood, was picked up by two plainclothes police from an internet cafe. Khaled, who was interested in computers and rap music, was suspected of being in possession of a small amount of marijuana. The cops began beating Khaled in an adjacent doorway, slamming his head against the wall and the steps. He was beaten to death there on the streets.

When his family went to the morgue to identify the corpse and collect the body of their beloved son and brother, they found his face was horribly disfigured by the police, his skull was fractured, jaw horribly dislocated, nose broken, and other signs of intense violence. His brother took a photo and shared it on social media.

The photo spread rapidly, and activists started a Facebook page publicizing what had been done to their loved one and calling for justice. A series of relatively small protests were called against the violence of the police, for the arrest of the officers, and eventually for the resignation of the governmental official in charge of the police. Seven months later, a call was put out for protests in the capital to coincide with National Police Day. In anticipation, the whole of the country's police force was deployed. Building on pent-up outrage, the protests exploded, and thousands came out and took to public squares.

Demonstrations spread throughout the country. Police attempted to force the people off the street using batons, water cannons, rubber bullets, and rounds and rounds of tear gas, but were met with heroic resistance and pitched battles in the street. People kept returning to the streets, and in greater numbers. Daily marches wound through the city, and if the throngs passed a police station, they would stop and chant the names of people killed by the police.[3] An open-ended occupation of several city squares began and was maintained and defended against police attempts at suppression. The slogans calling for the resignation of the head of police changed; the horizon was raised to a call for the fall of the entire government. After three days of defiant demonstrations and occupations of public space, the police literally disappeared from the streets. Various neighborhoods of the city created committees that implemented a "police curfew," establishing checkpoints to ensure that cops couldn't move freely throughout the city.[4] About half the police stations in the capital city were burned to the ground, and 60 percent were burned down in the city where Khaled was murdered.[5] Jails were opened and prisoners freed. Another turning point came when mass strikes in key sectors of the economy

An Ever-Raging Fire

broke out, building on each other in a domino effect until, just over two weeks after the protests began, the president resigned and the government fell. Celebrations erupted in the squares.

Examples and Lessons

These were the events of the 2010 police murder of Khaled Saeed, the 2011 Egyptian Revolution, and the downfall of the thirty-year reign of president Hosni Mubarak. I begin with this story because the events of the revolutionary process during the Arab Spring are not typically thought of as movements against the police. But this chapter will cover a series of struggles internationally that broaden the reference points for abolition and shed light on the kinds of movements and collective action that may be required to abolish the police. Imagining "a world without police" or rethinking "safety" are common refrains in movement literature and spaces in the US. In that creative endeavor, it serves us to have an expansive, international view. While the police of the US are particularly noxious, racist, and violent, policing is an international feature of capitalist states. One could argue that many international struggles against police have moved further toward the abolition of the police than struggles in the US, even though many of them were not self-consciously "abolitionist" in the way we may think of it in the US. While, in the end, these movements were defeated—a fact that shouldn't be glossed over—the lessons from both their high crests and their crashing falls are instructive.

Several revolutionary movements have contended powerfully with the police. Examples covered here include late 1960s Derry, Northern Ireland; Oaxaca, Mexico, in 2006; the events of the first wave of the Arab Spring in the 2010s; and the 1917 Russian Revolution. All these cases find people experimenting with the question of what "alternatives to the police" can be formed when a social struggle runs the police (sometimes literally) off the street, expanding its scope beyond individual campaigns or policy and opening up questions about the fundamental organization of society. Such revolutionary moments, it is important to mention, could only have built to these heights because of smaller campaigns building up to that point, creating networks, organizations, and movement cadre.

These examples underscore the arguments made in previous chapters about the relationship between capitalist states and the police. If "we are demanding that a carceral, racial capitalist state disarm itself," write abolitionists Mariame Kaba and Andrea Ritchie, "we are demanding that it stop performing its central functions."[6] What this means, they continue, is that "we need to fortify ourselves for a fight against a police state."[7] Even if they were not always conscious of it, the heroic movements detailed here, and many more, drew the profound and practical connection that the fight against the police is itself a fight against the state.

Last, although the focus here is on the role of antipolice organizing in these struggles, other grievances and causes helped set these revolutions ablaze as well. It is therefore important to situate these movement histories within the context of a web of conditions and grievances arising from the miseries of life under capitalism. Even so, organizing and mass insurgency against the police played an especially explosive role in igniting the fire of mass movements and propelling them forward.

Free Derry, Northern Ireland

For two significant periods between 1969 and 1972, large sections of the town of Derry, in Northern Ireland, were carved out as the autonomous Free Derry and operated with little interference from the state and its police.

An Ever-Raging Fire

Then as now, Northern Ireland was still a section of Ireland ruled by British colonialism. British rule involved a lack of voting rights, discrimination in housing, and other forms of oppression directed at the Catholic minority, who tended to side politically with independence from Britain and unity with the rest of Ireland. Beginning in the spring of 1968, a civil rights movement began to spring up against many of these conditions.[8] The movement picked up steam with various types of civil disobedience, including large marches from city to city that blocked roads. One of the organizations to play a key role was the Derry Housing Action Committee, in which several leaders and socialists in the movement, such as Bernadette Devlin and Eamonn McCann, were active.[9] In 1969, after increasing police brutality against the marches, the movement became more militant, and some of the marches began to fight back.[10] "The relationship between the civil rights struggle and the police," McCann told me, "was dictated and determined by the police themselves."[11] As such, the police had become, in the words of historian Niall Ó Dochartaigh, "*the* civil rights issue."[12]

Then, in August 1969, in response to rumors of a joint attack on a working-class neighborhood by the police and loyalist, pro-British organizations, activists formed the Derry Citizens Defence Association (DCDA) in preparation to defend the Irish republican, Catholic working-class neighborhood of Bogside. When the attack came, the police attempted to charge into the neighborhood. But the DCDA and the community were prepared with stones, sticks, and Molotov cocktails assembled the night before and were able to push the cops back. Historian Russell Stetler described what became known as the Battle of the Bogside as "a direct confrontation between *virtually a whole community* on one side and little more than the police on the other."[13] Barricades were erected with materials previously gathered and stowed, and within an hour they had blockaded every entrance to the Bogside.[14] The barricades stayed up after the police rout, and a mass meeting on the corner announced the creation of Free Derry. The level of organization within the movement was high, as McCann commented: "In every riot in Northern Ireland there is a person with a megaphone waiting for a meeting to start."[15] The iconic words "You Are Now Entering Free Derry" were painted on the walls at the corner, in what the painter, Liam Hillen, described as a declaration that "this is us, and you [the cops] are not in control . . . you are not coming into our territory and beating us up whenever you feel like it."[16]

This first iteration of Free Derry lasted only three months. But for that time, neither the police nor the British Army could enter the Bogside section of the city. To get a sense of size, Bogside encompassed about thirty thousand of the city's sixty thousand people, or about half of the city.

The DCDA grew rapidly to include representatives of various groups, tenants' associations, street committees, and, really, any individual who could "take a job that needed to be done."[17] Rooted in the organization of the movement, the DCDA displaced the authority of the established political parties. One police official sourly commented that the DCDA "were the defacto government of the area."[18] They issued demands for abolishing the B-Specials (a particularly notorious paramilitary police unit), disarming the police, and dissolving the Northern Ireland parliament.

In the absence of police, a group of unarmed activists, whose duty in the civil rights movement was to steward marches and keep them in control, put on armbands and took up the task of helping to manage conflict and the like. As a joke, the civil rights stewards took up the name of Free Derry Police.[19] Their role was largely negligible. McCann says that if they caught someone doing something they shouldn't, there wasn't any punishment aside from "a stern lecture about the need for solidarity."[20] "Which," he says, "seemed to work quite well." But without any particularly novel "alternative to the police," participants and observers noted that petty crime and disorder basically disappeared. This was attributed to the strong sense of the solidarity of mass struggle that infused all aspects of life in Free Derry. Everyone felt responsible for each other, McCann recounted, in the sense that if you violated the bonds of solidarity, you were letting the movement down, and that is what made crime basically disappear. "It was one of the most peaceful periods ever in Derry," he wrote.[21] Posters appeared all over the area, declaring that "barricades are nice."[22] Pubs stayed open all night long, Radio Bogside was established to tell stories of the movement, and a Free Derry *Fleadh Cheoil* (music festival) was organized.[23] Vacant houses were filled with people who needed housing, and collective meals were organized at the various local halls where the local assemblies of the DCDA met.

The first Free Derry ended when the barricades came down in October. But Free Derry would reemerge in a more substantial fashion two years later, in August 1971, when the British initiated a policy of internment and coordinated a wave of raids, mass arrests, and prolonged imprisonment. After the first night, in which 341 people from the Bogside were arrested, the barricades went back up, and Free Derry rose again. For a little over two weeks, the army tore down barricades and attempted to retake control with helicopters and armored cars. They found, however, that the barricades were "being erected as fast as the army was removing them." A combination of street

152   **Their End Is Our Beginning**

fights, mass protest, and sit-ins eventually forced the army and police out, and an "almost eerie calm" settled over the area.[24] This new iteration was a more serious endeavor and had even more mass support than the first Free Derry. The stones and Molotovs had been traded for guns, and the militias of the Official Irish Republican Army and the Provisional IRA (the Provos) took up roles in the movement. For a year, the police and the British Army remained largely expelled from the area. Residents stopped paying for rent and utilities, and the mail and milk were still delivered as some of the strong elements of solidarity and community organizing returned. Alternative public transit was organized through a repurposed fleet of taxis.[25] The Free Derry Police returned and largely carried out innocuous tasks like distributing cigarettes to the barricades and setting up the football goal on the pitch. As before, it wasn't so much that any organized alternative to the police mediated conflict or reduced so-called crime as it was social solidarity and the coherence of shared struggle. When I asked McCann what the Free Derry Police did, he told me: "I used to ask them that all the time: 'What are you fucking doing?'"

Perhaps even more than the guns or people throwing stones, the British ruling class saw the example of Free Derry and its existence outside the jurisdiction of the British state as an ominous threat. Any living example of people running society free from the parasitic control of capitalists and colonizers is a powerful symbol of the concrete possibility of a different world, and ruling classes always seek to crush them. That is exactly what the British set out to do, first with the "Bloody Sunday" massacre of a peaceful march in January 1972, and then with a coordinated attack in July of the same year that deployed tanks and thousands of British troops. In the largest British military operation in over fifteen years, the British moved in to destroy the barricades and re-establish their occupation.

The example of Free Derry shows that struggles can be politically radicalized through the issue of the police. A civil rights struggle about democracy and housing discrimination transformed into running the police from the street. In the Derry example, complicated alternative institutions were not needed to decrease crime and mitigate conflict.[26] The milk will still be delivered, and we will not have to pay rent to boot. "The idea of operating without any police force came naturally to people," said McCann. "It came as an act of defiance, but it was an act of defiance that didn't require anything of you other than you maintaining your defiance."[27]

Township Uprising, South Africa, 1984

In the long struggle to end the apartheid system in South Africa, one of the final chapters that contributed to the fall of formal white settler rule was an upsurge of popular struggle ascending in 1984 and lasting several years. These years have been referred to as the Vaal Uprising, or "insurrectionary period" of the anti-apartheid movement, and at its core were the township uprisings. During this period, large sections of townships—urban areas racially segregated by apartheid and designed to control and manage the Black working class—rose up in rebellion, repelled the police and the authorities of the apartheid government, and, in many areas, became police "no-go" zones. In the course of the struggle, "street committees" experimented with self-management of sections of the townships.

Since the 1960 Sharpeville massacre, the anti-apartheid movement had been in a period of retreat. But the course began to reverse, first with a massive wave of illegal strikes by Black

154   Their End Is Our Beginning

workers in Durban, in 1973, and then with the 1976 Soweto Uprising. In Soweto, school-age youth organized massive student demonstrations against the attempt to impose the Afrikaans language (largely spoken by whites) as the language for school classes. Police brutally attacked the march with tear gas, batons, and live rounds, killing youth as young as twelve in the street. In response, students rioted for days and burned down several government buildings. Black workers engaged in "stayaway" strikes in solidarity, with up to 75 percent of workers refusing to work in Johannesburg, the country's most populous city.[28] The struggle reverberated through the country and radicalized participants, as historian Noor Nieftagodien noted of Soweto: "At the start of the day students had set out to express their objections to Afrikaans. By the end of the day many had drawn the conclusion that the battle to be engaged was now against the apartheid system as a whole."[29]

Over the next several years, numerous struggles in a number of the townships began to spread and simmer until on September 3, 1984, in an industrial area just south of Johannesburg called the Vaal triangle, Black Africans demonstrated against an increase in rent and utilities in the townships. Before the increase, 58 percent of households in the Vaal were already in rent arrears.[30] These demonstrations also coincided with the opening of the Tricameral Parliament, a new system of separate and unequal legislative bodies for so-called Indians and so-called coloreds.[31] Black Africans were excluded from the new parliament and were instead relegated to Black Local Authorities, with limited administrative control of the townships through Black councilors. The cops responded to the demonstrations by shooting indiscriminately into the crowd, and once again police violence called forth an uprising.

An Ever-Raging Fire

Popular conflagrations in township after township saw youth armed with stones, makeshift weapons, and shields from trashcan lids, battling cops for control, while mass mobilizations pushed police off the streets. Government and police buildings were torched, and some of the detested Black councilors, collaborators who were responsible for administering apartheid rule over their own people, were killed. Hundreds of homes of Black policemen—who made up 50 percent of the South African police force—were firebombed in the first six months of the uprising.[32] To repel police from communities, organizations of youth in the Eastern Cape called *ambutho* used inventive strategies and homemade weapons, including digging Casspir traps, trenches that would trap police vehicles and allow the youth to pelt them with stones and Molotov cocktails.[33] The scenes were dramatic. As historian Franziska Rueedi describes, the crowds "acted as human barriers hindering police, the military and other government representatives from entering the townships."[34] The result was the creation of areas of liberated, police "no-go" zones, as the uprising effectively removed the sham Black Local Authorities and Black Africans took control of their own communities.[35] The *ambutho*, while inspired by the African National Congress's (ANC) armed wing—the *uMkhonto weSizwe* (MK)—organically grew out of initiatives from below, as the condition of exile severely inhibited the ANC's capacity to direct or lead the uprising in any real way.[36]

Rather, the uprising and the self-organization emerging from it were led by democratic street committees rooted in the neighborhoods. In the space created by the expulsion of the police and the administrative authorities, these street, block, and area committees began to organize around key social functions. Activist Tsietsi "Stompi" Mokhele described how, under the organization of street committees, "Streets were cleaned, often by youth who volunteered to become involved. Electricity and water meters were hacked and reconnected, parks were built and childcare facilities established."[37] Consumer boycotts and stayaway strikes were organized by committees as well. The goal, according to Mokhele, was to "make sure the communities run their own lives."[38] With schools closed, committees organized popular political education (*umrabulo*), covering themes such as the politics of the ANC, history of global revolutionary movements, and Marxism.[39]

Almost immediately after the onset of the rebellion, the government called off the rent increase. Patrick Noonan, in his eyewitness account of the rising, described how the concession resulted from negotiations carried out over the hood of a car with a line of riot police on one side and massive demonstration on the other.[40] But, at that point, the concession on rent did nothing to stifle a movement that had moved far beyond its initial demand. Indeed, the movement actually spread.[41] Mass rent strikes were organized so that only 18 percent of residents in the townships paid rent, and, by 1986, half a million households were on rent strike.[42] A central demand was the abolition of the police in the townships—in other words, the legal codification of what forces from below had already made a reality in many areas of the townships.

Experiments in popular courts were set up with the intent to manage communal conflict. Some of these focused on reparative action, centering "'collective justice' and caring community" and replacing punitive approaches with conciliatory ones with the "ultimate aim being social reintegration."[43] The experience of these courts, however, was decidedly mixed. Many became organs for settling scores, inherited some conservative and paternalistic ideas, wound up being punitive and violent, and were hardly an abolitionist model in themselves.[44] Still, they provide evidence that

An Ever-Raging Fire

experiments come to life when space is created, and show some glimmers of the possibilities when questions of social organization are not entirely encumbered by the baggage of capitalist society.

Of the liberated zones in the townships, senior policeman H. B. du Pleiss lamented: "I can tell you quite honestly that Port Elizabeth [one of the townships] was ungovernable." "The area and street committees," he worried, "exercised complete control over the masses."[45] There is little doubt that the hyperbole of "complete control" was a product of the ruling-class fear of democratic mobilization. ANC president Oliver Tambo's 1985 new year address called for these mobilizations to "render South Africa ungovernable" and to "challenge the apartheid authorities for control of these areas, emerging as the alternative power."[46] The clandestine ANC Radio Freedom sent out a stark broadcast: "The weapons are there in front of you, they are in the hands of the policemen themselves. Some of these policemen are coming back to sleep within our midst in the townships. We know where they live, let us break into their houses and take those guns that the apartheid regime gave them to kill us and turn those guns against them."[47]

During the battle for the townships, worker militancy was buoyed with new shop-floor organizing and an explosion of strikes, especially the political "stayaway" strikes. Nineteen eighty-seven saw the largest strike in the country's history, with 3.5 million miners going on strike as well as a two-day political strike of over 2 million workers.[48] The following year, another 3 million workers took part in a three-day political general strike. These examples are just a few highlights out of an overall wave that took off in 1985.

Fearing insurrection, the apartheid government carried out massive repression to quell the uprising, but due to its extent, the repression took time. A regional state of emergency was declared

158   **Their End Is Our Beginning**

in July 1985 and a national one in June 1986. The armed forces were sent into the townships on a campaign of mass arrest and targeted assassinations of leading activists. The street committees were not widespread or generalized enough to stand on their own as an alternative social power, despite romanticized overestimations of dual power by some commentators and ANC leaders.[49] By 1988, the uprising was over. Out of this context, negotiations emerged that led to the end of the system of racial apartheid.

Tragically, however, the end of racial apartheid did little to undo the system of racial capitalism. Today, a state headed by a Black government shoots down strikers just like the white-helmed state did.[50] "My sacrifice for the country," proclaimed Reid Mokoena, a prominent activist in the township uprising, "seems to have been for some people to have big cars and big houses."[51] Despite its tragic end, the township rebellion is an inspiring example of the possibilities of movements mobilized in opposition to a racist police state, and the creative capacities of community organization conducted even in difficult circumstances. Whole geographic areas were cleansed of the police, and the community organized rent strikes, free electricity and water, collective child-care, and even experiments in new forms of courts and democratic self-government. The rejection of the state and contestation with the police in the streets was an integral part that made that possible. It also showed that challenging apartheid would require an actual challenge against capitalism and the state itself.

Popular Mobilization of Oaxaca, Mexico, 2006

For five months, from June until October 2006, the southern Mexican city of Oaxaca operated with basically no police. A popular mobilization originating in a teachers' strike barricaded sections of the city and reorganized daily life. The state of

An Ever-Raging Fire

Oaxaca has one of the highest concentrations of Indigenous people in Mexico, with 48 percent of the total population belonging to one of the sixteen different, formally recognized Indigenous communities. The teachers' union in Oaxaca—Section 22 of the National Educational Workers Coordination (CNTE)—has a long history of militancy, and at the time it was common for the union to have one-year contracts. This meant that teacher strikes to bring the government to the table became an annual tradition, paired with an encampment of Oaxaca city's central square—the *Zócolo*—and the surrounding streets, which were filled that May with a festive but militant protest occupation and many hundreds of teachers and families from around the state.

On June 14, the governor sent the police with tear gas and batons to violently clear out the encampment. According to René González Pizarro, a participant in the mobilization I interviewed, the encampment and the police entered into a battle for the square starting at 5 a.m., which continued until 1 p.m. and resulted in victory for the encampment and the police literally running away.[52] In the context of mass dissatisfaction with the neoliberal policies of the governor, the outrage caused by cops attacking and tear gassing teachers and their families, combined with a newfound confidence after pushing back the police, triggered an escalation into a larger social struggle. Over 350 organizations joined the teachers' union, and large public assemblies, dubbed the Popular Assembly of the Peoples of Oaxaca (APPO), were convened to democratically organize the social mobilization.[53] These public assemblies were not spontaneously invented on the spot but were a strategy learned in previous labor struggles and fights to democratize the union.

Barricades were set up around the central square and surrounding streets. One innovative tactic for building the barricades involved older women activists boarding buses and announcing, "This vehicle is being requisitioned by the popular mobilization." After everyone was safely off the bus, it would be parked to block the street and then set on fire. As Pizarro recounted to me, the mobilization also appropriated giant construction vehicles and used them to pile up burned-out cars as barricades.

Chased off the street and still facing such a broad mobilization, the police gave the order not to leave their headquarters. Some of the smaller headquarters around the state were taken over by activists and the police evicted. Thousands of new barricades were established around the city to restrict movement by the police and the paramilitaries.[54] The governor fled the town, leaving no police, with the popular mobilization ostensibly in control of the city. Members of the popular mobilization covered the walls of the city with beautiful political graffiti, while others took over the radio station and used it to publicize mass actions and warn of the location of paramilitaries.[55]

In August, a women's *cacerolas* demonstration (banging of pots with spoons) marched on the state *Canal Nueve* TV station and demanded they present more balanced coverage than the anti-mobilization programing being aired. When the TV bosses refused the demands and shut down the station, the demonstration kidnapped them and forced them to turn the station back on. With the assistance of communications students from the university enlisted to the cause, the TV station was reopened under control of the mobilization. Under popular control, the station was used to broadcast political documentaries and share information about the mobilization. Many participants had been deprived of a political voice their whole lives by the oppression of the Mexican state, and they now used the popular TV station to talk about their lives, neighborhoods, and their struggles, truly giving voice to the voiceless.

An Ever-Raging Fire   161

The mobilization organized a series of mega marches to continue to galvanize support and spread their message. In interviews, activists who participated told me that the number was close to four hundred thousand for these marches, a number that exceeds the population of Oaxaca by one hundred thousand. People from around the state had traveled to participate and show solidarity. On August 18, a statewide general strike took place, and, in September, thousands marched the roughly 250 miles from Oaxaca to Mexico City.

"The Paris Commune made it 70 days. We have lasted more than 100," went one refrain of the mobilization.[56] For close to five months without police, despite the fever nightmares of the political right, the streets did not descend into criminality and chaos. An unarmed patrol—the *cuerpo de topiles*—walked the streets and checked the barricades, but their main function was looking out for possible attacks by the government and the right-wing paramilitaries, who made several attempts to attack activists. The *cuerpo* were descended from *la guardia* self-defense committees formed to protect the *Zócalo*. During the day, life proceeded. It was not as though petty crime simply went away—indeed, the movement was not able to reverse inequality in four short months. Pizzaro did note, however: "Definitely I can say that [crime] didn't go up. But the good thing is that the police were not doing it also." In other words, the criminal behavior of the police was entirely eliminated.

Sadly, stymied in their prior attempts to take back the city through police action, paramilitary raids, and a media smear campaign, the Mexican state made a concerted effort to remove the burgeoning social experiment. Beginning on October 29, the government launched a massive repressive campaign, attacking the mobilization with the full weight of the military, including

Their End Is Our Beginning

tanks, helicopters, live rounds, and chemical weapons. After a month of brutal state repression, the counterrevolution had its day: the barricades were taken down, the cops came back, and many activists were arrested.

Still, the popular mobilization of Oaxaca remains an inspiring example of how movements against the police can serve as a catalyst for larger social struggle. By running police off the streets and seizing control, organizers created space for new democratic institutions and ways of life to flourish.

MENA Intifada: Tunisia, Egypt, Syria, 2011

The events of the Egyptian Revolution described at the beginning of this chapter were part of a much broader wave of rebellions and revolutions that swept the Middle East and North Africa (MENA) region beginning in 2011.[57] Though seldom acknowledged as such, these revolutions represent one of the more powerful modern movements against police violence. Organizing against police brutality was an essential contributor to these uprisings that shook the region, toppled governments, inspired the globe, and kicked into gear a revolutionary process that found expression in a second wave of revolts and revolutions in 2019.[58] The generative force of organizing against state violence was a key dynamic that is often discounted in accounts of the rebellions. Moreover, for brief periods of time several of these revolutions achieved (in different ways) something akin to police abolition.

Years before the Egyptian Revolution, a prelude to the Arab Spring was brewing in Tunisia. Between January and July 2008, Tunisia's phosphate mining basin of Gafsa exploded in a wave of protests, sit-ins, street battles, and a general strike. The protests did not yet target the president and the state but swelled in response to unemployment, poverty, and corruption. One feature

An Ever-Raging Fire

163

of these protests was the fierce antagonism against the police. In one town, Redeyef, masked youth attacked a police station, and high schoolers and unemployed youth fought street battles against police—complete with fiery barricades.[59] The demonstrations exerted control over the streets, and, overwhelmed by the militancy, the police were forced to redeploy outside the city.[60] The protests and the general strike failed to spread, however, and eventually the Gafsa Rebellion was harshly suppressed with hundreds of arrests.[61]

With these events in recent memory, in 2010, in the Tunisian town of Sidi Bouzid, a vegetable peddler named Mohammed Bouazizi suffered continual police harassment for not having the right permits to sell his goods and was forced to pay bribes. In December of that year, the harassment escalated when a cop seized his wares and beat him up. He went to the city hall to retrieve his belongings and was refused entry. In desperate protest he doused himself in gasoline, proclaiming, "How do you expect me to make my living?" and set himself on fire. He died eighteen days later.

Within hours, protests began in Sidi Bouzid, soon spreading across the country. They were met with intense violence from the police, who killed dozens. The Tunisian General Labor Union (UGTT) called a rotating general strike around the country that culminated in mass demonstrations in Tunis, the capital.[62] While the military stood aside due to mass pressure and fear of mutiny, the movement overthrew the twenty-four-year reign of president Zine al-Abidine Ben Ali. Its gains included the beginning of a process for a new constitution, the first free elections, and the swift abolition of the State Security Department, which included the political police.

The spark that caused the conflagration was a brutal incident of police violence that ignited resistance. The success of the mass rebellion in Tunisia had a radicalizing effect and raised the aspirations of the peoples of the region. In the streets of Tunis, a chant was born that would soon be repeated by massive crowds in cities all over the Middle East and North Africa: "The people want the fall of the regime!"

In Egypt, similar seeds of revolt were sprouting, even before the movement for Khaled Saeed. As Hossam el-Hamalawy, a prominent activist in the revolution, recollected in an interview with me, the "turning point in dissent" began in June 2004, with the first protest explicitly being against the police and their widespread use of torture.[63] El-Hamalawy described how many of the individuals who organized this small protest of two hundred and faced repression by riot police ended up playing key roles in the movements that culminated in the fall of Mubarak.[64]

But it was the success of the Tunisian Uprising that gave flower to the dissent around police torture and the murder of Saeed and subsequently accounted for the explosion of protest in Egypt. "The popular support for the revolution was to a large extent motivated by antagonism toward the police," writes scholar Salwa Ismail.[65] According to el-Hamalawy, who was on the front lines during the National Police Day protest, when the cops were run off the streets they literally stripped off their uniforms on the spot and sprinted home in their boxers.

Their absence created the space for organizing the counterpower of the *al-lajaan al-sha'abiya*, the Popular Committees (PCs). The protests did not content themselves with demonstrations but began organizing. From the neighborhoods to the open-ended occupations of the revolutionary *maidan* (squares), activists turned public spaces into densely organized hubs, offering food, medical care, open political debate, cultural spaces,

An Ever-Raging Fire

and security established at the perimeter. The maidan, and, most important, Cairo's Tahrir Square, were places of refuge where people received aid they did not receive from the government; places of joyous celebration, with concerts at night and singing of revolutionary songs; and places of battle, requiring physical defense against attack by regime thugs (*baltagiyya*).

Referring to the period after the cops were forced to disappear and before their reinstatement, el-Hamalawy asserted confidently that without police on the streets, "Cairo was never safer than during those three months. Seriously, the safest three months in my whole life." "Things were amazing at that time," he remembered. The lack of crime and relative safety could partially be explained by the PCs, he told me, but, more important, "there was this feeling," independent of the political composition of the PCs, "where we felt like part of one big family where everyone is caring for and looking out for the other."[66] Safety was created through solidarity.

The first function of the PCs was to provide an alternative to the police in order to maintain order in the neighborhoods. However, due to their democratic functioning and the creative space carved out by the revolution, they were described in one study as follows:

> By mobilizing publicly, the local inhabitants gained voice and were able to exert pressure on the authorities to either finally implement projects they had approved years ago, or to react to the grievances of the inhabitants. . . . This included getting access to the gas network of the city, getting streets redone, having illegal garbage dumps removed, planting trees, restoring public recreation spaces, and setting up a new local library and a small youth center.[67]

The PCs also ensured that the movement progressed beyond the retreat of the police from the street into developing a counterpower against the state. Through the "police curfew" and the use of checkpoints to track or limit police movement, PCs prevented the police from being able to regroup or remobilize. This infrastructure played a key role in limiting the repressive capacity of the regime and ensuring that the sit-ins of the squares could be maintained. At the same time, as el-Hamalawy and others have pointed out, the role of the PCs can be overstated or glamorized. The PCs assisted with collective order, but they were formed on very practical grounds and not every PC even aligned politically with the revolution. While these committees perhaps serve as an example of the seeds of popular power, the PCs—even as the regime fell and the Egyptian state wobbled under pressure of the revolution—cannot yet be described as an alternative challenge to the existing state, rising to the level of a dual-power scenario. That advanced revolutionary situation—dual power—almost always occurs in times of deep political crisis and describes the development of some form of organized social force or counterpower to the point where it is contesting the existing capitalist state for control of society and the economy.[68]

The organization in the street and in the maidan was paired with a surge of workplace organizing. Five days into the revolution, workers organizing independent of the state established the Egyptian Federation of Independent Trade Unions. Many managers—"Mubaraks in the workplace"—were ousted by workers and some established committees to run their workplaces.[69] Self-organized workers set up liaisons across workplaces and regions, and, in February, a total of 200,000 workers engaged in 489 strikes across Egypt.[70]

An Ever-Raging Fire 167

One can imagine how the PCs, combined with workplace organizations, could have become the seeds of a dual-power alternative to the existing state, had they been able to develop further and had there been rooted left-wing organizations of sufficient size to influence the direction of the movement toward deepening democracy and working-class collective self-reliance.

The revolutionary movement culminated in the fall of Mubarak and persisted beyond his fall. Despite the later counterrevolution, the people of Egypt amplified the confidence generated by Tunisia and changed the politics of the world.[71] The Egyptian example buoyed confidence in Syria, where probably the most heroic and the most tragic of the struggles of the region occurred. Again, the Syrian revolution serves as an example about how police violence can be a detonator for larger social struggles and can even lead to revolutionary situations. After the revolutions in Tunisia and Egypt, some small protests emerged in Syria. But, in mid-February, a group of teenagers in the town of Deraa painted a wall with the words, "Your turn doctor," a reference to Syrian dictator Bashir al-Assad, who was an ophthalmologist before becoming a despot. Fifteen youths were rounded up by the police and tortured for the graffiti. Fierce protests erupted in Deraa, and by the time the youths were released in March, protests had spread throughout the country, fueled by a combination of increased confidence, outrage at the intense police violence directed at the demonstrations, and desperation spurred by the awareness that the struggle had life-or-death stakes.

The trajectory of the Syrian Revolution, subject as it was to the barbaric brutality of al-Assad's scorched-earth counterrevolution and a number of other factors, very quickly led to an armed conflict with complicated political dynamics.[72] However, similar to the Egyptian example, mass protests and armed resistance forced the state out of hundreds of newly liberated towns, and experiments in democratic self-governance flourished. Local Coordinating Committees (LCCs, or *tanseeqiyat*), organs first developed to coordinate the weekly protests, developed into alternative institutions to the state that managed the needs of the liberated areas. In many cases, the LCCs were modeled on the Egyptian Popular Committees as well as the work of Syrian anarchist organizer Omar Aziz—who was jailed by the regime in November 2012 and died three months later in prison. Continuing the international pattern, the organizing of the LCCs led in a number of instances to forcing the police out of the cities—contributing to their grassroots popularity and legitimacy.[73] Yasser Munif, who spent time doing research in the liberated town of Manbij, described to me in an interview how, as the protests swelled, the police in Manbij responded with repression and by kidnapping demonstrators, to which protests responded by demanding their release.[74] This constant cycle of confrontation culminated in a large protest at the police station. When the cops called for back-up, none came. The police gave up, removed their uniforms, and fled. "When people realize that the 'all powerful state' can't do anything," Munif said, "and realize that they massively outnumber the police, then the whole apparatus collapses. This was a surprise to all involved."[75] In the rush, untouched cups of coffee and tea were left behind by the cowards. After the inglorious exit of the police and other agents of the state repressive apparatus (*mukhabarat*), the towns organized by the LCCs were able to operate with almost no violence or theft, in what Munif described as "complete peace."[76] Revolutionaries opened the jails of Manbij and freed the prisoners, subsequently maintaining the empty jail as a memorial or site of pilgrimage for people to bear witness to the bowels of Assad's carceral state. In those months,

An Ever-Raging Fire   169

activists with the LCCs organized barricades and nightly patrols to prevent regime infiltration. They also maintained a presence at the market and bakery to de-escalate conflicts over bread, which, unfortunately, occurred with some regularity in the context of the regime's counterrevolutionary brutality.

Several months later, the community did eventually move to create a new police force to deal with minor incidents and make sure garbage was picked up. However, Munif contends that it was largely ineffective. The key difficulties of the city involved the militarization of the revolution and an influx of armed brigades, funded externally—mostly from Gulf countries—but the new "police" were incapable of handling these. As a body separate from the community tasked with maintaining "order," the new police proved useless. Rather, it was when the community stood together that the armed, often outsider, brigades were effectively contested. For example, when one of the armed groups attempted to control the flour mill that was vital for bread production for the whole region, the LCC issued statements, organized demonstrations, and showed that the entire population was behind them, forcing the return of the mill to the community.

As we now know, the early years of the Syrian Revolution turned to tragedy. Still, there is much to learn from these developments showing that, even in the most difficult of circumstances, revolutionary creativity and self-organization were able to flourish in the space opened up by the removal of the police. It was that very fact that made the revolution so dangerous— and why Assad, seeing the writing on the wall and anticipating his downfall, decided to bathe the country in blood.[77]

The various struggles of the MENA revolutions—especially in Tunisia, Egypt, and Syria—show how struggles against police violence can be the detonator for larger social struggle;

170 **Their End Is Our Beginning**

how, at their height, movements against the police lead to confrontations with the state; and how sweeping the police aside opens up space for the creation of new democratic institutions. The experiences of these revolutionary situations also suggest how new democratic organizing infrastructure could lay the groundwork for dual power or a counterpower to the capitalist state, built from below. Finally, these experiences also confirm Saint-Just's grim historical lesson: to make a revolution halfway is to dig your own grave.

Russian Revolution, 1917

Our final example jumps further back in history to the world-shaking revolutionary events of Russia, in 1917. From February to October, a revolutionary process unfolded in Russia that culminated, for the first time in history, in workers themselves taking power through the form of their highly democratic councils (or *soviets*, in Russian). In that year, their attempt to build a socialist society was carried out in the hopes of buoying further revolutions that could overthrow capitalist states and the capitalist system internationally.

The "soviet power" was described by Russian revolutionary Vladimir Lenin as "a new type of state without a bureaucracy, without police . . . that gives [working people] legislative and executive authority, that makes them responsible."[78] Quotes like this, from revolutionary socialists with key roles in the revolution, reflect a belief that police abolition was a key component of the struggle for socialism. It was, in fact, what the Russian Revolution enacted.

On International Working Women's Day, in February 1917, striking women workers launched what would become a revolution against the Russian tsar. Almost immediately, they were

An Ever-Raging Fire

171

confronted by the police, who attempted to break up the strike. The strikers fought back, joined in swelling waves by other workers, who went on the offensive and attacked police stations. By day three of the revolution, the police were ordered to cease all patrols, return to headquarters, and await orders. But no orders came. As the tsarist police came to find out, their superiors had changed into civilian clothes and escaped out the back door. Their underlings soon followed suit. "We simply went home, leaving police headquarters, which were burned down by the evening," writes one precinct police chief.[79]

Revolutionary workers set about burning police stations to the ground, setting court buildings on fire, and torching prisons after freeing those jailed within.[80] "The attacks on the prison," writes one authoritative historian of the revolution, "began establishing a sense of solidarity" between the revolutionary workers and rebelling soldiers.[81] The police "vanished,"[82] and, with them out of the way, the crowd marched, orchestra in the lead, to the royal palace.[83]

Socialists and liberals hotly debated many points in the course of the early negotiations to create a new provisional government for the country. But, as one moderate socialist wrote in his eyewitness account, the "abolition of the police" was one plank of the minimum program that had been easily agreed upon. While issues of elections and a Constituent Assembly were hotly contested, the abolition of the police was—perhaps astonishingly to the contemporary observer—uncontroversial, and even seen by the liberals as "moderate" and "good sense."[84]

Lenin and the Bolshevik Party he helped organize saw the importance of the efforts to abolish the police as essential to the successful completion of the revolution. Consequently, throughout the months that followed, the Bolsheviks organized against

Their End Is Our Beginning

the reinstatement of the police. In March 1917, Lenin wrote:

> In many other places the police force has been partly wiped out and partly dissolved. The [liberal provisional government] *cannot* either restore the monarchy or, in general, maintain power *without restoring* the police force as a special organization of armed men under the command of the bourgeoisie, separate from and opposed to the people. That is as clear as daylight.[85]

"Prevent the restoration of the police!" he implored, arguing that the creation of a people's militia was needed to prevent the re-establishment of the police, which he called the "anti-people's militia." Such proactive organization was essential for furthering the revolutionary movement "of every exploited toiler who cannot help hating the policemen." In May, Lenin argued that, to carry out any significant reforms, "one must not allow the police to be reinstated." Indeed, "no important radical reforms in favor of the working masses can be implemented through the police." Such plans, he insisted, were "objectively impossible."[86]

These arguments were carried through in the second revolution in October, when the revolutionary workers and soldiers replaced the bourgeois state with direct democratic control by the councils, which had proliferated over the course of the prior year into workplaces, neighborhoods, and army units.[87] After years of repression and police harassment, the new revolutionary government wasted no time. In the first month of the October revolution, the police and the courts were abolished by the Decree of the Soviet of People's Commissars Concerning the Courts No. 1.[88] Prisoners organized themselves into councils, too, and in part due to their petitions, thousands of imprisoned people were freed, irrespective of whether they were political or common-law prisoners.[89] Replacing the old carceral systems, the people established elected popular courts and attempted experiments with justice that moved beyond the notion of imprisonment as the only solution.[90]

Bolshevik legal theorists like Evgeny Pashukanis saw "the criminal jurisdiction of the bourgeois state [as] organized class terror"[91] and attempted to move beyond "the essentially incoherent notion that the severity of each crime can be weighed on a scale and expressed in months or years of imprisonment."[92] Pashukanis viewed the idea of punishment carried out through "deprivation of freedom" as a loathsome signature of a capitalist legal system that needed to be abolished.[93] Instead of guilt, he advocated the concept of "harm," and, instead of punishment, proposed to "substitute treatment, that is to say a concept of medical-health."[94] Pashukanis's questioning of punishment logics presaged current abolitionist conceptions of alternatives to punishment while also presenting an understanding of crime as a social problem to be solved collectively.

While many of the popular courts and tribunals were necessarily focused on countering sabotage and counterrevolution, even these cases were handled with an astonishingly restorative approach given the circumstances of the early months of the revolution. For better or worse, many members of the previous, deposed government and military were freed with nothing more than public censure and a verbal promise not to engage in counterrevolutionary activity.[95]

There is much more to be said about the Russian Revolution, and any lessons have to honestly reckon with the fact that, when international revolutions failed to provide a lifeline, the revolution degraded, as counterrevolution reared its head. The state repressive apparatus was not only repaired but also developed further into the apparatus that carried out Stalin's purges and the gulag. Assessing these developments would go beyond the scope of this chapter.[96] The defeat of Bolshevik abolitionism must ultimately be understood as one part of the defeat of the Russian Revolution itself. But, by turning a spotlight on certain features of the revolution, we can see how police abolition was an essential component of the overthrow of capitalism.

Conclusion: "Oh freedom, where are you? The police stand between us and you."[97]

Above are only a few examples—the histories of popular struggle are filled with the stories of ordinary people shedding long-held fears, unleashing creative energies, and inventing new nonpolicing institutions in moments of revolutionary upheaval. There are countless other instances of police abolition woven into revolutionary struggles against capitalism as a core and often decisive element.

In 1871, the working people of France undertook a valiant experiment in working-class self-rule during the seventy days of the Paris Commune. Over the course of two months, revolutionary workers expelled the government and ran the city under direct democratic control, removing the police in the process. "It was totally unthinkable," historian Alain Dalotel writes, "that a single cop might remain in Paris . . . the Communards abolished the police."[98] The old police headquarters were used by Communards to ferret out counterrevolutionary officers of the old order.[99] There were no murders in the Commune for those two months,[100] and, in the words of Karl Marx, "no more corpses at the morgue, no nocturnal burglaries, scarcely any robberies; in fact, for the first time since the days of February 1848, the streets of Paris were safe, and that without any police of any kind."[101]

An Ever-Raging Fire

For a week in 1919, militant workers during the Seattle General Strike took over and ran the city. Safety was maintained by the unarmed, arm-banded Labor War Veterans Guard, who—equipped only with persuasion and the prestige of the unions—patrolled the streets to preserve order "without the use of force."[102] The Major General of the Army brought in to suppress the insurrection admitted with surprise that he had "never seen so quiet and orderly a city."[103]

During the 1936–1937 Spanish Revolution, many cities abolished police for over a year and replaced them with armed worker defense committees and "control patrols" under the democratic control of barricade committees or village assemblies.[104] Similar to the Paris Commune, the main remit of the control patrols and defense committees was to prevent counter-revolution.[105] During the revolution, many prisons were closed and prisoners freed, such as the women's prison in the Raval neighborhood of Barcelona, left vacant under a banner reading, "This torture house was closed by the people, July 1936."[106]

From these and many more revolutionary struggles around the world, many important lessons can be drawn, related to the way police coalesce social anger, the relationship of police to the state, the contours of alternative social arrangements, and the challenge of defeat. First, the police often coalesce, focus, and sharpen much broader societal grievances. In many of the movements described above, the early demands revolved around issues of democracy, land, housing rights, union contracts, and the like, before a mass explosion. Keeanga-Yamahtta Taylor has pointed out this dynamic in connection with the 2020 George Floyd / Breonna Taylor Rebellion, in which overlapping economic and epidemiological crises created a wider condition of mass unemployment and the mass death caused by the Covid

176   **Their End Is Our Beginning**

pandemic. As Taylor stated on *Democracy Now*, "I don't believe these are just protests around or against police brutality."[107] We were witnessing, she concluded, "the convergence of a class rebellion with racism and racial terrorism at the center of it." The nexus of that convergence was police violence.

In other words, while the lineages of the revolts could be traced to a host of conditions imposed by global capitalism, struggles against police violence very often served as the catalyst for a qualitative shift in the movement, especially in cases in which state violence targets the movement and its actors during the course of other fights for social change. Police are the front-line managers and representatives of the state; far from friendly faces, they greet us with derision and scorn. For example, when our protests attempt to express themselves to a politician, it is the row of cops at the door that greets us, stops us, and stands in the way of our fight for change. In doing so, they become the target, which is precisely a result of their function.

Second, social movements against the police tend to quickly open up larger questions about the undemocratic character of the society the police are defending. Police are not the sole cause of the various miseries of life under capitalism, but they do represent the boundary that keeps the capitalist way of life together, the sharp point of the spear of the violence that underpins the world we live in. Ordinary people have basically no say in our workplaces or in our government, and we are forced to work often awful jobs to survive so that the ultrarich can continue to maximize profits and enjoy total control of society. The symbolic edge of this injustice is the ability of the state to physically attack and control working people with little pretense, to the point of gunning us down in the street. This is especially the case if you are Black or brown, as the

An Ever-Raging Fire 177

constant feature of US policing is the violent reification, reproduction, and maintenance of a racist order. But when neighbors or coworkers get organized and stand up for relief and
basic human dignity, whether in the workplace, the streets,
the tenant unions, or the prison cells, increasingly spectacular
police repression provides a forcible reminder of the limits of
our "democracy." The usual consent of society to a life determined by the market is frayed. When police act on their core
purpose, they show what it is they protect—and who it is they
serve. Cops coalesce, sharpen, and focus the manifold grievances created by this unequal and undemocratic system.

Third, revolutionary movements against the police and experiments with abolition show that truly posing a challenge to
police violence will quickly require challenging the capitalist
state and therefore capitalist rule. The police are not append-
ages to a state that is class neutral. Rather, the police embody
the monopoly of violence used by a capitalist state to maintain
racist class rule. The heroic struggles covered in this chapter—
especially those of the Arab Spring and in Russia—demonstrate that the level of struggle required to make a real impact
on state violence must be waged against not only the police but
also the state. Egyptian revolutionaries, for example, realized
that it was not just the Ministry of the Interior but the whole
regime that had to be taken on in order to address their basic
problems. Russian revolutionaries understood that, to actually
win, to have a chance to reorganize our social life, the state had
to be overthrown. That wider confrontation with the state, I
would argue, is how struggles become truly revolutionary. It is a
point taken up further in the concluding chapter.

Fourth, in the historical experiences described above, it was
not the alternatives to police themselves that pushed the police

Their End Is Our Beginning

out of the way or rendered them obsolete. In every instance, the police were first cleared out of the way, forced out of the street or out of their uniforms, and made to flee. The defeat of the police, at least for a time, was what created the necessary space that allowed for the possibility of alternatives to be created in a real way. Moreover, in many of the examples, it did not take complicated or intricately developed "alternatives" to facilitate people in struggle organizing their social life with relatively little crime and attending to the needs of the community. The social cohesion created by organizing oppositional counterpowers to the state in a common struggle can promote a feeling of community care, highlighted especially in the Egyptian and Irish examples. As people participate in struggles to change the world, we should not underestimate the way that people themselves are changed by that process. It is through these crucibles of collective action and mutual dependence that any community of people can become like Free Derry, where "operating without the police came naturally to people."[108] From many of these examples, it is clear that for alternative institutions to the police to be effective, they must seek not just to replace the police but to replace the state itself.

The US abolitionist movement continues to make tremendous contributions to the creative reimagining of new institutions while taking great care not to replicate carceral systems and thinking. In my interview with Hossam el-Hamalawy, he spoke to this directly in his reflections that abolitionist politics could have better equipped the Egyptian movement in the days after the fall of Mubarak for debates about police unions, the overwhelming focus of NGOs on "reforming" the police, and thinking through what alternatives are needed.

Last, there is a negative lesson to take from these cases in that they all, in the end, were defeated. Not just defeated but, especially in the examples of the Arab Spring and Russia, brutally crushed by counterrevolution in catastrophic fashion. In some ways that is unsurprising, because we haven't yet won our freedom from capitalism. In order to begin building a different kind of world, we will have to pry open our political and imaginative horizons and begin to lay the foundations of an international movement against global capitalism and the police states that uphold it. For now, we have yet to win our fight to abolish the police state.

It is this final question, about what it will take to win abolition, to which we now turn.

chapter 5
Revolutionary Abolitionism

Abolition requires that we change one thing: everything.
—Ruth Wilson Gilmore

We call communism the real movement which abolishes the present state of things.
—Karl Marx

Our dreams of abolition are born of a damnation of the sadistic, heartbreaking social order. How do we, all together, sculpt this vision into a physical world from the seemingly insufficient materials on hand, inherited from the past? In many ways, movement strategy discussions are evolving constantly through practical experience and theoretical insight. From the history and international experience of the police as presented in this book, many implications for organizing could be drawn. But we must start by grappling with the central fact of what police actually represent within the social order we live under: a primary guarantor of state authority and the linchpin of capitalist power. While making arrests and locking people up are part of the role of the cops, this is not their fundamental role. As Ben Brucato points out, in their work on racism and the origins of the police:

Their End Is Our Beginning

> Only a tiny fraction of police activity results in arrest, a minority of arrests result in criminal charges, fewer yet are prosecuted, and the majority of prosecutions do not end with prison sentences. In most cases officers and administrators alike prefer to respond to crime without recourse to the law and without making arrests. . . . Countless police engagements each year do not result in arrest but are necessary to the productive function of police in the fabrication of social order.[1]

This is the component of discretion that underlies the "situational despotism" of the police.[2] The cops and their ideologues are clear about this, as the blunt framing of police sociologist Egon Bittner spells out: "The police role is far better understood by saying that their ability to arrest offenders is incidental to their authority to use force."[3] "Police intervention," Bittner continues, "means above all making use of the capacity and authority to overpower resistance to an attempted solution in the native habitat of the problem."[4] Although perhaps not Bittner's immediate intention, we can understand the "attempted solution" to be that of capitalist order. Again, Sidney L. Harring's definition of the police is essential: "A full time, permanent force capable of continually asserting the power of the capitalist state," as they walk their beats, twirling their clubs of wood and law.[5]

More often, the threat of force alone serves as a reminder of their power. Their mandate is to produce compliance by threat or by force. Every command—"Move along," "Hands up," "Step back," "Keep your hands on the wheel"—is followed by the often silent imperative, ". . . or else." We are "policed," wrote political economist Adam Tooze—after witnessing the draconian and authoritative repression of student encampments

Revolutionary Abolitionism

against the genocide in Gaza, in April 2024—"not just abstractly but physically, guarded, bounded, out-muscled."[6] The threat of violence, sometimes held in reserve, is what gives states all their authority once the veil of "consent" is stripped away. It is not just the traffic stop: "Pay your taxes," "Follow the law," "Stop the strike," "Disperse your protest," "Leave this country" all carry the silent threat of eventual police violence behind them. In the words of foundational police theorist Patrick Colquhoun, the office of the police is not like other public offices: "It is, or ought to be constant, laborious, and without intermission."[7] The security of capitalist social order is dependent upon this monopoly of violence, this limitless, constant power without boundary or intermission, translated into human form as the cop. The police will never be obsolete for the ruling class. In organizing for abolition, we can't get around the fact that we are talking about depriving the state of its authority.

If the police are of essential importance to capitalist rule, and we can anchor our analysis in this fact, we are inevitably confronted by the strategic question: What is to be done? In our movement dreams and imaginings, at least partially, the police are already obsolete for the vast majority of people. It does not take a visionary to augur different solutions to the social problems cops are tasked with. But the challenge is how to bring that vision into being, to make that world—how, indeed, do we abolish the police?

No case against the police would be complete without discussing how to win: abolition and revolution, abolitionist revolution, or revolutionary abolitionism. The end of the police is inseparable from a new beginning and an abolitionist, socialist future. I do not presume to, nor am I positioned to, present a full strategic vision or complete cartography of the voyage from here to there. Drawing on the arguments made in the previous chapters, I will highlight a few critical points that need to be grappled with on our way to achieving our ultimate goal. There are two broad implications for our day-to-day work of building the movement that derive directly from the cops' centrality to capitalist class rule.

Firstly, the police's vital role in the overall capitalist system helps to explain why the strategy of reformism has been an abject failure and can even end up strengthening police power.[8] Second, a realistic appraisal of the intensity and centrality of the police state for capital suggests the ultimate futility of strategies that simply avoid the state. Scraping fugitive tunnels of escape or trying to "crowd them out" with the construction of alternative institutions downplays or evades the decisive question of class conflict, of power in society.[9]

As we have seen, organizing against the police is organizing against capitalist states. That means that attempts to abolish the police lead inevitably to conflict with states themselves, and vice versa. Conflicts with states, even those that begin with so-called peaceful protest, often come into confrontation with the cops. Resolving this requires revolutionary transformation, or rupture at the level of the state. The breaking of state power, and its replacement by democratic and popular rule, is necessary for the breaking of police power. They are indeed self-same.

The Police Fix for Social Crises

The long capitalist crisis that began in 2007–2008 has yet to resolve and has produced a deepening instability that has expressed itself through worsening living conditions and mass dissatisfaction the world over.[10] The recent troubling rise of far-right political forces is another product of this trend, as failures

Revolutionary Abolitionism

of left and left-liberal parties have ceded ground and paved the way for the center to move ever further to the right. While the names of Trump, Bolsonaro, Modi, and Netanyahu are the most prominent, a whole bevy of far-right forces are now in government or making unprecedented gains around the world. This economic and political crisis has also reverberated through the global order and the system of imperialism. The US still stands as the most dominant imperialist power, but it now faces an aspiring great power rival in China, another in Russia, and a host of regional powers, all of which are increasingly assertive of their own interests. We have thus entered what socialist activist Ashley Smith terms a "new asymmetric multipolar world order."[11] Conflict between states is on the rise and the US-helmed "rules-based international order" is now open disorder for them and disaster for us. Its delinquency is seen most vividly in the genocide of Palestinians in Gaza at the hands of the Israeli state—an atrocity carried out at best with the negligence, and at worst the culpability, of the world's states—with the mass slaughter of civilians occurring in full view of all the peoples of the world. Conflict between states will mean more arms buildup, externally through the military and internally through the police, less social spending, and the propagation of racist nationalism.[12] Additionally, conflict between states severely compromises the possibilities for multinational collaboration on the other great crises underway, as it did during the onset of the Covid pandemic (and will for epidemiological crises to come), including climate breakdown and global heating.

The epoch of the climate crisis, with its existential threat to humanity, is upon us. The Zetkin Collective has poignantly captured the way it chips away at the material foundations of society:

Heatwaves five or ten degrees hotter; wildfires roaring through regions for months on end; food provisioning systems at breaking point; storms pushing the sea dozens of kilometers inland—here there is little need to exercise the faculty of the imagination. It is portended in the science. Adaptation crisis would disrupt established stores and circuits of biophysical resources. Emergencies that put "peace, prosperity, functioning democracy, and domestic order" to the test are not, after all, quite so improbable—they are literally in the pipeline.[13]

These cataclysms are already profoundly exacerbating the inequalities within societies and between states as the "haves" cling more tightly to what they have and the desperation of the have-nots increases. Following the analyses of Geoff Eley and the Zetkin Collective, we can look forward to "fortress mentalities, idioms of politics organized by anxiety, *gatedness* as the emerging social paradigm."[14]

One of the most profound consequences of these developments is the phenomenon of mass migration.[15] In 2020, a total of 281 million people are living as migrants or refugees, displaced from their homes by the overlapping crises of climate, capitalism, and imperialism.[16] The world's states have responded with what Harsha Walia calls the construction of "bordering regimes."[17] As Walia methodically lays out in her book *Border & Rule*, this does not just mean the buildup of physical walls of concrete, steel, and razor wire, under surveillance from high-tech devices and drones, accompanied by highly militarized enforcement, and the interception of migrant boats. Bordering regimes operate far from the actual geographical borders themselves; they reach inside territories, through practices such as ICE raids in US cities, deporta-

Revolutionary Abolitionism

tion, immigrant detention camps, all of which are conducted by cops. Bordering regimes also reach beyond the territorial limits of the imperial center. Imperialist countries extend their bordering regimes into neighboring countries through compulsory aspects of trade deals and political agreements, as well as internal checkpoints. The US has Mexico crack down on migrant caravans coming from Central and South America, US Homeland Security officials declare that "the Guatemalan border with Chiapas is now our southern border," and Fortress Europe extends its bordering apparatus further afield to places like Sudan.[18]

Especially in the absence of any prominent noncapitalist alternative, the failure of liberal solutions to the overlapping crises gives space and creates conditions that foster the grotesque racism and xenophobia of the anti-immigrant and islamophobic far right, especially in the Global North.[19] Thinkers like Walia and the Zetkin Collective warn about the increasing danger of both "welfare nationalism" and eco-fascism or "fossil fascism."[20] In the coming cataclysms, these sadistic political forces openly call to sever hands holding onto the lifeboat, "using racial classifications to sort those deserving of survival from those to cut down."[21]

Expanding crisis has also been met with resistance. The year 2019 saw a global wave of revolt, then 2020 saw an uprising in the US that was the largest protest movement in the country's history.[22] The brutal Israeli genocide of Gaza, starting in October 2023, unleashed global waves of protests, mass marches in the millions, militant and disruptive actions that shut down infrastructure and weapons manufacturers, and a student encampment movement in the US unprecedented since the 1960s. Several comprehensive studies of trends in worldwide social movements from 2006 to 2020 found that global protests have steadily increased, eclipsing every historical wave of protest since the Second World War in both size and frequency.[23] Additionally, since 2016 the demands of the protests have moved from single-issue demands to what researchers label "'omnibus protests' (protesting on multiple issues) against the political and economic system. Polls world-wide reflect dissatisfaction with democracies and lack of trust in governments."[24]

Although to many it may feel as though the world is coming apart at the seams, these crises will most likely not culminate in the kind of social collapse of apocalyptic fiction, with small warring bands scavenging amid the ruins of a fallen world. Rather, as Jonathan Neale writes of climate collapse in *The Ecologist*, the state will not disintegrate but will "intensify": "It will not come in the form of a few wandering hairy bikers. It will come with the tanks on the streets and the military or the fascists taking power. . . it will take cruelty on an unprecedented scale to keep their inequality in place."[25] Deepening social crisis brings the intensification of state repression, the expansion of bordering regimes everywhere, the deepening of organized abandonment and deprivation (especially of communities of color), unprecedented cruelty, and the challenge of mass protests, riots, and unrest. For the ruling class, all the problems created by this tumultuous situation have one primary solution: more police. Ruling-class ideologues are quite clear about this and strategize about it with police "experts" at their conferences and in think tanks. As NYPD assistant commissioner Rebecca Weiner elaborated at the "Global Security Forum" conference in 2023, "evolving security challenges" include "widespread distrust, loss of faith in institutions, all sorts of institutions, all sectors, all vectors, and concerns about governance structures."[26] As these challenges increase with the coming crises, state reliance on repressive "solutions" has intensified and will continue to do so.

One marker of this trend is the continually increasing police budget.[27] A popular but false media narrative that police budgets were being defunded as a result of the 2020 uprising has been particularly prominent in conservative-aligned media outlets. To the contrary, one study found that 83 percent of the nation's police departments increased funding by more than 2 percent from 2019 to 2022, and 45 percent of departments increased funding by more than 10 percent.[28] Further preparation by the US ruling class to rely on repression can be seen in the proliferation of multimillion-dollar cop training academies from Chicago's "cop academy" to Atlanta's "cop city" to NYC's planned "public safety academy," announced at the end of May 2024. States are also increasing the flexibility of police for deployment in various contexts, through what is termed "interoperability" of different layers of policing nationally and globally. "Interoperability" plans include joint training, multiagency task forces, linked data gathering and analysis, and the spread of "fusion centers" around the country, which serve as hubs for integrating different agencies from the local to the federal.[29] The intensification of the police state is already underway.

The Paradox of Policing Reform

As long as police have existed, there have been attempts to curb their most violent behavior while retaining the hope of a friendly and professional police force rooted in communities. But the history of the police is riddled with attempts at wide-ranging expansive reform efforts that were not only ineffective but actually worked to expand police power and ability to do violence. "Police reform does not fail," writes prominent abolitionist scholar Naomi Murakawa, "it works—for the police."[30] The failure of reforms to muzzle the police generates the need for abolition.

190 **Their End Is Our Beginning**

Almost always, the first step in police reform efforts has been for the government to convene a commission or committee, usually in the wake of a blatant and odious act of police violence or, more likely, as a response to powerful movements and riots in the streets. The evidence, testimony proceedings, and findings produced by such commissions could fill whole libraries.[31] The first such investigation was carried out in 1894 by New York City's Lexow Committee. Their final report provoked breathless all-caps headlines in *The New York Times*—"THE ENTIRE DEPARTMENT CORRUPT"—and reported that "every occupation, almost every citizen was dominated by an all-controlling and overshadowing dread of the Police Department."[32] The report stated that the Lexow Committee "conclusively establishes an indictment against the Police Department of New York City as a whole."[33] In 1929, the federal Wickersham Commission attempted to generalize the work of the Progressive-era police professionalizers, like August Vollmer (discussed in chapter two), who co-authored the commission's report.[34] While it was critical of some of the crudest excesses of police brutality, Wickersham investigator E. Jerome Hopkins set out the commission's real goal, which was to "inculcate in [the criminal element] the *permanent submission* and genuine acceptance of society's authority."[35] This social education was to be achieved through a combination of imported colonial methods and social engineering. In the end, as Vollmer put it: "The public must drop its childish attitude of hostility and learn to appreciate this friendly, reassuring helpfulness . . . of the professionally trained policeman."[36] The 1960s saw three commissions, all in some ways dealing with the urban rebellions and explosion of resistance to racism and police violence: the 1965 Katzenbach Commission, the 1967 Kerner Commission, and the 1968 National Violence Com-

Revolutionary Abolitionism

mission.[37] The findings of these bodies, the Kerner Commission especially, identified the hostility toward police as the "primary cause" of the uprisings and linked that to the police being a symbol of the deeper racist inequalities of the system.[38] In the 1970s and 1980s, smaller commissions on the municipal level were convened following upswells on the streets, which all outlined problems of corruption, abuse, and lack of accountability in departments around the country.[39] Then, in 2014, reform efforts took a big step, going from a "commission" to a "task force," with president Barack Obama's Task Force on 21st Century Policing largely in response to the militant protests in Ferguson, Missouri. When Chicago cops killed seventeen-year-old Laquan McDonald in 2016, shooting him sixteen times as he walked away, public outcry compelled the convening of the Chicago Police Accountability Task Force, which concluded that "CPD's own data gives validity to the widely held belief the police have no regard for the sanctity of life when it comes to people of color."[40]

Dozens of regularly convened committees of experts have nevertheless yielded a situation today in which police are more deadly, more militarized, more legally protected, and equipped with palantír-style surveillance capabilities. And they are certainly better funded. From 1977 to 2017, state and local spending on the police skyrocketed from $42 billion to $115 billion dollars, adjusted for inflation.[41] These figures do not include the hundreds of millions paid out per year—$300 million in 2019 alone—for police-admitted misconduct settlements.

Perhaps the most substantial change from police reform efforts has been to increase the legitimacy and normalcy of the fundamentally violent institution in the eyes of the public. It is notable that, in the recent past, mass protests have most often erupted in response to cops killing people, the apotheosis of their regular violence. Yet, historian Elizabeth Hinton points out that during the previous wave of urban rebellions in the 1960s and 1970s, the detonators of the protests were usually "everyday policing practices" as opposed to the *exceptional* instances of police violence"—murder—"a sign that the status quo has become accepted, however bitterly. In this sense at least, national and local authorities won the War on Crime."[42] Compare this, too, with the early history recounted in chapter one, where the very creation and existence of the police resulted in riots and protest. Whereas reform commissions have worked to normalize and expand police, the politics of abolition offer a recentering of social norms by disavowing the new status quo of policing. Rejecting and delegitimizing this status quo means getting back to, frankly, raging at and rejecting their very presence.

Some advocates of police reform would argue that many good recommendations that resulted from these committees were not enacted, or that the right reforms have not yet been attempted. There is something to this: historians have outlined how many of the recommendations to address structural inequality were abandoned, while all the recommendations to increase policing were enacted.[43] Federal consent decrees—legal orders to municipal police departments to enact reforms—are routinely met with delays, dodges, and exercises of minimal effort on the part of police departments. Chicago's 2019 consent decree, for example, which resulted from the killing of McDonald, has been in effect under three separate mayors, and based on the city's own reporting had only achieved 6 percent compliance as of March 2024.[44] In the same time period, Chicago's cops had killed at least twenty-eight more people, while the bureaucracy lumbers on.[45]

Revolutionary Abolitionism

Even when recommendations are enacted, there is hardly any noticeable difference in policing. The Minneapolis Police Department was known as the national poster child for police reform.[46] The MPD was selected as one of six cities by the federal government to enact Obama's reforms, spending millions of dollars to pursue a shift toward what former police chief Janeé Harteau called "MPD 2.0: A New Policing Model," with a community policing focus and training on implicit bias and crisis intervention. The MPD even held listening sessions with the community and offered yoga and meditation to cops.[47] Then, Derek Chauvin—a twenty-year veteran of the force, with four medals of valor and commendation as well as eighteen prior complaints, including shooting three people and killing one— placed his knee on George Floyd's neck. And the city burned. A journalist in the local *Star-Tribune* remarked, "Minneapolis did everything Barack Obama asked it to."[48] None of those changes were able to stop the killing of Floyd, nor the others the MPD killed in the same time period.[49] The "new policing model" turned out to be a rebranding of the same violence.

The reforms under discussion range from the thoroughly discredited body cams to better training, reporting, oversight, and strategies like "community policing."[50] Police training has taken up much (paid) time but yielded few results. The Chicago police—remember, the ones with "no regard for the sanctity of life"—require nine hundred hours of training for new recruits to help promote "a solid ethical foundation."[51] On the ethical foundation created by so much training, CPD has become the number one department in the nation in the killing of children.[52] Kim Potter, the Minnesota cop who executed Daunte Wright in 2021, was a professional police trainer who "mistook her gun for a taser." Potter murdered Wright five years after Minnesota funneled twelve million dollars into training in the wake of the 2016 killing of Philando Castile during a traffic stop. To paraphrase a formulation of Marx, it is not changes in how cops think that determine their social role, but, on the contrary, their social role that determines their way of thinking. The police role, described in chapter three, as a uniquely repressive hyper-disciplinary avatar of the state, trumps whatever training they receive.

If training doesn't work, what about better policy around use of force, profiling, reporting, and oversight? While the removal of some legal protections, such as qualified immunity of the police, is long overdue, the police break policy and laws routinely. Eric Garner and others were killed by an "illegal" move, for example. More troubling, as Naomi Murakawa points out, legal regulations can wind up serving as instructions. As one example, she cites a 1985 Supreme Court hearing that established the conditional clause of lethal violence being permissible if the cops "feared for their life."[53] Now this clause has been the watchword ad nauseam of every police defense, establishing the legal script for justifying their brutality. In order to fulfill their essential function under capitalism, cops require an extremely high level of discretionary despotism, so reforms that attempt to limit this discretionary power will always run up against the core mission of policing and lose out.

In light of these failures, police reformers often resort to advocating for a larger reset of police-community relations. "Community policing" posits the everyday problem of police misconduct as one of a "crisis of trust between cops and the Black community."[54] The strategy to restore these relations has been deployed by many departments around the country since the Houston Police Department was first credited with its use, and over forty years of attempts don't seem to add up to anything other than a public relations stunt for the police. Seen in a different way, community policing, the notion of collaboration between police and community, is hardly a reform but rather a core practice of policing throughout its history, including the colonial constabulary, Peel's notion of "democratic police," and others described in chapter one. The problem is not communication or trust but cops' violent mission. "Their very presence is an insult," writes James Baldwin, "even if they spent their entire day feeding gumdrops to children."[55]

Another long-standing movement strategy calls for community *control* of the police. These demands seek to establish democratically elected review boards that can oversee police complaints, hiring and firing, and policy. While in general more democracy is better, in most circumstances—however well intentioned—this perspective is limiting. Advocates of these boards, like those in Chicago who won the Empowering Communities for Public Safety (ECPS), argued that winning these boards was necessary to defund the police. However, it is not at all clear that simply adding another body creates more democracy. In most cities, budgeting and police policy are established by some combination of the mayor's office and city council. These seats are presumably democratically controlled, yet they generally carry on the ruling-class investment in their loyal shock troops. If the elections of those seats have not yielded robust reforms of police anywhere in the country, let alone concrete abolitionist steps, what would be different about another elected body?

Unfortunately, in the Chicago example, the compromise ordinance that passed even dropped a key component of the democratic process. Instead of being directly elected to a body,

Their End Is Our Beginning

ECPS elects a "pool" that then are appointed by the mayor. Additionally, community control would essentially turn elections of civilians, presumably coming from the movement ranks but also perhaps competing with pro-police candidates, into police administrators working to change police policy from within. The problems with this approach are outlined in an excellent essay by a number of authors in *The Forge*, who point out a crucial danger: "Leading the community into close involvement with the police is more likely to deliver us into their hands than the other way around."[56] As a consequence, organizers are left in a situation that closely resembles other compromised movement strategies, as described by Chicago activist Jayda Van, who organized for community control but was critical of ECPS. She writes:

> To quote the ordinance: "People who trust the police department are more likely to cooperate with the police department, and public cooperation with the police department helps to reduce and solve crime." Those words sound nothing like the chants that drove millions of us to the streets to fight for change and for an end to the racist and violent system of policing in the United States.[57]

Let's look at the limitation of reform another way: cops' murdering of citizens is often—with good reason—the focus of many police reform issues. Does it tell us anything about the police if we look at places where that is not as prevalent? The US—along with Brazil and South Africa—is in many ways an outlier globally in the murderousness of its cops. Contrast that with somewhere like Sweden. Sweden has a reputation for Scandinavian exceptionalism, or liberalism and progressivism, and is seen even by some on the US socialist left and some prison reformers as a

Revolutionary Abolitionism

model, or as "the most humane social system ever constructed."[58] Compared to the US, Sweden's policing record is certainly an improvement. In the past thirty-one years, there have been forty-four fatal shootings by police in Sweden, with a population of ten million.[59] In the US, in 2023, there were thirty-seven killings per ten million people, roughly similar every year.[60] Per capita, US police killings *per year* are approaching the same rate as for Swedish police *over three decades*. However, this does not mean that the Swedish police are the ideal. In Sweden, too, the core police function is still in operation, albeit with less lethal violence. The Afro-Swedish activist Ibbi Chune has described Swedish policing realities: "We are constantly being stopped and harassed by police and security officers, and often using violent measures." "Over-policed neighborhoods," Chune says, "do not make us feel safe, but rather the opposite."[61] Riots ripped through Stockholm's suburbs in 2013 against police brutality, and again in 2020, when the George Floyd rebellion inspired protests in Sweden against their own racist police. Cops attacked these demonstrations with batons and pepper spray.

Sweden's veneer of progressivism has been peeling away for decades, anti-immigrant sentiment is on the rise, new prisons are being constructed, and an ascendent far-right—in the form of the neo-Nazi Sweden Democrats party—is, as of 2022, the second-largest party in parliament. Even in a country perceived to be as "functional" and "humane" as Sweden, and with a police force that is less lethal, the role of the police is the same; they are still a problem, and people still protest and riot against them. In Sweden, too, the social crisis is driving an increase and intensification of policing in line with global trends.

Police reforms are bound to fail because they do not affect the main purpose and inalterable role the cops play under capitalism.

Their End Is Our Beginning

To attempt to change this core function would be akin to trying to reform firefighters so that they stop fighting fires. If that were accomplished, then they wouldn't be "firefighters'" any longer but something qualitatively different—and the same is true for the police. You can't transform a pig into a pony. Keeanga-Yamahtta Taylor describes the police as a cake that has already been baked with a racist batter. "We cannot," she writes "go back now and decide to take out this or that thing. The whole cake has to be discarded."[62] Neither the violence nor the racism, both essential ingredients cooked into the institution, can be reformed away.

A movement for abolition recognizes police themselves as the problem and, as a start, seeks changes to limit their size, funding, and power. Generally speaking, abolitionist demands address the underlying purpose of policing head on and include demands to limit the number of cops on the street, get them out of schools and off campuses, reduce their budget and their access to weaponry, prevent the rehiring of fired cops across municipalities, withhold pension and pay from violent cops, and eliminate qualified immunity. These demands can blunt the violence and have real benefits for the populations most targeted by policing.[63]

Demands to defund and reduce public expenditures for cops are especially important because they are tied to broader fights to adequately fund the public services needed to solve the social crises into which cops are dangerously inserted. As many have pointed out, "defund" must be paired with funding that meets community needs. In short: we need more teachers and social workers, not more cops; we need to close prisons and open schools; we need more jobs and health care, not more taxpayer-funded military gadgets for bullies in blue. If politicians were actually concerned about so-called crime, these are the things they would invest in. Removing police alone does nothing to dis-

Revolutionary Abolitionism 199

appear the broader conditions of privation and misery. Luckily, among abolitionists, absolutely no one argues with that, despite claims by the right wing and even some erstwhile socialist allies.

For an example of the latter, see Cedric Johnson's book *After Black Lives Matter* (and elsewhere), in which he constructs a false dichotomy to argue for an "abolition of a different sort," whereby instead of abolishing police and prisons, we need the "abolition of the conditions" that give rise to the social problems to which the police are purportedly the response.[64] His insistence on this dichotomy is especially curious, because he must be aware that all of the serious abolitionist thinkers are quite clear about their anticapitalism and the need to abolish the conditions of capitalism that breed so-called crime. Even more inexplicably, Johnson discusses the "promising policy agendas" to change the conditions while, at the same time, wondering to himself "*if* there is an anti-capitalist" politics to Black Lives Matter.[65] Meanwhile, in the year Johnson's book came out, two thousand people gathered together in the city where he lives to discuss "abolition communism."[66] His conclusions are to argue that cops are just alienated workers, that the focus on anti-Black racism is divisive for the working-class movement, and that pedestrian automotive fatalities should be seen as a "more pervasive, looming peril" in society than police murder.[67]

Organizing around demands related to defunding the police and funding other public services is a key component of building the fighting capacity, self-activity, and confidence of ordinary working people. From Stop Cop City to Treatment Not Trauma nonpolice mental health response, the abolitionist movement has been built by activists doggedly organizing important campaigns, often in unfavorable circumstances. Here, though, we should be clear that movements being "strong" in the sense of size, level of organization, or embeddedness alone is not the goal in itself. Often, the goal is talked about as "building power," a phrase in social movement circles that can serve as a stand-in for strategy, with ambiguous content. Building power is not valuable for its own sake—insofar as that power is being used, we must ask how it should be wielded, and for what purpose. The phrase "building power" can sometimes obscure the fact that we are organizing in opposition to violent structures that currently hold power over society and act constantly against our movements. The ruling class and their state are never passive actors. Our struggle against cops and cages, as Ruth Wilson Gilmore reminds us, is, after all, class war.[68]

Once we have differentiated between the problems with attempts at reforming the police and strategies with abolitionist or transformative demands, there remains the question of the relationship between the struggle for abolitionist demands and the task of abolition itself. When abolition is class war, how do we grapple with the decisive question of class conflict, of states, and of power in society?

"It Is Our Duty to Win"[69]

What could it look like to abolish the conditions that give rise to cops and cages? We fight for a society in which there are no rich capitalists hoarding wealth, an end to inequality, and the free access to resources needed to survive and lead full lives. All of us should be able to democratically control our society and how it distributes resources. Housing and health care would not be commodities to be bought and sold but simple components of being a part of society—a "right," to use a liberal formulation. The land would be decolonized rather than owned by individuals. In a world free of capitalist deprivation, one could quite easily imagine there being little need for theft and other activities associated with crime. Without the atmosphere of stress, trauma, and the forced competition of "all against all" blaring at every level as in our current society, it isn't hard to imagine that dangerous situations like mental health crises and domestic violence would dramatically decrease. While there would certainly be emergencies, conflicts, and instances of harm, the vast majority of these would be prevented. Without the material structures that buttress, reify, and reproduce racism and sexism, it will be easier to root out and transform individual prejudice.

Would community safety require coercion or compulsion by some individuals to control the actions of others? Perhaps, but one need not insist that the form of the police is required. States operate with police as key agents to institute coercion, acting as a body with separate interests from the general populace. These separate interests are not random but conditioned by the goal of promoting the general interests of the whole capitalist class, to secure positive conditions for business and profitability. It is not difficult to imagine a way of living together in a world with access to the full and total benefits of social organization, which could free up greater capacity to resolve conflicts in different ways. In a society democratically organized from bottom to top, there is no need for a separate entity with separate interests, to resolve such conflicts. Any potential compulsion in such a society should be understood in a collective sense, where the self-interests of safety and community are paramount and accessible to all, and carceral violence is recognized as detrimental to collective safety. As Guy Aitchison points out: "Compliance is more likely where each person has the prospect of influencing the future direction of society on equal terms with others," and real democracy "would lead people to feel less alienated from social institutions and less inclined to defect from the rules when it is in their short-term interest."[70] In this kind of world, the notion of the police and prisons would indeed be wholly obsolete. But how do we get there, and how do we deal with the inevitable barriers that arise along the way?

One path is described by abolitionist Charmaine Chua as "procedural abolition."[71] In this scenario, strong social movements are able to pressure the government to enact abolitionist demands, also described as "non-reformist reforms," a concept first coined by philosopher André Gorz.[72] These demands or concessions may, for example, close a prison, prevent the building of a new one, or win moratoriums on construction, defund and reduce the number of police, or deprive them of weaponry. Movements could push to create alternative institutions to promote actual public safety, like public teams of nonpolice mental health responders, diverting 911 crisis calls to be handled by these teams. All are demands that can reduce the scope, power, and legitimacy of the police state, which makes them "non-reformist," in that they "unravel rather than widen the net of social control through criminalization."[73] These nonreformist reforms could also be seen as ways to "extract resources from the state." These fit into the abolitionist framework of "divest/invest" in relation to the cops: defunding the police and funding schools, healthcare, and transformative justice programs that would address some of the root causes of crises that the police are currently assigned to respond to. To contribute to a lasting and growing movement, these reforms should also play a role in creating what Amna Akbar has described as "pathways for building ever-growing organized popular power. Such movement wins, however small, aim to shift power away from elites and toward the masses of people'" and "new centers of democratic power."[74]

Revolutionary Abolitionism

Chua terms another proposed strategic path, "autonomist abolition."[75] Similar to the procedural path, the aim is to limit and strip away the ability and reach of the police state, while building up alternative forms of popular power. What is different here is that instead of pressuring the state to be the initiator, vessel, or funder of these new forms, this strategy is primarily focused on building structures "outside the state." Some examples could include projects of mutual aid that aim to provide for community needs (such as those that flowered during the height of the Covid pandemic), prisoner support networks like Black & Pink, Cook County Community Jail Support, or the Todos Para Todos organizing in Chicago that sought to facilitate the horizontal self-organization of refugee asylum seekers in a Chicago warehouse instead of the city-constructed carceral tent camps.[76] These projects seek to better organize on the individual, neighborhood, and community level, to respond effectively to crisis situations and thereby "chip away at how police shape our understanding of the world and the solutions to the problems we face."[77] It may look like organized community intervention and violence interrupter efforts by self-organized grassroots networks able to help support conflict and crisis on that level. It could also look like some of the examples in chapter four, in which liberated zones are claimed during the heights of social struggle, such as during the 2020 rebellion, when, in Minneapolis, a Sheraton hotel was claimed by activists and turned into a houseless shelter, mutual aid hub, and community center, dubbed the Share-a-ton.[78]

Scaled up, some of these experiments could create what Geo Maher calls "liberated territory, [an] embryonic world without police."[79] In this framework, if communities were organized enough, those communities would have no need for police intervention. Grassroots networks fully taking care of houseless people, organizing neighborhood conflict resolution, and intervening and supporting mental health emergencies would in a way render the police obsolete *for our communities and movements*.

The two strategies—procedural and autonomist abolition—are not necessarily mutually exclusive and sometimes work in tandem, both organizing communities autonomously while also mobilizing to "liberate state resources for housing, healthcare," and various other social supports "without policing," as described by Kaba and Ritchie.[80] Underlying both strategies of nonreformist reforms and of autonomous movement organizing is a reliance on community as an alternative or replacement for the police. As Geo Maher argues, "The only antidote to the police is community, community, and more community."[81] In these twinned strategies, the police become obsolete for our communities because we can take care of ourselves. But both strategies also present their own contradictions and challenges, especially when we take into account the core function of the police of enforcing capitalist order on behalf of the state.

The Question of Police Obsolescence

The procedural and autonomist abolition approaches converge in a strategy of attrition: we abolish the police by stifling the institution's growth and chipping away at its foundations so that it crumbles over time.[82] For some, if we are able to organize new networks and new institutions (either through the state or on a grassroots basis) that take over the space occupied by prisons and the police, then prisons and police become increasingly unnecessary, such that they shrink and wither into their eventual disappearance.[83] There is truth to this analysis, but it also raises

Revolutionary Abolitionism

the question: unnecessary or obsolete for whom? Whatever reliance we may have on the police—a consequence of our having few other options—the cops do not depend on us for their existence and purpose. The police will never be obsolete for a capitalist state that relies on them to enforce its order in the market and on the street, and abolitionist strategies should be able to account for that fact.

What this means in terms of strategy is simple, if daunting: to take on the police is to take on the capitalist state. While nonreformist reforms to the cops and efforts to organize our own infrastructure can free up our power, organize our side, and prepare us to organize a different kind of society, attempts to gradually chip away at the police state will sooner or later provoke a reaction by the ruling class.

Even André Gorz—the theorizer of the nonreformist reform—acknowledges that there can be no incremental or gradual transition away from capitalism. He writes:

> The economic power of the bourgeoisie will not be whittled away by a slow process of erosion, nor destroyed by a succession of partial reforms, each one apparently innocuous and acceptable to capitalism, but which cumulatively would amount to a discrete siege of the enemy by a secret and masked socialist army, advancing soundlessly, under cover of night, until one fine morning it would find itself in power.[84]

The police state is not an inert, neutral edifice that we can chip away until its collapse. Rather it acts with purpose. In seeking the abolition of cops and capital we must recognize that we are in a struggle against a well-organized class that actively opposes us. That class possesses a state machine—with cops at the core—built for its purposes: the war engine of capital. There is a red line, a limit to how much the ruling class and the state will give up or cede, and transgressions of that line are always met with violent resistance.

Consider, for example, if we were to somehow pass a law to disband the police, or strip them of their guns, or to "liberate resources," not just in the sense of redistributing tax dollars but in the form of expropriating capitalists. Consider if our hypothetical liberated territories or mutual aid projects were to grow to the point where it started having an impact on capital's ability to realize profit, and our efforts posed real threats to the operation of the capitalist system. The cops are the built-in mechanism that capitalism (and its system of states) have to address such dangers—with coercive force and violence. Any move to get rid of the police or severely suppress their ability to act deprives the capitalist class of that tool. Similarly, if our goal is to abolish the conditions of inequality that the police uphold, it would mean upending the system of capitalism.

In that context, it would be naïve to expect that the ruling class will simply give up their stolen wealth and power to rule without a furious fight. The ruling class are not going to simply let go of their gold or their coppers. They stole the wealth and positioned themselves in power with bloodshed and will defend it the same way. We see indications of this every day, through counterinsurgency and counterrevolution.

Democratic norms are tossed to the side when they don't serve the interest of states and capital. We saw that in 2020, when unelected state bureaucrats blocked the Minneapolis City Council's vote to disband the police.[85] We saw it in the struggle to stop construction of Atlanta's Cop City, with the local ruling

Revolutionary Abolitionism

class flaunting mass support and record attendance at city council meetings, blocking the public referendum, and implementing draconian repression of protest, including terrorism charges for advocates, racketeering charges for supporters, and outright murder ("*viva viva* Tortuguita").[86] We saw the ruling-class disregard for democracy in the violent crackdown by riot police on dozens of colleges, when students peacefully camped on their own campuses in solidarity with Gaza. These are relatively minor setbacks for capital, but their response was violence and murder. If we should strike closer to the heart of their power and wealth, we can only expect a heavier hand of repression. We know the ferocity they are capable of because they threaten us with it daily, and some already weather its blows.

State and Counterrevolution

With the central importance of the police to capitalism in mind, we can return to the question of strategy and the two paths to abolition, outlined above.

Many parts of the abolitionist movement pursue some kind of "procedural abolition," that is, nonreformist reforms passed through the government. What would it take for procedural abolition to win a cop-free world? Undoubtedly, something as significant as the abolition of the police will not be won by Democrats and Republicans debating an Abolishing Cops Absolutely Bill (ACAB) on the floor of Congress. Instead, let us imagine that the movement has powerfully built up power in the sense of movement capacity, legitimacy, and mass support through local organizing, mass mobilization, and general strikes. In this scenario, perhaps there have even been some cutbacks to local police departments, and nonpolice mental health crisis response infrastructure is widespread. Backed by a strong movement, a new socialist abolitionist party wins a majority in Congress and perhaps even the executive branch of the government (here we must note that this hypothetical itself is problematic because it assumes a level of democracy that is perhaps more fantastical than the situation itself). In this case, are we within the realm of possibility where the passage of ACAB could be achieved?

To play out the scenario further: now our party is at the helm of the capitalist state apparatus and thus must contend with all the constraints set by profitability and the maintenance of the state itself, which present a massive gravitational pull toward accommodation and collaboration with the capitalist class. The efficacy of any ACAB legislation would require a massive restructuring of the economy to resolve the social problems to which the police are a supposed response. Restructuring the economy to suit human needs rather than market dependence would inevitably mean a direct threat to the capitalist class's private property and a fundamental challenge to capitalist social relations. This scenario replicates the dilemma of social democracy. In the words of British socialist Ian Birchall, "To challenge the pursuit of profit makes reform impossible; but to leave profit unchallenged means that no significant progress can be made towards equality."[87]

The alternative to this conundrum would be to take steps to upend capitalist social relations, and that means upending private property, along with its police protectors. The reason why capitalism cannot meet human needs is not an issue of distribution but of social relations: when private property is held by the few, the many are forced to trade their labor on the market in order not to starve. The existence of private property (or private ownership of the means of production) continuously recreates

Revolutionary Abolitionism

the same dynamics of inequality in wealth and power as long as markets exist. That is why the state can't simply be used as a fiscal and bureaucratic tool to redistribute. Its activity emerges from capitalist social relations, and relations between classes are a blueprint of the structure of states.[88] The bounds of a legality created by the capitalist state will not allow for a direct confrontation with the capitalists and their cops. The problem with the police is that they are designed to manage and enforce this reality and are a core component of the state that would be used in attempts against them.

These are the structural limits to larger reforms such as nationalization through the legal channels of the state and why so many attempts to carry it out are met with either capital flight (capitalists just take their money and leave or wait it out) or violent coups, in which the state is dissolved or taken over by forces friendlier to the capitalists (counterrevolution). To attempt to create a fully self-sustaining, nonmarket system in a globalized world of competing imperialist powers means one of two options are available: either engage with the market and thus be subordinated to the requirements of capitalist competition, or flip over the moneychangers' table entirely. One path leads to accommodation to the market and private property and thus fails to end capitalism and the cops. The other approach would require actually moving to break the hold of capitalist social relations and the state (cops), which transgresses beyond what states can achieve as an institution. To put our society in the collective hands of the people requires the power of the people's collective hands, a social force broader and more powerful than state institutions. They who would be free—as the slogan of the early abolitionists went—must strike the first blow; self-emancipation is not a value but a necessity.

210   **Their End Is Our Beginning**

The trajectory of "autonomist abolition" plays out differently but also poses new challenges. Let us imagine that a powerful movement has been able to organize liberated neighborhoods as police no-go zones, and grassroots mutual aid networks have achieved a broad reach across some sections of major cities. In these areas, well-organized community networks have dense structures of crisis response, restorative and transformative justice, and community healthcare clinics. While these steps are crucial to save lives and minimize contact with the state, they also implicitly accept certain aspects of the status quo. Chua points out how these strategies can risk legitimating governmental abandonment while taking on the huge tasks of social organization, but without the full productive capacity of the society being organized. A strategy of scaling up mutual aid to the level of society at large rapidly encounters the question of power. "Such acts of care," Chua writes astutely, "do not sidestep the question of the state—and the state doesn't ignore them, either."[89]

People with few resources can do heroic things at the margins to take care of each other. However, if we move beyond the task of better redistribution of limited resources and take steps toward the control of the means of creating the resources, the equation begins to change: not just getting more diapers and redistributing them more equitably, but taking over the diaper factory. Here, again, it is clear that in terms of meeting human needs, the problem of capitalism is not just a problem of distribution but of the social relations of private property. The capacity to actually meet the needs of the community (and eventually, the whole society) requires bottom-up efforts to expropriate private property, land, food, medication, and even the productive capacity inherent in something like a factory, a

Revolutionary Abolitionism

hospital, or a transportation hub. These sorts of efforts will necessarily garner responses from states. Community self-defense could perhaps hold off state crackdowns for some time, but as the "islands" of abolitionist mutual aid encroach on capitalist profits and social relations, state repression will scale up as well. Many of the examples in chapter four clearly demonstrate this challenge. A chief lesson is that our movements cannot simply go around the state; you can't create a new society on the side that poses a serious challenge to the operation of capitalism and its states and not expect those who benefit from capitalist extraction and state repression to retaliate. Achieving abolition (or socialism) will require taking seriously the question of counterrevolution.[90]

Counterrevolution will not be defeated without destroying the means for counterrevolution to be carried out, which will mean breaking apart the police state, the cops and repressive apparatus, and seizing the means of production. As outlined in chapter four, running the police off the street and burning their precincts is just the beginning. The subsequent tasks, in the words of Ernest Mandel, can only be "called socialist revolution and it cannot be accompanied by any respect for private property or servility to bourgeois legality."[91]

Revolutions arise out of situations of severe political crisis. Such crises present themselves as an inability of the ruling class to maintain their rule as they have, a refusal of the oppressed to continue living as they have been, and a surge in activity of people in struggle, fighting to change those conditions.[92] Of this notion of crisis, French communist Daniel Bensaïd writes:

> The crisis that affects a determinant social formation does not become revolutionary until a subject works

towards its resolution; this is accomplished through attacking the State. The State is the strategic target, the connecting point which maintains the relation between capitalist relations of production and the forces of production. After having located the principal object of the crisis [the State], it still must be defeated.[93]

The weakness of the procedural and autonomist paths is that they both leave open the question of what to do about the "principal object of the crisis"—the state—and are thus unable to push beyond the crisis and transition to a different kind of world. There is a third path to abolition: social revolution. Abolishing the police requires the overthrow of the state. Achieving this goal requires, as Lenin wrote, "revolutionary mass action strong enough to break the old government which never, not even in a period of crisis, 'falls' if it is not toppled over."[94] At a fundamental level, states are bodies of armed men with separate, counterposed interests to the people living in a society because they serve the needs of capital: rebellion control, market dependence, and social order. The state's primary agent of coercive force and violence is the police. Because of their nature within the capitalist state, the real alternative to the police is democratic control over all of society from below. Rather than power being abstracted, power is manifest in the collective will of the people. If history is any indicator, that democratic control will likely be exercised through some sort of council or assembly-based system, determined by the popular movements themselves.[95] With direct democratic control over social decisions and resources, we would have no need for a separate entity to guarantee contracts and private property, defend its barriers, and enforce subordination to the market for survival. The only way to truly break

Revolutionary Abolitionism

police power is to deprive the state of its monopoly of coercive violence floating as a separate force above society.

Democratic control over society is premised on a densely organized society. It is for this reason that discussions of overthrow or revolution are far from some kind of guerrilla-style armed struggle, carried out by a small group acting on behalf of the masses of people. Such a military approach to social change has no hope of success against the advanced repressive state, especially in the United States. Thankfully, that is not what revolution will rely on. Instead, a social revolutionary process always involves masses of people, and the source of the movement's power is its ability to shut down society through workplace strikes, street mobilizations, and protecting ourselves and our communities. Revolution undoubtedly will require self-defense, probably with arms, but its mass character and self-organization should be its defining traits. The aim of abolitionist movements is to meet the needs and establish real safety for all. It will take a revolution to achieve these things in any lasting form. Blocking that path are the cops, and behind them the capitalist state. The struggle for police abolition thus targets the chief adversaries of human flourishing,. the main weapon of the owning class, and the linchpin of the capitalist system. Their power must be broken for us to be able to create and nurture a new world of repair, collective care, and liberation.

Preparation, Organization, and an Abolitionist Horizon

The new world dwells already in our hearts, whispering amid the smoldering rubble and ashes of police precincts. It may be hard to make out its murmurs in the face of the enormity of the task. We do, after all, seek not just to close a prison or two, or decrease the police budget, or achieve passable healthcare, but to

214　　　　　　　**Their End Is Our Beginning**

change everything. "Our demands most moderate are," wrote the Irish revolutionary James Connolly, "We only want the earth." This book does not present a full map for how we can enact that change. There are components not fully explored, such as the question of imperialism and the other special bodies of armed men that enact states' interests in external, international capitalist competition and domination. But this, at least, should be clear: in the struggle for revolutionary transformation of society, the fight against the police will play a central role. In turn, the struggle to abolish the police will require a revolutionary challenge to the capitalist state. Both historically and today, capitalism as a system relies on the institution for the maintenance and recreation of its racist and unequal order. Police forcibly maintain capitalist rule by violently containing the symptoms of organized abandonment, protecting the obscene hoarding of society's wealth, and standing on guard to repress any resistance. The weapon of the police is a central component of the capitalist state, and neither of them can be reformed or repurposed for our use.

We also must be honest that social revolution is not an immediately realizable task, nor is it the main question confronting abolitionists and socialists right now. To say otherwise substitutes sloganeering for politics. "History," writes Stuart Hall, "sets the terrain, it establishes the parameters, within which struggle and survival take place."[96] In the current parameters history has set for us, building a fighting movement that is international, antiracist, and intersectional is vital, as any hope of seizing a moment of historical upsurge will depend on the strength of our organizations and movements. The most powerful organizing efforts are infused with what Daniel Bensaïd called an "urgent patience," which understands the current terrain of the struggle but is grounded in the actuality of rev-

Revolutionary Abolitionism

olution amid changing conditions.[97] As abolitionist organizer Dean Spade clearly puts it: "Can we work on abolition even if we disagree about taking over or getting rid of these governments? We can, up to a point. . . . Disagreement will influence our approach to the work."[98] The points of debate within social movements are many: what demands do we fight for, the question of electoral activity in its emphasis and its purpose, what methods are most effective, and many more. But, as historical and international struggles have made clear, at the point when our power becomes a serious threat to capitalist rule, the struggle can take on a directly confrontational, insurrectionary character against the cops and the state. Until then, through our many campaigns and movements, we must organize, we must prepare. Alongside the patient building of movement organizations and other infrastructures of dissent and contention, political organizations with a revolutionary vision and perspective are also needed. Specifically, to alter our terrain in favor of abolition, moments of severe political crisis call for an organization or strategic actor capable of initiative and decision—perhaps we call it a party. Tobi Haslett describes such a formation as "not simply something that offers a 'line' that you can chain yourself to, but that the organization serves as both a place for struggles to meet and a repository for movement history. The party cultivates a sense of memory, and can offer a *coordinated*, partisan counter to bourgeois discourse."[99] As we have seen, such an organization or party will need to coordinate a counter not just to bourgeois *discourse* but also to capitalist *power*. What is needed is a political vision rooted in the real, vital organizing and struggle of the movement for immediate gains that, as Italian communists Antonio Gramsci and Palmiro Togliatti put it in the 1920s, can simultaneously

> link every demand to a revolutionary objective; make use of every partial struggle to teach the masses the need for general action and for insurrection against the reactionary rule of capital; and seek to ensure that every struggle of a limited character is prepared and led in such a way as to be able to lead to the mobilization of the proletariat, and not to their dispersal.[100]

The larger political questions like revolution have important ramifications for the day-to-day organizing work we do to cohere, deepen, and prepare our forces. Within the swirling clouds of future conflict and crisis lurks the potential for eruptions. These explosions can burst forth when people reject the violence of the police and fight back, as they have before, surging and powerful in the streets of Ferguson and Minneapolis, Cairo and Sidi Bouzid, Oaxaca and Soweto, Derry and Petrograd. Resistance is inevitable, but those examples also show us that winning is not. Actually achieving a post-capitalist and post-police society requires us to be prepared to move from resistance to revolutionary abolitionism, from social movement to social revolution.

Hope lies unshakable in the tremendous creativity of people in struggle. What seemed impossible yesterday can rapidly shift to be what is necessary today. The possibility for a liberated future will only be built in a world free of police and free from the rubble of capitalist states. Their end is our beginning.

acknowledgments

Before recognizing the many people who have impacted the creation of this book, I want to start by paying respect to the hope and heroism of the Palestinian struggle. The writing of this book was put on pause for four months after the beginning of the events of the al-Aqsa Flood. Writing and organizing to stop the genocide being carried out by the Zionist entity in Gaza and escalation of settler colonialism in the occupied West Bank had greater importance. As the unrelenting atrocity, the number martyred, and steadfast resistance continued, and having blown past my deadline, I made a decision to finish this book. This decision did not come without guilt. This was mitigated by the many deep connections between the abolitionist struggle here in the US and that of the liberation of Palestine. The egregious cop crackdown on the student encampments for divestment in some ways underlined the connection between cops here and imperialism and settler colonialism abroad. With that in mind, I hope this work makes a modest contribution to one component of that fight while holding to the others. Free Palestine.

With that, I turn to the many, many individuals to whom I am indebted for both this book itself and the politics that it contains. All my thanks:

To my friend, comrade, editor Sean Larson. Sean's collaboration is more that of a co-thinker and co-writer than editor.

He has tirelessly edited the vast majority of everything I have written for the past several years, rendering my often gnarled prose and confused thoughts comprehensible. This book would not have been possible without him, and for that I have nothing but boundless gratitude.

To Keeanga-Yamahtta Taylor, comrade, friend, and (you will hate my use of this term!) mentor, who has influenced and honed my politics around anti-racism and socialism more than anyone.

To Eric Kerl, my fellow Appalachian abolitionist, for guiding this project into a reality, for valuable contributions thinking through the politics of the book, and for asking the good questions. And to the rest of the good people at Haymarket who do the good work. To Maria Isabelle Carlos for early on helping me focus and clarify my voice. To Caroline Luft for the vital final polish.

To Nisha Atalie, for initially pitching the idea for this book to me, especially with its internationalist bent, and for her stalwart support, friendship, and critical insights.

To Mary, for their consistently good advice, smart edits, and incalculable support and love.

To those who graced me by being interviewed for the book, gifting me their experiences: Hossam el-Hamalawy, Eammon McCann, Afsaneh Moradian, Yasser Munif, René González Pizzaro, Aldo Cordeiro Sauda.

To Shireen Akram-Boshar, Rick Elmore, Ruby Healer, and Naomi Murakawa for reading various chapters of the book and giving invaluable feedback.

To my friend and comrade Charlie Aleck for sharing laughter and, more important, blessing this book with their stunning artwork.

acknowledgments

To the many individuals, some of whom I have known for years and some only for months of pitched struggle, who all in some way have influenced these politics through discussion, debate, and organizing: Ariel Atkins, Anderson Bean, Will Calloway, Charlene Carruthers, Rachel Cohen, Anton Ford, Mariame Kaba, Brian Kelly, James Manos, Page May, Jason Metter, Jasson Perez, Haley Pessin, Khury Petersen-Smith, Jim Plank, Charlie Post, Aislinn Pulley, Ashley Smith, Debbie Southern, Todd St Hill, Lee Sustar, Natalia Tylim, Joe Weiss, David Whitehouse.

And, last, to those who struggle, those who fight, those who know that it is always right to rebel, and to those who "feel like they are living in a world without any possible escape—in which there is nothing but to fight for an impossible escape." Solidarity.

notes

introduction

1. Quoted in David Peisner, "Little Turtle's War," *The Bitter Southerner,* January 20, 2023, https://bittersoutherner.com/feature/2023/ little-turtles-war-cop-city-atlanta.
2. Sam Levin, "'A Talented Goofy Kid': Family of Ryan Gainer, Autistic Teen Killed by Police Speaks Out," *Guardian*, March 21, 2024; Sam Levin, "California Sheriff Releases Video Showing Killing of Boy, 15, Holding Garden Tool," *Guardian*, March 13, 2024.
3. Elizabeth Hinton, *An Unjust Burden: The Disparate Treatment of Black Americans in the Criminal Justice System* (New York: Vera Institute of Justice, 2018).
4. Justin Wolfers, David Leonhardt, and Kevin Quelly, "1.5 Million Missing Black Men," *New York Times,* April 20, 2015.
5. Christopher Ingraham, "14 Baltimore Neighborhoods Have Lower Life Expectancies than North Korea," *Washington Post*, April 30, 2015.
6. Alex Soth, "The Great Divide," *New York Times*, August 5, 2020.
7. Mariame Kaba, *We Do This 'Til We Free Us* (Chicago: Haymarket, 2021), 96.
8. For one, see Mariame Kaba, "Police 'Reforms' You Should Always Oppose," *Truthout*, December 7, 2014.
9. "Welcome the World Through My Eyes," T Nichols Photography, https://thiscaliforniakid2.wixsite.com/tnicholsphotography/about.
10. "Tyre Nichols 10," posted August 11, 2010, by Austin, YouTube, https://www.youtube.com/watch?v=i_hZGVI2U-4.
11. "Video 3," posted January 27, 2023, by City of Memphis, Vimeo, https://vimeo.com/793455761.
12. I tend to use simply *capitalism* rather than *racial capitalism*—often used in some quarters—throughout. I do so, following Keeanga-Yamahtta Taylor, who points out that you can't talk about racism and

221

222 Their End Is Our Beginning

capitalism as separate, as there "is no period" in US history when "race and ethnicity were not completely bound up with the exploitation of labor and exploitation of the lands resources by the capitalist class" (Taylor "Capitalism: Naming the System Behind Systemic Racism," *Spectre* 5 (Spring 2022): 16–17.) Thus, she argues, there is no such thing as a nonracial capitalism. *Racial capitalism* is descriptive and useful in the regard that it very clearly highlights that connection, especially as that connection is sometimes contested in some socialist thought. It also has a particular historic origin and context as a term (South Africa specifically) and, per Taylor, still requires development. So, my choice of terms is mostly out of simplicity although I, like Taylor, think that racial capitalism is perhaps an unneeded supplement, in that Marxism can explain the essential racist quality of capitalism properly; I have no particular critique of the term.

13. Angela Davis, "Angela Davis on the Struggle for Socialist Internationalism and Real Democracy," interview by Astra Taylor, *Jacobin*, October 31, 2020.

14. Mariame Kaba, "Towards the Horizon of Abolition," interview by John Duda, *Next System Project,* November 9, 2017.

15. Ruth Wilson Gilmore, "A World to Win: Seizing the State," interview by Grace Blakely, *Jacobin Radio*, September 21, 2022.

16. Robin D. G. Kelley, "Abolition Communism," panel presentation, Socialism 2023 Conference, Chicago, September 3, 2023.

17. Vincent Bevins, *If We Burn: The Mass Protest Decade and the Missing Revolution* (New York: PublicAffairs, 2023), 275.

18. Throughout this book I use the term *socialism* to describe what we replace the capitalist system with. I just as easily could perhaps have also used the term *communism*. Folks like Marx and Lenin used both terms at different times throughout their lives, based on the political context. In my usage of the term, I conceive of either socialism or communism as something distinct from either the social-democratic, market-based, mixed economy of Scandinavia, or the similarly state-centric, often authoritarian systems like the ex-USSR, China, or places like Cuba or North Korea. Though there are pages of debates about the nature of the latter states that are not relevant for this work, I would consider the notion of "state capitalist" as the generally correct label, except for China—which has the second-most billionaires in the world after the US. But what is key in this distinction is that democracy and the self-activity of the masses of people are essential to socialism or communism; indeed, only through that can we create this new world. It can be

notes **223**

encapsulated by borrowing two oft-used phrases of Marx, a world "from each according to their ability and to each according to their need," which comes into realization through the "self-emancipation" of the working class. I tend to not use the term communism only because of my assumption of a typical association with Stalinism and the states I mentioned associated with it that I do not hold up as examples.

19. Ruth Wilson Gilmore, "The Worrying State of the Anti-Prison Movement," in *Abolition Geography: Essays Towards Liberation*, ed. Ruth Wilson Gilmore (London: Verso, 2022), 453.

20. Marx paired this, the uprising of John Brown and a revolt of the enslaved in Missouri, with a peasant rebellion in Russia. Karl Marx, "Letter to Friedrich Engels, from January 11, 1860," *Collected Works*, vol. 41 (Lawrence & Wishart, 2010), 4.

21. V. I. Lenin, *What Is to Be Done?* (International Publishers, 1969), 80. Italics mine.

22. Peisner, "Little Turtle's War."

23. "Forest Defender," quoted on *Democracy Now*, January 20, 2023.

24. Mariame Kaba and Andrea Ritchie, *No More Police: A Case for Abolition* (New York: New Press, 2022), 220.

25. Nia Prater, "What We Know About the Police Shooting of a Man Who Was Wielding Scissors," *New York Magazine*, March 28, 2024.

26. David Correia, "Poisoned and Policed to Death," in *Violent Order: Essays on the Nature of Police*, ed. David Correia and Tyler Wall (Chicago: Haymarket, 2021), 79.

27. Ariel Parrella-Aureli, Kelly Bauer, Mack Liederman, Quinn Myers, "Dexter Reed Shot Cop Before Officers Returned Fire 96 Times, Watchdog Says as Video Released," *Block Club Chicago*, April 9, 2024.

28. Ben Brucato, *Race and Police: The Origin of Our Peculiar Institution* (New Brunswick, NJ: Rutgers University Press, 2023), 198.

29. Mark Neocleous, *A Critical Theory of Police Power: The Fabrication of the Social Order* (London: Verso Books, 2021), 3.

chapter 1: Origins of a Violent Order

1. Quoted in Sally E. Hadden, *Slave Patrols: Law and Violence in Virginia and the Carolinas* (Boston: Harvard University Press, 2003).

2. Quoted in Audrey Farrell, *Crime, Class and Corruption: The Politics of the Police* (London: Bookmarks, 1992), 54–55.

3. Quoted in Brucato, *Race and Police: The Origin of Our Peculiar Institution* (New Brunswick, NJ: Rutgers University Press, 2023), 190.

4. In this book, I make reference to the modern police. I use this term

to describe police institutions that emerged in the early to mid 1800s. I term them *modern* because the word *police* was used in earlier eras to describe concepts, institutions, and officials that resembled the institution we see today in important, foundational ways. In police historiography, some scholars pinpoint the modernity of the institution, and thus modern police, as corresponding at later points in time with the professionalization of the institution, August Vollmer's 1909 assumption of the position of chief of police of Berkeley being one such marker. In my use of the term, I am mostly motivated by distinguishing when the word police came to describe the institution with core similarity to the force that exists today. I would define the modern police—building off the work of Kristian Williams—as 1) uniformed, 2) operating round-the-clock both night and day; 3) having the ability to make arrest without a warrant and the capacity to use force; 4) public, ostensibly accountable to government, and paid a publicly funded salary and 5) typically having a preventative orientation.

5. Karl Marx, *Capital*, vol. 1 (London: New Left Review, 1976), 876.

6. Marx, *Capital*, 915.

7. See Jairus Banaji, *A Brief History of Commercial Capitalism* (Chicago: Haymarket, 2020), for an expansive view of this process globally.

8. Chris Harman, *A People's History of the World: From the Stone Age to the New Millennium* (London: Verso Books, 2017), 141.

9. Colin Barker, "Revolutionary Reflections: Value, Force, Many States and Other Problems: Part 3," *rs21*, June 7, 2019.

10. This attribution of Marx, quoted in Tony Cliff, "Marxism at the Millenium," chapter 1, is actually a paraphrase of Marx (*Capital*, vol. 1, chapter 10, section 2) in Max Weber, *General Economic History*, chapter 4 (1923), trans. Frank Knight (Greenberg, 1927).

11. Chris Wickham, *Medieval Europe* (London: Yale University Press, 2016), 124; Harman, *A People's History of the World*, 142.

12. Harman, *A People's History of the World*, 144.

13. See Marx, *Capital*, vol. 1, chapter 10, section 2.

14. Marx, *Capital*, vol. 1, chapter 10, section 2.

15. Wickham, *Medieval Europe*, 121. There are a series of debates on this transition from feudalism to capitalism. For our purposes, the central point is that this transition resulted in the creation and increased centrality of towns and urban areas and dependence on the market for survival.

16. Wickham, *Medieval Europe*, 130. For comparison, the populations of Paris and Milan were about two hundred thousand people in 1300; London had eighty thousand.

notes   225

17. David McNally, *Against the Market: Political Economy, Market Socialism, and the Marxist Critique*, (London: Verso, 1993), 17.
18. Marx, *Capital*.
19. Marx, *Capital*, 896; Peter Linebaugh and Marcus Rediker, *The Many-Headed Hydra* (Boston: Beacon, 2000), 294.
20. Marx, *Capital*, 896–900.
21. Dario Melossi and Massimo Pavarini, *The Prison and the Factory* (London: Palgrave, 2017), 31.
22. Marx, *Capital*, 895.
23. Mr. Bishton, *Report on Shropshire*, cited in McNally, *Against the Market*, 19.
24. Quoted in Neil Davidson, *How Revolutionary Were the Bourgeois Revolutions* (Chicago: Haymarket, 2017), 39.
25. Harman, *A People's History of the World*, 181; Melossi and Pavarini, *The Prison and the Factory*, 41.
26. Melossi and Pavarini, *The Prison and the Factory*, 32.
27. Aimé Césaire, *Discourse on Colonialism* (New York: Monthly Review Press, 2000), 33.
28. Robbie McVeigh and Bill Rolston, *Ireland, Colonialism, and the Unfinished Revolution* (Chicago: Haymarket, 2023), 56.
29. Walter Rodney, *How Europe Underdeveloped Africa* (London: Verso Books, 2018), 180.
30. Davidson, *How Revolutionary Were the Bourgeois Revolutions*, 52.
31. Davidson, *How Revolutionary Were the Bourgeois Revolutions*, 52.
32. C. L. R. James, *The Black Jacobins* (New York: Vintage, 1989), 86.
33. Eric Williams, *Capitalism & Slavery* (Chapel Hill: University of North Carolina Press, 1994), 52.
34. Marx, *Capital*, 925.
35. Harman, *A People's History of the World*, 234.
36. Harman, *A People's History of the World*, 318.
37. David Whitehouse, "The Origins of the Police," *Libcom*, December 2014.
38. The section is very indebted to the important scholarship of Mark Neocleous.
39. Mark Neocleous, *A Critical Theory of Police Power: The Fabrication of the Social Order* (London: Verso Books, 2021), 67.
40. Quoted in Neocleous, *A Critical Theory of Police Power*, 58.
41. This quote is most likely apocryphal, but I will let the historians decide.
42. René Lévy and Jean-Marc Berlière, *History of the Police in France: From the Old Regime to the Present Day* (New World Editions, 2011); David Garrioch, "The People of Paris and Their Police in the Eighteenth

Century. Reflections on the Introduction of a 'Modern' Police Force," *European History Quarterly*, 24 (1994): 511–35.

43. Quoted in Neocleous, *A Critical Theory of Police Power*, 59.

44. Santiago Legarre, "The Historical Background of the Police Power," *Journal of Constitutional Law*, vol. 9 (2006): 750. It is not a coincidence that Queen Anne was also the English monarch who carried out the absorption of Scotland into the British monarchy and was also responsible for greatly expanding the British slave trade through securing the contract (*asiento*) to supply enslaved Africans to the Spanish colonies in 1713.

45. Legarre, "The Historical Background of the Police Power," 750.

46. Neocleous, *A Critical Theory of Police Power*, 86.

47. Neocleous, *A Critical Theory of Police Power*, 86.

48. Neocleous, *A Critical Theory of Police Power*, 97.

49. Jill Lepore, "The Invention of the Police," *The New Yorker,* July 20, 2020.

50. Letter, Thomas Jefferson to James Madison, July 26, 1780, *Founders Online,* National Archives.

51. Kristian Williams, *Our Enemies in Blue: Police and Power in America* (Oakland, CA: AK Press, 2015), 56.

52. Brucato, *Race and Police*, 122.

53. Brucato, *Race and Police*, 124.

54. Garrioch, "People of Paris."

55. Clive Emsley, *Policing and Its Context 1750–1870* (London: Macmillan, 1983), 12.

56. Clive Emsley, "A Typology of Nineteenth Century Police," *Crime, History, and Societies* 3, no. 1 (1999): 29–44.

57. Major-General Lord Blayney, quoted in Emsley, *Policing and Its Context*, 40, my emphasis.

58. Emsley, *Policing and Its Context*, 41.

59. Emsley, "A Typology of Nineteenth Century Police."

60. S. H. Palmer, *Police and Protest in England and Ireland, 1780–1850* (Cambridge: Cambridge University Press, 1988), 148.

61. Hadden, *Slave Patrols*, 13.

62. Brucato, *Race and Police*, 100.

63. Hadden, *Slave Patrols*, 11.

64. "N o 329. An ACT for the Governing of Negroes," May 1667, in William Rawlin, *The Laws of Barbados Collected in One Volume by William Rawlin, of the Middle-Temple, London, Esquire, and Now Clerk of the Assembly of the Said Island*, 137, http://name.umdl.umich.edu/A30866.0001.001.

65. Brucato, *Race and Police*, 100; Rawlin, *The Laws of Barbados*, 140.

66. Bradley J. Nicholson, "Legal Borrowing and the Origins of Slave Law

notes

in the British Colonies," *American Journal of Legal History* 38, no. 1 (January 1994): 38–54.

67. Rawlin, *The Laws of Barbados*, 137; Jerome S. Handler, "Freedman and Slaves in the Barbados Militia," *Journal of Caribbean History* 19 (1984): 1–25.
68. Hadden, *Slave Patrols*, 12.
69. William Dickson, *Letters on Slavery* (London: printed and sold by J. Phillips and sold by J. Johnson and Elliot and Kay, 1788), 97.
70. Hilary Beckles, *The First Black Slave Society: Britain's "Barbarity Time" in Barbados, 1636-1876* (Kingston, Jamaica: University Press of the West Indies, 2016), 133.
71. Quoted in Theodore W. Allen, *The Invention of the White Race: Volume II: The Origin of Racial Oppression in Anglo America* (London: Verso Books, 2012), 198.
72. Allen, *Invention of the White Race*, vol. 2, 198.
73. North Carolina directly paid patrols. In the other southern states, the patrol was compensated sometimes with leniency on taxes, exemption from militia duty, and other perks. Hadden, *Slave Patrols*, 37.
74. Brucato, *Race and Police*, 40.
75. Saidiya V. Hartman, *Scenes of Subjection: Terror, Slavery, and Self-Making in Nineteenth-Century America* (Oxford: Oxford University Press, 1997), 69.
76. Hadden, *Slave Patrols*, 55.
77. Hadden, *Slave Patrols*, 150.
78. Brucato, *Race and Police*, 202.
79. Hadden, *Slave Patrols*, 72, 97.
80. Hadden *Slave Patrols*, 90.
81. Keri Leigh Merritt, *Masterless Men: Poor Whites and Slavery in the Antebellum South* (Cambridge: Cambridge University Press, 2017), 180.
82. Merritt, *Masterless Men*, 253–55.
83. Hartman, *Scenes of Subjection*, 79–80; Dorothy Roberts, *Killing the Black Body: Race, Reproduction, and the Meaning of Liberty* (New York: Vintage, 1999), 29–31; Angela Davis, *Women, Race, and Class* (New York: Vintage, 1983), chapter one.
84. Davis, *Women, Race, and Class*, chapter one.
85. Merritt, *Masterless Men,* 210.
86. Frederick Douglass, *Life and Times of Frederick Douglass* (Boston: De Wolfe, Fisk, & Co., 1895), 224.
87. Merritt, *Masterless Men*, 225–26.
88. Ruth Wilson Gilmore, "Race, Prisons, and War," in *Abolition*

Geography: Essays Towards Liberation, ed. Ruth Wilson Gilmore (London: Verso, 2022), 188.

89. Edmund Morgan, *American Slavery, American Freedom* (New York: W.W. Norton & Company, 1975), 331.

90. Barbara J. Fields, "Slavery, Race, and Ideology in the United States of America," in *Racecraft: The Soul of Inequality in American Life*, ed. Karen E. Fields (London: Verso, 2012), 128.

91. Brucato, *Race and Police*, 198.

92. See chapter 1 in Julius Scott, *The Common Wind: Afro-American Currents in the Age of the Haitian Revolution* (New York: Verso, 2018).

93. Peter Linebaugh, *The London Hanged* (London: Verso, 2006), 334–38; Peter Linebaugh, "Say Their Names!," *Counterpunch*, June 5, 2020.

94. Linebaugh, *The London Hanged*, 348.

95. Aviah Sarah Day and Shanice Octavia McBean, *Abolition Revolution* (London: Pluto Press, 2022), 93.

96. Linebaugh, *The London Hanged*, 347.

97. Linebaugh, *The London Hanged*, 333.

98. Emsley, *Policing and Its Context*, 28; Linebaugh, *The London Hanged*, 358.

99. Emlsey, *Policing and Its Context*, 29.

100. Day and McBean, *Abolition Revolution*, 95.

101. John McGowan, "The Emergence of Modern Civil Police in Scotland: A Case Study of the Police and Systems of Police in Edinburghshire 1800–1833," PhD thesis, The Open University, 1997, 91.

102. Brucato, *Race and Police*, 135.

103. Brucato, *Race and Police*, 181.

104. Peter Linebaugh and Marcus Rediker, *The Many-Headed Hydra: The Hidden History of the Revolutionary Atlantic* (London: Verso, 2012), 206–10.

105. Quoted in Brucato, *Race and Police*, 174. Also see Linebaugh and Rediker, *The Many-Headed Hydra*.

106. Sidney L Harring, *Policing a Class Society: The Experience of American Cities, 1865–1915* (Chicago: Haymarket Books, 2017), 33.

107. Whitehouse, "The Origins of the Police."

108. Garrioch, "People of Paris," 515.

109. Garrioch, "People of Paris," 515.

110. Eric Hobsbawm, "The Machine Breakers," *Past & Present* 1, no. 1 (February 1952): 57–70.

111. Samuel Chapman and Col. T. Eric St. Jonson, *The Police Heritage in England and America* (East Lansing: Michigan State University Press, 1962), 13.

112. Scott, *The Common Wind*, 194.

notes 229

113. Scott, *The Common Wind*, 194.
114. Robert S. Starobin, *Industrial Slavery in the Old South* (New York: Oxford University Press, 1970), 11.
115. Errol Henderson, "Slave Religion, Slave Hiring, and the Incipient Proletarianization of Enslaved Black Labor: Developing Du Bois' Thesis on Black Participation in the Civil War as a Revolution," *Journal of African American Studies* 19, no. 2 (June 2015): 192–213.
116. Sylviane A. Diouf, *Slavery's Exiles* (New York: New York University Press, 2014), 37, 206.
117. Scott, *The Common Wind*, 199.
118. Scott, *The Common Wind*, 191.
119. David Whitehouse, "The Denmark Vesey Rebellion (Part 1)," *Tempest*, January 2, 2023.
120. Starobin, *Industrial Slavery in the Old South*, 3.
121. The revolt of Nat Turner, confined to an isolated rural environment without the aim of connecting to the cities, was an outlier of the trend of the latter period of revolt, as David Whitehouse and others have pointed out.
122. Quoted in Whitehouse, "Denmark Vesey Rebellion."
123. Whitehouse, "Denmark Vesey Rebellion."
124. Williams, *Our Enemies in Blue*, 78.
125. Alex S. Vitale, *The End of Policing* (London: Verso Books, 2017), 46.
126. Paul Mason, *Live Working or Die Fighting* (Chicago: Haymarket, 2020) 23.
127. Mason, *Live Working or Die Fighting*, 12; Emsley, *Policing and Its Context*, 47.
128. Mason, *Live Working or Die Fighting*, 14.
129. E. P. Thompson, *The Making of the English Working Class* (New York: Vintage Books, 1966), 681–91; J. L. Lyman, "The Metropolitan Police Act of 1829: An Analysis of Certain Events Influencing the Passage and Character of the Metropolitan Police Act in England," *Journal of Criminal Law, Criminology, and Political Science* 55 (1964): 148.
130. Thompson, *Making of the English Working Class*, 695.
131. Mason, *Live Working or Die Fighting*, 25.
132. Lyman, "The Metropolitan Police Act of 1829."
133. Thompson, *Making of the English Working Class*, 82.
134. David Robinson, "The Local Government of the Metropolis," *Blackwood's Edinburgh Magazine* 29 (January–June 1831): 83.
135. Quoted in Melossi and Pavarini, *The Prison and the Factory*, 56.
136. Quoted in Linebaugh, *The London Hanged*, 360.
137. Harring, *Policing a Class Society*, 15.
138. David Whitehouse, "Origins of the Police," *Libcom*, December 24, 2014,

230   **Their End Is Our Beginning**

139. It is from his name that police get their colloquial sobriquet "bobbies."
140. Robert Peel, House of Commons proceedings, March 11, 1817, vol. 35, 980–93.
141. Peel, House of Commons proceedings.
142. Robert Peel, quoted in Tanzil Chowdhury, "From the Colony to the Metropole," *Abolishing the Police*, ed. Koshka Duff (London: Dog Section Press, 2021).
143. Emsley, *Policing and Its Context*, 69.
144. Marx, *Capital*, vol. 1, chapter 29.
145. Harring, *Policing a Class Society*, 13; Neocleous, *A Critical Theory of Police Power*, 81.
146. Quoted in Audrey Farrell, *Crime, Class & Corruption* (London: Bookmarks, 1992), 53.
147. Chapman and Johnston, *Police Heritage in England and America*, 14.
148. Poster, April 6, 1850, accessed at https://british-police-history.uk/f/ aberystwyth.
149. Farrell, *Crime, Class & Corruption*, 15.
150. Friedrich Engels, *The Condition of the Working Class in England*, 157.
151. Farrell, *Crime, Class & Corruption*, 54.
152. Chartism was a mass political movement based in England roughly from 1837 to 1860. Organized around a political platform—the People's Charter—the movement fused democratic rights with betterment of working conditions for workers. The movement was broad and its activity consisted of everything from petitions to general strikes to armed insurrection. Eventually suppressed with the help of the new institution of the police, it involved and influenced individuals like Marx and Engels, and many of its cadre and spirit would re-emerge in the socialist labor movement. The editor of the Chartists' main newspaper would be the first to publish the *Communist Manifesto*.
153. Emsley, *Policing and Its Context*, 69; Farrell, *Crime, Class & Corruption*, 56–57.
154. Quentin Deleurmoz, "Police Forces and Political Crises: Revolutions, Policing Alternatives and Institutional Resilience in Paris, 1848–1871," *Urban History* 43, no. 2 (May 2016): 240.
155. Deleurmoz, "Police Forces and Political Crises"; the renovation of Paris was carried out by Georges-Eugène Haussmann.
156. Seán William Gannon, "The Black and Tans in Palestine—Irish Connections to the Palestine Police 1922–1948," *The Irish Story*, February 20, 2020.
157. Seán William Gannon, "The Royal Irish Constabulary and Colonial

Policing: Lessons and Legacies," *Raidió Teilifís Éireann*, 2020.

158. Gannon, "The Royal Irish Constabulary and Colonial Policing."

159. David Arnold, "The Police and Colonial Control in South India," *Social Scientist* 4, no. 12 (July 1976): 5.

160. Hossam el-Hamalawy, "In Egypt, the Police Are the Soldiers for the Regime," *Rosa Luxemburg Stiftung*, January 24, 2024.

161. El-Hamalawy, "In Egypt, the Police."

162. Thomas H. Holloway, *Policing Rio de Janeiro: Repression and Resistance in a Nineteenth-Century City* (Palo Alto: Stanford University Press, 1993), 29, 50.

163. Holloway, *Policing Rio de Janeiro*, 89, 91, 233.

164. Holloway, *Policing Rio de Janeiro*, 270.

165. Deniz Kocak, "The Historical Origins of Community Policing in 19th Century Britain and Imperial Japan," *Rethinking Community Policing in International Police Reform: Examples from Asia*, SSR paper 17 (London: Ubiquity Press, 2018), 19.

166. Roxanne Dunbar-Ortiz, *An Indigenous Peoples' History of the United States* (Boston: Beacon Press, 2014), 126–27.

167. Roxanne Dunbar-Ortiz, *Loaded: A Disarming History of the Second Amendment* (San Francisco: City Lights, 2018), 51; Kelly Lytle Hernández, *Migra!: History of the U.S. Border Patrol* (Berkeley: University of California Press, 2010), 20.

168. Eugene Barker, *The Life of Stephen F. Austin, Founder of Texas, 1793–1836: A Chapter in the Westward Movement of the Anglo-American People* (Nashville: Cokesbury Press, 1926), 256.

169. Dunbar-Ortiz, *An Indigenous Peoples' History of the United States*, 127.

170. Hernández, *Migra!*, 20; Dunbar-Ortiz, *Loaded*, 52.

171. According to Hernández's history, the "father of the U.S. Border Patrol" was Jefferson Davis Milton, an ex-Texas Ranger who, in an instance of the ironic poetry of history, was named for the president of the slavers' Confederacy.

172. Williams, *Our Enemies in Blue*, 114.

173. Egon Bitner, *The Functions of the Police in Modern Society* (Chevy Chase, MD: Center for Studies in Crime and Delinquency, 1970), 15.

174. Quoted in Matthew Guariglia, *Police and the Empire City: Race and the Origins of Modern Policing in New York* (Durham, NC: Duke University Press, 2023), 24.

175. John P. Senning, "The Know-Nothing Movement in Illinois 1854–1856," *Journal of the Illinois State Historical Society (1908-1984)* 7, no. 1 (April 1914): 11.

232   Their End Is Our Beginning

176. Sam Mitrani, *The Rise of the Chicago Police Department: Class and Conflict, 1850-1894* (Urbana, IL: University of Illinois Press, 2013), 18.
177. Mitrani, *The Rise of the Chicago Police Department*, 19.
178. Harring, *Policing a Class Society*, 156.
179. Harring, *Policing a Class Society*, 150.
180. Quoted in Harring, *Policing a Class Society*, 152.
181. Mitrani, *The Rise of the Chicago Police Department*, 15.
182. Mitrani, *The Rise of the Chicago Police Department*, 15.
183. Mitrani, *The Rise of the Chicago Police Department*, 24.
184. Report of police inspector John A. Bonfield after the Chicago Police Department attacked a strike and murdered six workers in the lead-up to the 1886 Haymarket affair.
185. Harring, *Policing a Class Society*, 254.

chapter 2: "Bullies in Blue Suits"

1. Alexander "Clubber" Williams was a nineteenth-century New York City cop who was one of the first police investigated for misconduct by the 1894 Lexow Committee. Quoted in David Correia and Tyler Wall, *Police: A Field Guide* (London: Verso Books, 2018), 40.
2. These were some of the last words spoken by Sandra Bland, recorded by a bystander during a routine traffic stop of Bland by police in Texas in 2015. After her arrest, Bland was taken to a local jail, where she died under suspicious circumstances. Many believe the police are responsible.
3. The police also made false statements about packages for Glover being delivered to Taylor's home to justify the obtaining of the warrant.
4. Patrick Radden Keefe, "The Family That Built an Empire of Pain," *New Yorker,* October 23, 2017; see also Sam Quinones, *Dreamland: The True Story of America's Opiate Epidemic* (London: Bloomsbury Press, 2015).
5. Keefe, "The Family That Built an Empire of Pain"; National Institute on Drug Abuse, "Drug Overdose Death Rates," National Institutes of Health, June 30, 2023, https://nida.nih.gov/research-topics/trends-statistics/overdose-death-rates.
6. Nicole Colson, "Overwhelmed by a Sea of Despair," *Socialist Worker,* April 6, 2017.
7. Tom McArthur, "Purdue and Sackler Family Agree $7.4bn Opioid Settlement," BBC News, January 23, 2025, https://www.bbc.com/news/articles/ceq97nvjv0wo.
8. Micol Seigel, *Violence Work: State Power and the Limits of the Police* (Durham, NC: Duke University Press, 2018), 14.
9. Kristian Williams, *Our Enemies in Blue* (Oakland, CA: AK Press,

notes

233

2015), 109.

10. Josiah Quincy, *Remarks on Some of the Provisions of the Laws of Massachusetts Affecting Poverty, Vice, and Crime* (Cambridge: University Press by Hilliard and Metcalf, 1822), 4.

11. Emsley, *Policing and Its Context*, 121.

12. Mitrani, *The Rise of the Chicago Police Department*, 27.

13. Mitrani, *The Rise of the Chicago Police Department*, 31; Holloway, *Policing Rio de Janeiro*, 210–12; Emsley, *Policing and Its Context*, 121; see also Eric Makknonen, "A Disorderly People? Urban Order in the Nineteenth and Twentieth Century," *Journal of American History* 68, no. 3 (December 1981): 539–59, for more on trends in the US.

14. Letter, Theodore Roosevelt to Winthrop Murray Crane (Governor of Massachusetts), October 22, 1902, in Elting E. Morrison, ed. *The Letters of Theodore Roosevelt, Vol. III* (Cambridge: Harvard University Press, 1951), 360.

15. Quoted in Williams, *Our Enemies in Blue*, 180.

16. Williams, *Our Enemies in Blue*, 182.

17. David Correia, *Set the Earth on Fire: The Great Anthracite Coal Strike of 1902 and the Birth of the Police* (Chicago: Haymarket Books, 2024), 13.

18. Correia, *Set the Earth on Fire*, 109.

19. John C. Groom, letter to Governor Pennypacker, quoted in Correia, *Set the Earth on Fire*, 185–86.

20. Stuart Schrader, *Badges Without Borders: How Global Counterinsurgency Transformed American Policing* (Oakland, CA: University of California, 2019), 74.

21. Quoted in Schrader, *Badges Without Borders*, 67; Center for Research on Criminal Justice, *The Iron Fist and the Velvet Glove: An Analysis of the U.S. Police* (Berkeley, CA: Center for Research on Criminal Justice, 1982), 33.

22. Schrader, *Badges Without Borders*, 67.

23. Quoted in Julian Go, "The Colonial Origins of the UChicago Police," *Rampant,* June 6, 2023.

24. Go, "Colonial Origins of the UChicago Police."

25. Matthew Guariglia, *Police and the Empire City: Race and the Origins of Modern Policing in New York* (Durham, NC: Duke University Press, 2023), 74–79.

26. Simon Balto, *Occupied Territory: Policing Black Chicago from Red Summer to Black Power* (Chapel Hill, NC: University of North Carolina Press, 2019), 166, 159.

27. Balto, *Occupied Territory*, 156.

28. Balto, *Occupied Territory*, 166.

234   **Their End Is Our Beginning**

29. Balto, *Occupied Territory*, 163.
30. Balto, *Occupied Territory*, 163.
31. Mariame Kaba, *Resisting Police Violence in Harlem*, pamphlet (Chicago: Project NIA, 2012), 12.
32. Quoted in Elizabeth Hinton, *America on Fire: The Untold History of Police Violence and Black Rebellion Since the 1960s* (New York: Liveright Publishing, 2021), 13.
33. Marie Gottschalk, *Caught: The Prison State and the Lockdown of American Politics* (Princeton: Princeton University Press, 2014), 147; Center for Research on Criminal Justice, *Iron Fist and the Velvet Glove*, 50.
34. Martin Luther King, Jr., *Autobiography of Martin Luther King, Jr.* (New York: Grand Central Publishing, 2001), 291.
35. Quoted in Seigel, *Violence Work*, 23.
36. Hinton, *America on Fire*, 10.
37. Elizabeth Hinton, *From the War on Poverty to the War on Crime* (Cambridge: Harvard University Press, 2016),106.
38. Hinton, *From the War on Poverty*, 107.
39. Hinton, *From the War on Poverty*, 106.
40. Balto, *Occupied Territory*, 216.
41. Keeanga-Yamahtta Taylor, *From #BlackLivesMatter to Black Liberation* (Chicago: Haymarket Books, 2016), 54.
42. Taylor, *From #BlackLivesMatter to Black Liberation*, 46–47; Hinton, *From the War on Poverty,* 127.
43. Ruth Wilson Gilmore, *Abolition Geographies: Essays Towards Liberation* (London: Verso Books, 2022), 324.
44. Gilmore, *Abolition Geographies*, 325.
45. Gilmore, *Abolition Geographies*, 326.
46. Loïc Wacquant, *Punishing the Poor: The Neoliberal Government of Social Insecurity* (Durham, NC: Duke University Press, 2009), 114, 125.
47. Hinton, *America on Fire*, 204.
48. Ruth Wilson Gilmore, *Golden Gulag: Prisons, Surplus, Crisis, and Opposition in Globalizing California* (Berkeley, CA: University of California Press, 2007), 20.
49. Friedrich Engels, "Condition of the Working Class in England," *Marx and Engels Collected Works, vol 3* (Moscow, Progress Publishers; 1975), 393–94.
50. Gilmore, *Golden Gulag*, 28.
51. The stats of the Substance Abuse and Mental Health Services Administration (SAMHSA) national surveys report use of "illicit" drugs at just a percentage point higher for Blacks than whites, although "heavy alcohol use" trends strongly white. The Hamilton

notes   235

Project/Brookings Institute report white use at slightly higher rates than Black use. Whichever way you cut it, the difference is statistically small, especially in comparison with the grossly disproportionate rates of arrest. Peter Ikeler and Calvin John Smiley, "The Racial Economics of Mass Incarceration," *Spectre,* November 8, 2020.

52. brian bean, "How the Workers Stole Christmas," *Rampant,* December 21, 2021.

53. Sam Dean, "Retailers Say Thefts Are at a Crisis Level, the Numbers Say Otherwise," *Los Angeles Times,* December 15, 2021.

54. "U.S. Companies Are Stealing Pay from Low Wage Workers, Report Says," CBS News, May 4, 2021.

55. Alexia Elejalde-Ruiz, "Chicago to Create Office to Enforce City's Minimum Wage," *Chicago Tribune,* October 31, 2018.

56. Engels, "Condition of the Working Class," 514.

57. Evgeny Pashukanis, *Law and Marxism: A General Theory* (London: Pluto Press, 1989), 173.

58. Naomi Murakawa, *The First Civil Right: How Liberals Built Prison America* (New York: Oxford University Press, 2014), 3.

59. Michelle Alexander, *The New Jim Crow: Mass Incarceration in the Age of Colorblindness* (New York: New Press, 2012), chapter 1; Khalil Gibran Muhammad, *The Condemnation of Blackness: Race, Crime, and the Making of Modern Urban America* (Cambridge: Harvard University Press, 2010); Angela Davis, "Race and Criminalization," in *Abolition: Politics, Practices, Promises vol.1,* ed. Angela Davis (Chicago: Haymarket Books, 2024), 76–91.

60. Taylor, *From #BlackLivesMatter to Black Liberation,* 207–10.

61. Muhammad, *Condemnation of Blackness.*

62. Robert Peel's "9 Principles of Policing" accompanied the creation of the London Metropolitan Police. The first principle was "to prevent crime and disorder, as an alternative to their repression by military force and severity of legal punishment."

63. John Moore, "Protecting the Property of Slavers: London's First State Funded Police," *Abolitionist Futures,* August 11, 2021.

64. Linebaugh, *The London Hanged,* 417; Moore, "Protecting the Property."

65. Linebaugh, *The London Hanged,* 430.

66. Patrick Colquhoun, *The Treatise on the Police of the Metropolis,* quoted in Mark Neocleous, *A Critical Theory of Police Power: The Fabrication of the Social Order* (London: Verso Books, 2021), 125.

67. Colquhoun, *Treatise on Indigence,* quoted in Neocleous, *Critical Theory of Police Power,* 128.

236   **Their End Is Our Beginning**

68. Quoted in Linebaugh, *The London Hanged*, 428.
69. Neocleous, *Critical Theory of Police Power*, 154.
70. Robin D. G. Kelley, "The Black Poor and the Politics of Opposition in a New South City, 1929–1970," in *The "Underclass" Debate: Views from History*, ed. Michael B. Katz (Princeton; Princeton University; 1992), 301.
71. Ruth Wilson Gilmore, "A World to Win: Seizing the State," interview by Grace Blakeley, *Jacobin Radio* podcast, September 21, 2022.
72. David McNally, *Against the Market: Political Economy, Market Socialism and the Marxist Critique* (London: Verso Books, 1993), 34.
73. Both Neocleous and Linebaugh expound on this point in the works cited above.
74. These programs have been explicitly designed as police propaganda, from racist Los Angeles police chief William H. Parker's consulting on *Dragnet* in 1951 to one of the current longest-running dramas, *Law and Order*. Rick Porter, "How Network TV Depends on Cop Shows," *Hollywood Reporter*, June 20, 2020; Mike Davis and Jon Weiner, "How LAPD Police Chief William H. Parker Influenced the Depiction of Policing on the TV Show Dragnet," *Verso* blog, June 6, 2020.
75. In London, detectives were implemented earlier, but still it took fourteen years before the London Metropolitan Police added the role. See Emsley, *Policing and Its Context*, 76.
76. Sean Goodison, "Local Police Department Personal; 2020," report, *Bureau of Justice Statistics*, November 2022.
77. Shayne Kavanagh and Jennifer Park, "Rethinking Police and Public Safety Budgeting," *PM Magazine*, April 1, 2021.
78. Egon Bittner, *The Functions of the Police* (Chevy Chase, MD: National Institute of Mental Health, 1970), 38.
79. Bittner, *The Functions of the Police*, 42.
80. Schrader, *Badges Without Borders*, 12.
81. Also known as "snitching." Additionally, it could be pointed out that the police metric for a crime being solved is called the clearance rate. Per the FBI, the clearance rate for violent crime is less than 50 percent, and for nonviolent crime the clearance rate is less than 20 percent.
82. Jack R. Greene and Carl Klockars, "What Do Police Do?" in *Thinking About Police: Contemporary Readings*, ed. Carl Klockars and Stephen Mastrofski (New York: McGraw-Hill, 1991), 273, 275.
83. Audrey Farrell, *Crime, Class and Corruption: The Politics of the Police* (London: Bookmarks, 1992), 25.
84. Reports available on FBI Crime Data Explorer at http://cde.ucr.cjis.gov.
85. Shima Baughman, "Police Solve Just 2% of All Major Crimes," *The*

notes

237

Conversation, August 20, 2020.

86. "Research and Resources," Innocence Project, innocenceproject.com

87. Alex S. Vitale, *The End of Policing* (London: Verso Books, 2017), 31.

88. Farrell, *Crime, Class and Corruption*, 32.

89. Rebecca Neusteter and Megan O'Toole, *Every Three Seconds: Unlocking Police Data on Arrests* (Brooklyn, NY: Vera Institute of Justice, January 2019).

90. Balto, *Occupied Territory*, 3.

91. Robin D. G. Kelley, "Thug Nation: On State Violence and Disposability," in *Policing the Planet: Why the Policing Crisis Led to Black Lives Matter*, ed. Jordan T. Camp and Christina Heatherton (New York: Verso Books, 2016), 25–26. Also, for more on the the the racist assumptions of Kelling and Wilson and the influence of Edward Banfield, see chapter two in Bernard Harcourt, *Illusion of Order* (Cambridge: Harvard University Press, 2001).

92. Hinton, *From the War on Poverty to the War on Crime*, 21.

93. See Camp and Heatherton, *Policing the Planet*.

94. Wacquant, *Punishing the Poor*, 260.

95. Wacquant, *Punishing the Poor*, 263.

96. Alice Speri, "NYPD Is Still Stopping and Frisking Black People at Disproportionate Rates," *The Intercept*, June 10, 2021; Corey Kilgannon, "N.Y.P.D. Anti-Crime Units Still Stopping People Illegally, Report Shows," *New York Times*, June 5, 2023.

97. Harcourt, *Illusion of Order*, 51–52.

98. Pascal Sabino, "The New Stop and Frisk? Chicago Police Make Millions of Traffic Stops While Searching For Guns," *Block Club Chicago*, March 30, 2023.

99. Quoted in James Forman Jr., *Locking Up Our Own* (New York: Farrar, Straus, and Giroux, 2017), 170.

100. Dara Lind, "Why You Shouldn't Take Any Crime Statistics Seriously," *Vox*, August 24, 2014.

101. Richard Vargas, Chris Williams, Phillip O. Sullivan, Christina Cano, "Capitalizing on Crisis: Chicago Policy Responses to Homicide Waves, 1920–2016," *University Chicago Law Review* 89, no. 2 (March 2022), 406; Hinton, *From the War on Poverty*, 6–7.

102. Amber Jean, Aryssa, Samhitha, Troy Bolton, brian bean, "Science in the Service of Cops," *Rampant,* October 9, 2020.

103. Thomas B. Marvell and Carlisle Moody, "Specification Problems, Police Levels, and Crime Rates," *Criminology* 34, no. 4 (2006): 609–646.

104. YongJei Lee, John Eck, Nicholas Corsaro, "Conclusions from

the History of Research into the Effects of Police Force Size on Crime—1968 through 2013: A Historical Systematic Review," *Journal of Experimental Criminology* 12 (2016): 431–51.

105. John Worrall, Tomislav Kovandzic, "COPS Grants and Crime Revisited," *Criminology* 45, no. 1 (2007): 183.

106. John Eck and Edward R. Maguire, "Have Changes in Policing Reduced Violent Crime? An Assessment of the Evidence" in *The Crime Drop in America*, ed. Alfred Blumstein and Joel Wallman (New York: Cambridge University Press, 2006).

107. Aaron Chalfin, Benjamin Hansen, Emily K. Weisburst, Morgan C. Williams Jr., "Police Force Size and Civilian Race," *American Economic Review* 4, no. 2 (2022): 139–58.

108. Shaila Dawan, "'Refund the Police?' Why It Might Not Reduce Crime," *New York Times*, June 22, 2023.

109. Jackie Wang, *Carceral Capitalism* (South Pasadena, CA: semiotext(e), 2018), 231.

110. Camp and Heatherton, *Policing the Planet*, 5.

111. Wacquant, *Punishing the Poor*, 253–54.

112. Wacuant, *Punishing the Poor*, 255, also see Harcourt, *Illusion of Order*.

113. Quoted in Harcourt, *Illusion of Order*, 179.

114. Tyler Wall, "Inventing Humanity, Or the Thin Blue Line as Patronizing Shit," from *Violent Order: Essays on the Nature of Police*, ed. David Correia and Tyler Wall (Chicago: Haymarket Books, 2021), 15.

115. Christopher M. Sullivan and Zachary P. O'Keefe, "Evidence That Curtailing Proactive Policing Can Reduce Major Crime," *Nature* 1 (2017): 730–37.

116. Rob Arthur, "What Happened After Chicago Police Cut Down on Busting Drug Possession and Prostitution," *Vice News*, December 5, 2019.

117. Hannu Takala, *The Police Strike in Finland* (Helsinki: Oikeuspoliittinen tutkimuslaitos, 1979); T. Makinen; H. Takala, "1976 Police Strike in Finland," in *Policing Scandinavia*, ed. Ragnar Hauge (Oslo: Universitetsforlaget; 1980), 87–106.

118. Yoav Gonen and Eileen Grench, "Five Days Without Cops: Could Brooklyn Policing Experiment Be 'Model for the Future,'" *The City*, January 3, 2021.

119. Interview conducted by author with Brazilian activist and lawyer Aldo Cordiero Sauda on March 6, 2024.

120. Arkady Petrov, "Prominent Ceará Senator Is Shot While Challenging Striking Police Officers," *El Pais*, February 20, 2020.

121. Sam Cowie, "Brazil Sends Armed Forces to North-east to Quell

notes 239

Violence from Police Strike," February 21, 2020.

122. Rory Fanning, "Why Was Stephon Watts Killed?," *Socialist Worker*, February 27, 2012.

123. D. Fuller, *Overlooked in the Undercounted: The Role of Mental Illness in Fatal Police Encounters* (Alexandria, VA: Treatment Advocacy Center, December 2015).

124. Kimberly Kindy, Julie Tate, Jennifer Jenkins, Ted Mellnik, "Fatal Police Shooting of Mentally Ill More Likely in Small and Midsize Areas," *Washington Post*, October 17, 2020.

125. Lindsey Bailey, "Chicago Needs Treatment Not Trauma," *Rampant*, November 20, 2020.

126. Julia Cardi, "15 Months into STAR Program. No Calls Directed to Civilian-led Teams Resulted in Arrest," *Denver Gazette*, October 28, 2022; Thoma Dee and Jaymes Pyne, "A Community Response to Mental Health and Substance Use Decreased Crime," *Science Advances*, June 8, 2022.

127. Mariame Kaba and Andrea J. Ritchie, *No More Police: A Case for Abolition* (New York: The New Press, 2022), 155–58.

128. Kaba and Ritchie, *No More Police*, 150.

129. Jeff Asher and Ben Horwitz, "How Do the Police Actually Spend Their Time?," *New York Times*, November 8, 2021.

130. Cited in Robert Hampton, "Domestic Violence and Homicide of Black Women," *Facts About Domestic Violence and African American Women*, ed. Robert Hampton, Joyce Thomas, Trisha Bent-Goodley, and Tameka Gilium (St. Paul, MN: University of Minnesota Press, 2015).

131. INCITE!, *The Critical Resistance-INCITE! Statement on Gender Violence and the Prison-Industrial Complex* (Incite-national.org, 2008). One other recent trend to note is that during the Covid-related lockdowns, there was a significant rise in domestic violence rates worldwide, per several reports.

132. American Civil Liberties Union, *Responses from the Field: Sexual Assault, Domestic Violence, and Policing*, report (New York: ACLU Foundation, 2015).

133. Interrupting Criminalization, "Police Responses to Domestic Violence: A Fact Sheet," https://www.interruptingcriminalization.com/resources-all/police-responses-to-domestic-violence-a-fact-sheet.

134. Derecka Purnell, *Becoming Abolitionists: Police, Protests, and the Pursuit of Freedom* (New York: Astra House, 2021),175.

135. Aya Gruper, "How Police Became the Go-to Response for Domestic Violence," *Slate*, July 7, 2020.

240   **Their End Is Our Beginning**

136. Brit Schulte, "We Won Clemency for Cyntoia Brown—Now Let's Free All Survivors," *In These Times*, January 15, 2019.

137. Connor Friersdorf, "Police Have a Much Bigger Domestic Violence Problem Than the NFL Does," *The Atlantic*, September 19, 2014; Joshua Klugman, "Do 40% of Police Families Experience Domestic Violence?" *Temple University* (blog), July 20, 2020; Geo Maher, *A World Without Police: How Strong Communities Make Cops Obsolete* (London: Verso Books, 2021), 58.

138. Sarah Cohen, Rebecca R. Ruiz, and Sarah Childress, "Departments Are Slow to Police Their Own Abusers," *New York Times*, November 23, 2012.

139. Purnell, *Becoming Abolitionists*, 186.

140. Purnell, *Becoming Abolitionists*, 186–87.

141. Philip Matthew Stinson, Robert W. Taylor, and John Liederbach, "The Situational Context of Police Sexual Violence: Data and Policy Implications," *Family and Intimate Partner Violence Quarterly* 12, no. 4 (2020): 59–68.

142. Sam Levine, "Police Killed Niani Finlayson Seconds after Responding to Her 911 Call, Video Shows," *Guardian*, December 29, 2023.

143. Critical Resistance-INCITE! Statement on Gender Violence and the Prison-Industrial Complex, https://incite-national.org/wp-content/uploads/2018/08/CR-INCITE-statement-2008discussion.pdf

144. Kaba and Ritchie, *No More Police*, 83.

145. Kaba and Ritchie, *No More Police*, 83.

146. Chris Michael, "US Breaks Record for Single Year after Weekend Murders," *Guardian*, December 5, 2023. The Gun Violence Archive, another recorder of this data, defines "mass shooting" differently, defining a mass shooting event as when multiple people are shot, regardless of numbers of deaths. Their number for 2023 is 603, more than one per day.

147. brian bean, "Cops Are Cowards, But We Don't Want Them Brave," *Rampant*, May 30, 2022.

148. Jillian Peterson, James Densley, Gina Erikson, "Presence of Armed School Officials and Fatal and Nonfatal Gunshot Injuries During Mass School Shootings, United States, 1980–2019," *Journal of the American Medical Association Network Open* 4, no. 2 (2021): e2037394; my emphasis.

149. In breathless headlines, it was claimed that an attempted 2023 shooting at a Jewish school in Memphis, Tennessee, by an ex-student, James Bowman, was "averted" by the police. However, the shooter

notes **241**

attempted to gain access to the school and left. The police then apprehended him at a traffic stop. Obviously, it is conjecture what would have happened after that point, but the specific violence that didn't occur at the school at that moment was not averted because of police involvement. In a strange but perhaps unsurprising irony, the attempted shooter of the school had witnessed his father killed by police twenty years prior, during a mental health crisis. The family filed a wrongful death lawsuit against the Memphis police because of police using lethal means against someone who "posed no threat to anyone other than himself." James Bowman suffered extensive trauma because of this. It is yet another instance in which the trauma of the police can be traced as boomeranging into more violence.

150. Larry Buchanan and Laura Leatherbey, "Who Stops 'A Bad Guy With A Gun'?," *New York Times*, June 22, 2022.
151. Buchanan and Leatherbey, "Who Stops 'A Bad Guy With A Gun'?,"
152. Akela Lacy, "Cops Didn't Stop the Uvalde School Shooting," *The Intercept*, May 25, 2022.
153. bean, "Cops Are Cowards."
154. ACLU Foundation, *War Comes Home: The Excessive Militarization of American Policing*, report (New York: ACLU Foundation, June 2014).
155. Gilmore, *Abolition Geography*, 147–48; Sean Larson, "The Political Economy of 'Gun Culture,'" *Socialist Worker*, March 1, 2018; Jeff Sparrow, "'When the Burning Moment Breaks': Gun Control and Rage Massacres," *Overland*, August 6, 2012.
156. Kendrick Lamar, "Alright," song, *To Pimp a Butterfly* (2015).
157. John Gramlich, "What the Data Says about Crime in the U.S.," Pew Research Center, April 24, 2024, https://www.pewresearch.org/short-reads/2020/11/20/facts-about-crime-in-the-u-s/
158. Wacquant, *Punishing the Poor*, 125.
159. Maria Woelfell and Tina Sfondeles, "POLL - Chicago Voters Feel Unsafe from Crime, Unhappy with Police Relations—and Seek a Candidate to Fix Both," *Chicago Sun-Times*, February 9, 2023; The Harris Poll, "Reimagining Public Safety in Chicago," MacArthur Foundation, June 3, 2021.
160. Tahman Bradley, Peter Curi, "Poll: Chicagoans Support Policies to Address Root Cause of Crime," *WGN9*, April 10, 2023.
161. The National Institute of Justice defines "use of force" or the proper determination for police to use violence as "amount of effort required by police to compel compliance by an unwilling subject."
162. Amina Khan, "Getting Shot by Police Is a Leading Cause of Death for

Young Black Men in America," *Los Angeles Times*, August 16, 2019.

163. Taylor, *From #Blacklivesmatter to Black Liberation*, 213.

164. Patrick Ball, "Violence in Blue," *Granta*, March 4, 2016.

165. Christopher Cannon, Alex McIntyre, Adam Pierce, "The Deadliest Jobs in America," *Bloomberg*, May 30, 2015.

166. 2023 Police Violence Report, Mappingpoliceviolence.org.

chapter 3: The Police State and Its Functionaries

1. W. E. B. Du Bois, "My Evolving Program for Negro Freedom," in *What The Negro Really Wants*, ed. Rayford Logan (Chapel Hill, NC: University of North Carolina Press, 1944).

2. Friedrich Engels, *The Origin of the Family, Private Property and the State*, chapter 9, "Barbarism and Civilization," Marx/Engels Internet Archive, https://www.marxists.org/archive/marx/works/1884/origin-family/ch09.htm.

3. Christopher Uggen, Ryan Larson, Sarah Shannon, and Robert Stewart, "Locked Out 2022: Estimates of People Denied Voting Rights," Sentencing Project, October 25, 2022; Kevin Morris, Coryn Grange, Zoe Merriman, "The Impact of Restrictive Voting Legislation," Brennan Center for Justice, April 5, 2022; "Democracy Defended," Thurgood Marshall Institute, September 2, 2021; Alexander Keyssar, "We Still Need to Abolish the Electoral College," interview by Chris Maisano, *Jacobin*, October 13, 2020.

4. "Did Money Win?" *OpenSecrets*, April 1, 2021; Karl Evers-Hillstrom, "Most Expensive Ever: 2020 Election Cost $14.4 Billion," *OpenSecrets*, February 11, 2021.

5. Quoted in Kim Moody, "The Class Ceiling: Political Money and The Primary Election," *Spectre*, no. 6 (Fall 2022): 37.

6. Moody, "The Class Ceiling."

7. Martin Gillens and Benjamin I. Page, "Testing Theories of American Politics: Elites, Interest Groups, and Average Citizens," *Perspectives on Politics* 12, no. 3 (2014): 564–81.

8. I return to the question of "community control" over the police in chapter five of this book.

9. For one example of this, see Olúfẹ́mi O. Táíwò's discussion of multinational institutions in *Elite Capture: How the Powerful Took Over Identity Politics (And Everything Else)* (Chicago: Haymarket Books, 2022), 27.

10. See V. I. Lenin, *The State and Revolution*. I intentionally leave the gender masculine although, of course, in contemporary society, the

police, while still predominantly cis male, have a sizable number of cis women and even transgender cops.

11. Mark Neocleous, *A Critical Theory of Police Power: The Fabrication of the Social Order* (London: Verso Books, 2021), 46.

12. Leon Trotsky, *History of the Russian Revolution* (Chicago: Haymarket Books, 2017), 80.

13. This often quoted definition, paired with the further description of "objective, territorially bounded set of institutions," comes from Ruth Wilson Gilmore and Craig Gilmore, "Restating the Obvious," in *Abolition Geography: Essays Towards Liberation*, ed. Ruth Wilson Gilmore (Verso Books, 2008): 262–63.

14. Hal Draper, *Karl Marx's Theory of Revolution Volume One: State and Bureaucracy* (New York: Monthly Review, 1977) 260.

15. Fred Block, "The Ruling Class Does Not Rule: Notes on the Marxist Theory of the State," *Socialist Revolution*, no. 33 (May–June 1977): 6–28.

16. As Lenin writes in *State and Revolution*: "Engels elucidates the concept of the 'power' which is called the state, a power which arose from society but places itself above it and alienates itself more and more from it."

17. See Draper, *Karl Marx's Theory of Revolution*, 321–24, on why "the exuberance of internal hostilities makes it difficult for any individual capitalist to be trusted as executor for the class as a whole."

18. Stuart Easterling, "Marx's Theory of Economic Crisis," *International Socialist Review* 32 (November–December 2003); Michael Goldfield, "Worker Insurgency, Radical Organization, and New Deal Labor Legislation," in *The American Political Science Review* 83, no. 4 (1989): 1257–82; Kim Moody, "Worker Insurgency and the New Deal," *Tempest*, December 20, 2022.

19. See Block, "The Ruling Class Does Not Rule."

20. Examples would include the *New York Times, Wall Street Journal, Financial Times*, and so on.

21. Draper, *Karl Marx's Theory of Revolution*, 324.

22. Block, "The Ruling Class Does Not Rule."

23. See, for example, Robert Brenner, "The Problem of Reformism," *Against the Current* 43 (May–June 1993).

24. Block, "The Ruling Class Does Not Rule."

25. One example of this was the reformist social democratic program in France under Mitterand in the early 1980s. See Jonah Birch, "The Many Lives of François Mitterrand," *Jacobin*, August 19, 2015.

26. Colin Barker, "States in Capitalism: Reflections on Value, Force, Many States and Other Problems," *Revolutionary Reflections* (June 2019), 45.

27. Barker, *States in Capitalism*, 30.
28. Barker, *States in Capitalism*, 41.
29. Neil Davidson, *Nation-States: Consciousness and Competition* (Chicago: Haymarket Books, 2016), 245.
30. Noura Erakat, "The Boomerang Comes Back," *Boston Review*, February 5, 2025.
31. Harsha Walia, *Border & Rule: Global Migration, Capitalism, and the Rise of Racist Nationalism* (Chicago: Haymarket Books, 2021), 206.
32. Barker, *States in Capitalism*, 37.
33. Neocleous, *A Critical Theory of Police Power*, 221.
34. Evgeny Pashukanis, *Law and Marxism: A General Theory* (London: Pluto; 1989), 149
35. Barker, *States in Capitalism*, 13.
36. Barker, *States in Capitalism*, 19.
37. These changes were due largely to the anomaly of the postwar economic boom that remains unparalleled in the history of capitalism, which allowed the state more leeway to cede gains to workers. See Kim Moody, "The Making of Business Unionism," in *In Solidarity: Essays on Working Class Organization* (Chicago: Haymarket Books, 2014).
38. Sam Levin, "2023 Saw Record Killings by US Police. Who Is Most Affected?" *Guardian*, January 8, 2024.
39. Jack Poulson, "Reports of a Silicon Valley/Military Divide Have Been Greatly Exaggerated," *Tech Inquiry*, July 7, 2020.
40. Hope O'Dell, "The US Is Sending More Troops into the Middle East. Where in the World Are US Military Deployed," *Global Affairs*, April 5, 2024.
41. For more on the dimensions of US military globalization, see Jonathan Ellis and brian bean, "Rebuilding the Anti-Imperialist Movement in a New Era," *Rampant*, March 17, 2021. Sanctions list pulled from "Sanctions Program and Country Information" list from the US Department of Treasury Office of Foreign Asset Control website in September 2024.
42. Sean Goodison, "Local Police Departments Personnel," Bureau of Justice Statistics, November 2022.
43. "Budget of the US Government: Fiscal Year 2022," Office of Management and Budget, Whitehouse.gov.
44. "Civilian Personnel in the DoD," Office of Diversity, Equity, and Inclusion, https://diversity.defense.gov/Portals/51/Documents/Resources/Docs/Civilian%20Employment/Civilian%20Employment.pdf.
45. Henry Taylor, "Who Is the World's Largest Employer? The Answer Might

notes

245

Not Be What You Expect," World Economic Forum, June 17, 2015.

46. Federal Bureau of Prisons, bop.gov/about/agency; US Customs and Border Protection, cbp.gov/about; Federal Bureau of Investigation, https://www.fbi.gov/about/faqs/how-many-people-work-for-the-fb; estimates for CIA and NSA from Wikipedia, as numbers are not officially disclosed; notably, this does not include civilian contractors, so undoubtedly this number is a conservative estimate. All numbers accessed September 2024.

47. Goodison, "Local Police Departments Personnel."

48. Karl Marx, *The Civil War in France*, marxists.org.

49. Stuart Hall, Chas Critcher, Tony Jefferson, John Clarke, *Policing the Crisis: Mugging, the State, and Law and Order* (London: Palgrave, 1978), 346, 347.

50. Sean Larson and Tyler Zimmer, "Who Runs Chicago?," *Rampant*, February 23, 2020.

51. David McNally, *Global Slump: The Economics and Politics of Crisis and Resistance* (London: PM Press, 2018), 118.

52. Brenden Beck, "The Role of Police in Gentrification," *The Appeal*, August 4, 2020.

53. Beck, "Role of Police in Gentrification."

54. Sean Larson, "The Abolitionist Road to Socialism," *Rampant*, July 23, 2020.

55. See Stuart Hall's treatment of "hustling" in *Policing the Crisis*, 351–58.

56. Sudhir Alladi Venkatesh, *Off the Books: The Underground Economy of the Urban Poor* (Cambridge: Harvard University Press, 2006), 4.

57. Venkatesh, *Off the Books*, 10–12.

58. For the latter, a prominent example was the use of the image of the Black "welfare queen" to drive through cuts to welfare in the 1980s and 1990s. Black women were used as a stand-in for the typical welfare recipient, a population of whom white women were the majority.

59. Gilmore, *Abolition Geography*, 451.

60. Fields, "Slavery, Race, and Ideology in the USA," 117.

61. Larson, "The Abolitionist Road to Socialism."

62. Gilmore, *Abolition Geography*, 265.

63. Ceebo the Rapper, "Fuck Tha Police," YouTube.com, August 2014.

64. The example of Ferguson, Missouri, is illustrative. The extent that the city used their police force to exert fines and fees upon the Black citizenry was exposed in the Department of Justice report completed after the killing of Michael Brown and made national news. However, in this extreme case, in 2015, city income from fees and fines collected

by the police amounted to $3 million (23% of the total income), while the police budget was $5.5 million (42% of expenditure). https://www.cnn.com/2015/03/06/us/ferguson-missouri-racism-tickets-fines/index.html; https://www.fergusoncity.com/DocumentCenter/View/1849/2016-COFM-Budget-Main-Final-Version. The work of Jackie Wang deserves exploration on this point, specifically her book *Carceral Capitalism* (Semiotext(e), 2018), that takes up the relationship of municipal finance and debt and connection to the police.

65. E. P. Thompson, "The Peculiarities of the English," *Socialist Register* (1965).

66. Ellen Meiksins Wood, *Democracy Against Capitalism: Renewing Historical Materialism* (Cambridge: Cambridge University Press, 1995), 82.

67. Thompson, "Peculiarities of the English," 11.

68. Leon Trotsky, "The Only Road," in *The Struggle Against Fascism in German* (New York: Pathfinder Press, 1971), 370.

69. Robin D. G. Kelley, "Insecure: Policing Under Racial Capitalism," *Spectre* 1, no. 2 (Fall 2020).

70. Williams, "Police Force Size and Civilian Race," 221.

71. Correia and Wall, *Violent Order*, 13.

72. Trotsky, "What Next? Vital Questions of the German Proletariat," in *The Struggle Against Fascism in Germany* (New York: Pathfinder Press, 1971), 190.

73. James Baldwin, "Report from Occupied Country" in *Collected Essays* (New York: Penguin Random House, 1998), 734.

74. National Border Patrol Council, https://bpunion.org/about-nbpc/union-faq/.

75. Reade Levinson, "Across the U.S., Police Contracts Shield Officers from Scrutiny and Discipline," *Reuters*, January 13, 2017.

76. Much more has been and can be written about actual connections between the police and fascist organizations. This serves as more evidence of the points made here.

77. Cedric G. Johnson, *After Black Lives Matter: Policing and Anti-Capitalist Struggle* (London: Verso Books, 2023), 321, 314.

78. Johnson, *After Black Lives Matter*, 317.

79. Jarrod Shanahan and Tyler Wall, "'Fight the Reds, Support the Blue': Blue Lives Matter and the US Counter-subversive Tradition," *Race & Class* 63, no. 1 (2021): 70–90.

80. Dan Berger, "In the Fight for Justice, the Police Can Only Be on One Side," *Defector*, May 3, 2023.

81. There is more to be said about the difference between the police and the military that should be compared fully elsewhere.

notes 247

82. Seals was later murdered in 2016 and his body put in a car and then set on fire, part of a mysterious similar string of deaths of prominent Ferguson activists.

83. Dan Collyn, "Bolivian Police in La Paz Join 'Mutiny' against Evo Morales," *Guardian*, November 9, 2019.

84. Jeffery Webber, "The Eighteenth Brumaire of Macho Camacho," interview by Ashley Smith, *Verso* blog, November 15, 2019.

85. Leon Trotsky, "What Next? Vital Questions for the German Proletariat," 190.

86. KRS-ONE, "Black Cop," song, *Return of the Boom Bap*, 1993.

87. Lauren Leatherby and Richard Oppel Jr., "Which Police Departments Are as Diverse as Their Communities," *New York Times,* September 23, 2020.

88. Goodison, "Local Police Departments Personnel."

89. Leatherby and Oppel, "Which Police Departments Are as Diverse as Their Communities."

90. Kwame Ture and Charles V. Hamilton, *Black Power, the Politics of Liberation* (New York: Vintage Books, 1967), 46.

91. "Petitions Statement for Community Control of the Police" *The Black Panther*, June 14, 1969; Bobby Seale, "Community Control of Police Was on the Berkeley Ballot in 1969," *San Francisco Bay View*, August 13, 2015. Also see the demands of the 1967 Newark Black Power Conference described in Robert Allen's *Black Awakening in Capitalist America: An Analytic History* (Trenton, NJ: Africa World Press, 1990), 157–58.

92. Taylor, *From #BlackLivesMatter to Black Liberation*, 83.

93. For example, Bernie Sanders's "Justice and Safety for All" platform called to "diversify police forces . . . and incentivize officers to live and work in the communities they serve." See berniesanders.com/issues/criminal-justice-reform. This is also a component of the George Floyd Justice in Policing Act of 2021 (H.R. 1280), text accessible at congress.gov/bill/117th-congress/house-bill/1280/text.

94. Tamar Sarai Davis, "The False Promise of Black Police Chiefs," *Capital B News*, January 30, 2022.

95. Matthew Guariglia, *Police and the Empire City: Race and the Origins of Modern Policing in New York* (Durham, NC: Duke University Press, 2023), 201.

96. Tom Jacobs, "Black Cops Are Just as Likely As White Cops To Kill Black Suspects," *Pacific Standard*, August 9, 2018.

97. See Department of Justice reports of Chicago and Baltimore police departments after the murders of Laquan McDonald and Freddie Gray, respectively. Dallas is fifth highest in the number of police

248   **Their End Is Our Beginning**

murders in the country and has had a series of public incidents of racism in the department.

98. "Q & A: Dallas Police Deputy Chief Malik Aziz on Being a Black Cop," *Dallas Morning News*, July 16, 2016, https://www.dallasnews.com /opinion/commentary/2016/07/16qa-dallas-police-deputy-chief-malik -aziz-black-cop.

99. Kim Barker, "The Black Officer Who Detained George Floyd Had Pledged to Fix the Police," *New York Times*, September 15, 2020.

100. Tim Haines, "Chicago Mayor Lightfoot: FOP President Is 'Attempting to Induce an Insurrection' by Opposing Vaccine Mandate," *Real Clear Politics*, October 18, 2021.

101. For one example, see Maher, *A World Without Police*, 216.

102. Hassan Kanu, "Prevalence of White Supremacists in Law Enforcement Demands Drastic Change," Reuters, May 12, 2022.

103. Alice Speri, "Unredacted FBI Document Sheds New Light on White Supremacist Infiltration of Law Enforcement," *The Intercept*, September 29, 2020.

104. Henry Goldman, "NYC Police Say de Blasio's Words, Not Policies, Betray Them," *Bloomberg*, December 30, 2014.

105. Eric Kerl, "Four Theses on American Fascism," *Rampant*, November 2, 2020.

106. Hall, *Policing the Crisis*, 320.

107. Barker, *States in Capitalism*, 37.

108. Colin Barker, "The State as Capital," *International Socialism* (July 1978): 16–42.

chapter 4: An Ever-Raging Fire

1. Quoted in Philip Marfleet, *Egypt: Contested Revolution* (London: Pluto Press, 2016), 4.

2. V. I. Lenin, "The Tasks of the Proletariat in the Present Revolution," *Collected Works*, vol. 24 (Moscow: Progress Publishers, 1964), 19–26.

3. Ahmed Saleh, "The Popular Committees: The Local, The Ordinary, and The Violent in The Egyptian Revolution," masters thesis, Central European University, 2016, 54.

4. Saleh, "The Popular Committees."

5. Asef Bayat, *Revolution without Revolutionaries: Making Sense of the Arab Spring* (Palo Alto: Stanford University Press, 2017), 157.

6. Mariame Kaba and Andrea Ritchie, *No More Police: A Case for Abolition* (New York: New Press, 2022), 220.

7. Kaba and Ritchie, *No More Police*, 221.

notes   249

8. Simon Basketter, "October 1968: When Derry Dared to Revolt against British Imperialism," *Socialist Worker* (UK), October 2, 2018.

9. In October 1968, many on the left (including Devlin, McCann, and others) also formed the socialist organization People's Democracy (*Daonlathas an Phobail*).

10. See Part 2 of Eamonn McCann, *War and an Irish Town* (Chicago: Haymarket Books, 2018), for a description of the early civil rights movement and police repression.

11. Eamonn McCann, "Operating without the Police Came Naturally to People," interview by brian bean, *Rampant*, March 16, 2022.

12. Niall Ó Dochartaigh, *From Civil Rights to Armalites: Derry and the Birth of the Irish Troubles* (Cork: Cork University, 1997), 312. Emphasis in original.

13. Russell Stetler, *The Battle of the Bogside: Politics of Violence in Northern Ireland* (London: Sheed & Ward, 1970), chapter 3. Italics mine.

14. Eamonn McCann, "The Battle of the Bogside," *Socialist Worker* (UK), August 11, 2009.

15. McCann, *War and an Irish Town*, 88.

16. Quoted in Freya McClements, "You Are Now Entering Free Derry: 50 Years On," *Irish Times*, January 5, 2018.

17. McClements, "You Are Now Entering Free Derry," 90.

18. Ó Dochartaigh, *From Civil Rights to Armalites*, 134.

19. McCann, "Operating without the Police."

20. McCann, "Operating without the Police," 94.

21. McCann, "The Battle of the Bogside."

22. Ó Dochartaigh, *From Civil Rights to Armalites*, 134.

23. Ó Dochartaigh, *From Civil Rights to Armalites*, 134.

24. Ó Dochartaigh, *From Civil Rights to Armalites*, 274–75.

25. Ó Dochartaigh, *From Civil Rights to Armalites*, 280.

26. An astute reader might notice that, in this short section about Derry, I do not mention the nonprofit Community Restorative Justice (CRJ) organization. In some literature, such as the excellent books by Kristian Williams and Geo Maher that I cite several times in this book, CRJ is discussed as an alternative to the police in Northern Ireland, albeit with some criticism. I do not spend time discussing it, as the assessment of CRJ did not seem to come directly from the struggle of Free Derry but rather as a component of Sinn Féin's peace process with the British state, inaugurated with the 1998 Good Friday agreement. One anonymous comrade from Derry whom I interviewed stated that "what is on paper about them is not the reality." Their

perspective was that the CRJ connection with Sinn Féin is apparent, and most people see them as not doing much except as a job source for Sinn Féin supporters. Additionally, their existence prepared the ground for Sinn Féin to eventually join the police instead of just doing quasi-policing (Williams and Maher are clear about this), as CRJ now exists as a networked community/police partnership as opposed to a clear alternative *to the police*. McCann—in an interview conducted by me on February 17, 2022—described how CRJ is well regarded by the state because of its ability to settle disputes that they could not settle, but always with a decision in the state's interest. In one example, a conflict between an individual and a landlord was handled by CRJ instead of applying pressure on the landlord. He somewhat mournfully described how "the people who manned the barricades of Free Derry and so on, their equivalence now in 2022 have got walkie-talkie communication with the cops."

27. McCann, "Operating without the Police."

28. Noor Nieftagodien, *The Soweto Uprising* (Athens, OH: Ohio University Press, 2014), 129.

29. Nieftagodien, *The Soweto Uprising*, 103.

30. Franziska Rueedi, *The Vaal Uprising of 1984 & the Struggle for Freedom in South Africa* (Suffolk: James Currey Publishing, 2021), 104.

31. The Koornhof Bills were the package of legislation that simultaneously established these two measures as well as degrading the citizen rights of Black South Africans.

32. Humphrey Tyler, "South Africa's Black Police: Focus of Black Civilian Hostility," *Christian Science Monitor,* April 9, 1985.

33. Janet Cherry, *Spear of the Nation (uMkhonto weSizwe)* (Athens, OH: Ohio University Press, 2011), 90–92.

34. Rueedi, *The Vaal Uprising of 1984*, 128.

35. Cherry, *Spear of the Nation*, 87.

36. Rueedi, *The Vaal Uprising of 1984*, 188–89; Cherry, *Spear of the Nation*, 88–89.

37. Quoted in Rueedi, *The Vaal Uprising of 1984* , 171.

38. Rueedi, *The Vaal Uprising of 1984*, 172.

39. Rueedi, *The Vaal Uprising of 1984*, 181.

40. Patrick Noonan, *They're Burning the Churches* (Sunnyside; Jacanna Media; 2003) 73

41. Claire Ceruti, "The End of Apartheid in South Africa," in *Revolutionary Rehearsals in the Neoliberal Age*, ed. Colin Barker, Gareth Dale, Neil Davidson (Chicago: Haymarket Books, 2021), 103.

notes 251

42. Ceruti, "End of Apartheid in South Africa," 103; Rueedi, *The Vaal Uprising of 1984*, 160.

43. Sandra Burman and Wilfried Schärf, "Creating People's Justice: Street Committees and People's Courts in a South African City," *Law & Society Review* 24, no. 3 (1990): 724; Tom Lodge, "Rebellion: Turning the Tide," in *All, Here, and Now: Black Politics in South Africa in the 1980s*, ed. Tom Lodge and Bill Mason (New York: Ford Foundation– Foreign Police Association, 1991), 137.

44. Lodge, "Rebellion: Turning the Tide," 135–39.

45. Quoted in Cherry, *Spear of the Nation*, 88–89.

46. Quoted in Alex Callinicos, "Politics of the ANC," *Socialist Worker Review*, no. 79 (September 1985): 18–19.

47. From a transcript of proceedings of the Truth and Reconciliation Commission, July 27, 1999, day 2, case of Mzixholo Stokwe, accessed at https://www.justice.gov.za/trc/amntrans/1999/99072629_ pe_990727pe.htm.

48. Ceruti, "End of Apartheid in South Africa," 105; numbers pulled from Congress of South African Trade Unions, South African History Online.

49. Ceruti, "End of Apartheid in South Africa," 108; Callinicos, "Politics of the ANC."

50. One example is the 2012 Marikana massacre of striking gold miners, carried out under the presidency of Jacob Zuma, who was once a prominent anti-apartheid leader, political prisoner, and member of the ANC's armed wing.

51. Quoted in Rueedi, *The Vaal Uprising of 1984*, 196.

52. This section relies on interviews by the author with René González Pizzaro, an organizer-participant in the events described, conducted on May 15, 2022.

53. B. Gloria Martínez González and Alejandro Valle Baeza, "Oaxaca: Rebellion against Marginalization, Extreme Poverty, and Abuse of Power," *Monthly Review*, July 1, 2007.

54. Robert Joe Stout, "Awakening in Oaxaca," *Monthly Review*, July 1, 2010.

55. Gerardo Rénique & Deborah Poole, "The Oaxacan Commune: Struggle for Autonomy and Dignity," *NACLA Report on the Americas* 41, no. 3 (2008): 24–30.

56. Barucha Peller, "Self-Reproduction and the Oaxacan Commune," *ROAR Magazine*, no. 1 (Spring 2016): 7.

57. Almost every country in the region experienced major uprisings in this period; four heads of state (Egypt, Libya, Tunisia, Yemen) with a

252   **Their End Is Our Beginning**

combined one hundred and eighteen years in office were ousted, and others came close.

58. In 2019, another regional wave of revolts swept the region, which ousted two more heads of state with a combined fifty years in office (Algeria and Sudan) and several governments in Lebanon and Iraq.

59. Joel Beinin, *Workers and Thieves: Labor Movements and Popular Uprisings in Tunisia and Egypt* (Palo Alto: Stanford University Press, 2016), 87–88.

60. Eric Gobe, "The Gafsa Mining Basin between Riots and a Social Movement: Meaning and Significance of a Protest Movement in Ben Ali's Tunisia," working paper, HAL sciences humains et sociales, 2010.

61. Beinin, *Workers and Thieves*, 89.

62. Gilbert Achcar, *The People Want: A Radical Exploration of the Arab Uprising* (Berkeley, CA: University of California Press, 2013), 145.

63. Hossam el-Hamalawy, interview by author, conducted on March 17, 2024.

64. Many of the individuals came through the Kefaya movement. See Hossam el-Hamalawy, "In Pursuit of the Domino Theory," *3rabawy*, November 2, 2023.

65. Salwa Ismail, "The Egyptian Revolution against the Police," *Social Research* 79, no. 2, (Summer 2012): 435–62.

66. El-Hamalawy, interview March 17, 2024.

67. Cilja Harders and Dina Wahba, "New Neighborhood Power: Informal Popular Committees and Changing Local Governance in Egypt," in *Arab Politics Beyond the Uprisings. Experiments in an Era of Resurgent Authoritarianism*, ed. Thanassis Cambanis and Michael Wahid Hanna (New York: Century Foundation Press), 400–419.

68. First coined by Lenin in "The Dual Power," *Pravda,* April 9, 1917.

69. Marfleet, *Egypt: Contested Revolution*, 36.

70. Beinin, *Workers and Thieves*, 110.

71. The revolt spread from Tunisia and Egypt and made immediate parallels with the capital occupation in Wisconsin, the "movement of the squares" in Greece, the *indignados* in Spain, and the Occupy movement, then resurfaced again in 2019 in Algeria, Sudan, Iraq, and Lebanon.

72. See Robin Yassin-Kassab and Leila Al-Shami, *Burning Country: Syrians in Revolution and War* and Joseph Daher, *Syria After the Uprisings: The Political Economy of State Resilience* (Chicago: Haymarket Books, 2019).

73. Yasser Munif, *The Syrian Revolution: Between the Politics of Life and the Geopolitics of Death* (London: Pluto Press, 2020), 147.

74. Yasser Munif, interview by author, March 14, 2024.

75. Munif, interview March 14, 2024.

notes   253

76. Munif, interview March 14, 2024. In Manbij, the LCC was called the Revolutionary Committee; I have continued referring to it as LCC for simplicity of understanding.

77. As this book was being edited, in December 2024, the Assad regime in Syria finally fell. His military melted away in the face of an offensive driven by a number of pro-revolution militias, most notably that of Hay'at Tahrir al-Sham. A new chapter, its conclusion far from decided, has opened in Syria.

78. V. I. Lenin, "Report on the Review of the Program and on Changing the Name of the Party," *Collected Works*, vol. 27 (Moscow: Progress Publishing, 1964), 133.

79. Tsuyoshi Hasegawa, *The February Revolution, Petrograd, 1917* (Leiden: Brill, 2018), 295.

80. Hasegawa, *The February Revolution*, 283–87.

81. Hasegawa, *The February Revolution*, 286

82. N. N. Sukhanov, *The Russian Revolution 1917: A Personal Record* (Princeton: Princeton University Press, 1984), 16.

83. Hasegawa, *The February Revolution*, 290.

84. Sukhanov, *The Russian Revolution 1917*, 122, 125.

85. V. I. Lenin, "Concerning a Proletarian Militia," Third Letter, Letters from Afar, March 11, 1917, Marxists Internet Archive, https://www.marxists.org/archive/lenin/works/1917/lfafar/third.htm.

86. V. I. Lenin, "They Have Forgotten the Main Thing." *Collected Works*, vol. 24 (Moscow: Progress Publishers, 1964), 350–53.

87. For more on this condensed history, see *The History of the Russian Revolution* by Leon Trotsky.

88. Декрет о суде, 22 ноября (5 декабря) *1917 г.* [Decree of the Court 1917], Decrees of the Soviet Government, State Publishing House of Political Literature, 1957, Moscow State University, http://www.hist.msu.ru/ER/Etext/DEKRET/o_sude1.htm.

89. Victor Serge, *Year One of the Russian Revolution* (Chicago: Haymarket Books, 2015), 103.

90. Marcel Liebman, *Leninism Under Lenin* (London: Merlin Press, 1985), 326.

91. Evgeny Pashukanis, *Law and Marxism: A General Theory* (London: Pluto Press, 1989), 173.

92. Pashukanis, *Law and Marxism*, 185.

93. Pashukanis, *Law and Marxism*, 180.

94. Pashukanis, *Law and Marxism*, 158, 179.

95. Liebman, *Leninism Under Lenin*, 311–13; Adele Lindenmeyer, "The

254 **Their End Is Our Beginning**

First Soviet Political Trial: Countess Sofia Panina Before the Petrograd Revolutionary Tribunal," *The Russian Review* 60, no. 40 (October 2001): 505–25.

96. For this question, see Anthony Arnove et al, *Russia: From Workers' State to State Capitalism* (Chicago: Haymarket Books, 2003); Victor Serge, *From Lenin to Stalin*, trans. Ralph Manheim (New York: Pathfinder, 1973); Tony Cliff, *The Revolution Besieged: Lenin 1917–1923* (Chicago, Haymarket Books, 2012); Moshe Lewin, *Lenin's Last Struggle* (Michigan University Press, 2005); among a number of other works that seriously engage with the question without falling into the trap of seeing the Russian Revolution's turn to the Stalinist party-state as inevitable.

97. Chant from a 2004 protest against torture in Egypt mentioned in my interview with Hossam el-Hamalawy. The Arabic reads: يا حرية فينك فينك أمن الدولة بينا وبينك. I have translated what is literally "State Security," the name of the body that included the police in Egypt at the time, to simply "police."

98. Alain Dalotel, "The Paris Commune 1871," transcription of a video by O. Ressler in collaboration with Rebond pour la Commune, recorded in Paris, France, 25 min., 2004.

99. Quentin Delarmouz, "Police Forces and Political Crises: Revolutions, Policing Alternatives and Institutional Resilience in Paris, 1848–1871," *Urban History* 43, no. 2 (May 2016): 244.

100. Donny Gluckstein, *The Paris Commune: A Revolution in Democracy* (Chicago: Haymarket Books, 2011), 10.

101. Karl Marx, *The Civil War in France* (New York: International Publishers, 1968), 67.

102. Kristian Williams, *Our Enemies in Blue: Police and Power in America* (Oakland, CA: AK Press, 2015), 371.

103. Harvey O'Connor, *Revolution in Seattle: A Memoir* (Chicago: Haymarket Books, 2009), 138.

104. Pierre Broué and Émile Témine, *The Revolution and the Civil War in Spain* (Chicago: Haymarket Books, 2008), 140. Agustín Guillamón, *Ready for Revolution: The CNT Defense Committees in Barcelona* (Oakland, CA: AK Press, 2014), 71, 82.

105. Guillamón describes the work of the control patrols as contradictory. They both served a purpose for the revolution but, he argues, also served as means for the controlling of the July Revolution in Catalonia. Guillamón, *Ready for Revolution*, 246.

106. Chris Ealham, *Anarchism and the City: Revolution and Counter Revolution in Barcelona, 1898–1937* (Oakland, CA: AK Press, 2010), 185.

notes 255

107. Keeanga-Yamahtta Taylor, interview *Democracy Now!*, June 1, 2020.
108. McCann, "Operating without the Police."

chapter 5: Revolutionary Abolitionism

1. Ben Brucato, *Race and Police: The Origin of Our Peculiar Institution* (New Brunswick, NJ: Rutgers University Press, 2023), 43.
2. This term comes from Stuart Schrader, *Badges Without Borders: How Global Counterinsurgency Transformed American Policing* (Oakland, CA: University of California, 2019).
3. Egon Bittner, *The Functions of the Police* (Chevy Chase, MD: National Institute of Mental Health, 1970), 38.
4. Bittner, *Functions of the Police*, 40.
5. Sidney L Harring, *Policing a Class Society: The Experience of American Cities, 1865–1915* (Chicago: Haymarket Books, 2017), 15.
6. Adam Tooze, "The State as Blunt Force—Impressions of the Columbia Campus Clearance," *Chartbook Newsletter*, no. 280, May 1, 2024.
7. Patrick Colquhoun, *A Treatise on the Police of the Metropolis Containing a Detail of the Various Crimes and Misdemeanors by which Public and Private Property and Security are, at Present, Injured and Endangered: and Suggesting Remedies for their Prevention* (London: Baldwin & Son, 1800).
8. Mariame Kaba, "Police 'Reforms' You Should Always Oppose," *Truthout*, December 7, 2014; see also Mariame Kaba and Andrea Ritchie, *No More Police: A Case for Abolition* (New York: New Press, 2022), 132–35.
9. One example: "The creation of new institutions that lay claim to the space occupied by the prison can eventually start to crowd out the prison so that it would inhabit increasingly smaller areas of our social and psychic landscape," Angela Davis, *Are Prisons Obsolete?* (New York: Seven Stories Press, 2003), 107–8.
10. Michael Roberts, *The Long Depression: Marxism and the Global Crisis of Capitalism* (Chicago: Haymarket Books, 2016).
11. Ashley Smith, "Imperialism and Anti-Imperialism Today," *Tempest*, May 24, 2024.
12. Richard Seymour, *Disaster Nationalism: The Downfall of Liberal Civilization* (London: Verso Books, 2024).
13. Andreas Malm and the Zetkin Collective, *White Skin, Black Fuel* (London: Verso Books, 2021), 241–42.
14. Malm and the Zetkin Collective, *White Skin, Black Fuel*, 242; Geoff Eley, *Nazism as Fascism: Violence, Ideology, and the Ground of Consent in Germany 1930–1945* (London: Rutledge, 2013), 217.
15. It is important to understand here the category of "migrant" not as

some unified social group but as a grouping created through "state-regulated relations of governance and difference." Harsha Walia, *Border & Rule: Global Migration, Capitalism, and the Rise of Racist Nationalism* (Chicago: Haymarket Books, 2021), 2.

16. United Nations International Order of Migration, *World Migration Report 2024* (Geneva: IOM Publications, 2024).

17. Walia, *Border & Rule*, 77.

18. Walia, *Border & Rule*, 79–92.

19. See Malm and Zetkin Collective, *White Skin, Black Fuel*, chapter two.

20. Walia, *Border & Rule*, 209–11. There is an interesting debate about differences between these terms as to how "green" fascism can be and its relation to fossil capital. The Zetkin Collective take this up extensively in the work cited here.

21. Malm and the Zetkin Collective, *White Skin, Black Fuel*, 245.

22. Larry Buchanan, Quoctrung Bui, Jugal Patel, Black Lives Matter May Be the Largest Movement in U.S. History," *New York Times*, July 3, 2020.

23. Samuel Brannen, Christian Haig, Katherine Schmidt, "The Age of Mass Protest: Understanding and Escalating Global Threat," *Center for Strategic International Studies,* March 2020.

24. Isabel Ortiz, Sara Burke, Mohamed Barrada, Hernán Saenz Cortéz, *World Protests: A Study of Key Protest Issues in the 21st Century* (New York: Palmgrave Macmillan, 2021).

25. Jonathan Neal, "Social Collapse and Climate Breakdown," *The Ecologist*, May 8, 2019.

26. Rebecca Weiner, "Evolving Security Challenges and Threat Landscapes," panel at Global Security Forum, March 28, 2023.

27. In the wake of the 2008 economic crisis, police spending temporarily dipped; it has subsequently rebounded.

28. Grace Manthey, Frank Esposito, and Amanda Hernandez, "Despite 'Defunding' Claims, Police Funding Has Increased in Many U.S. Cities," ABC7, October 19, 2022.

29. Kevin Pope, "Advancing National and Global Security: Four Pillars for Enhanced Interoperability," *Police1*, January 31, 2024.

30. Naomi Murakawa, "Three Traps of Police Reform," in *Abolition for the People*, ed. Colin Kaepernick (Chicago: Haymarket Books, 2023), 146.

31. The Lexow Committee findings alone consist of over ten thousand pages of information.

32. Lexow Committee, "LEXOW COMMITTEE REPORT; New-York's Police Described as Allies of Criminals. . .," *New York Times*, January 18, 1895.

notes 257

33. Lexow Committee, "LEXOW COMMITTEE REPORT," January 18, 1895.

34. Center for Research on Criminal Justice, *The Iron Fist and the Velvet Glove: An Analysis of the U.S. Police* (Berkeley, CA: Center for Research on Criminal Justice, 1982), 36–39.

35. Quoted in *Iron Fist and the Velvet Glove*, emphasis mine.

36. August Vollmer, "Aims and Ideals of the Police," *Journal of Criminal Law and Criminology* 13, no. 2 (August 1922).

37. The President's Commission on Law Enforcement and Administration of Justice; National Advisory Commission on Civil Disorders; and U.S. National Commission on the Causes and Prevention of Violence, respectively.

38. National Advisory Commission on Social Disorders, *Report of the National Advisory Commission on Social Disorders* (New York: Bantam Books, 1968), 157.

39. See Geo Maher, *A World Without Police: How Strong Communities Make Cops Obsolete* (London: Verso Books, 2021), 76–78.

40. Police Accountability Task Force, *Recommendations for Reform: Restoring Trust Between the Chicago Police and the Communities That They Serve: Executive Summary* (Chicago: Police Accountability Task Force, 2016), 8.

41. Keeanga-Yamahtta Taylor, "We Should Still Defund the Police," *New Yorker*, August 14, 2020.

42. Elizabeth Hinton, *America on Fire: The Untold History of Police Violence and Black Rebellion Since the 1960s* (New York: Liveright Publishing, 2021), 15.

43. See the work of Hinton in *America on Fire* and *From the War on Poverty to the War on Crime* as two examples.

44. Heather Cherone, "5 Years After Chicago's Consent Decree Took Effect, Little Urgency Surrounds Reform Push," WTTW, March 4, 2024.

45. See https://mappingpoliceviolence.us/cities.

46. Jarrod Shanahan and Zhandarka Kurti, *States of Incarceration: Rebellion, Reform, and America's Punishment System* (London: Reaktion Books, 2022), 23.

47. Maher, *A World Without Police*, 90.

48. Andy Mannix, "Killing of George Floyd Shows that Years of Police Reform Fall Far Short," *Star Tribune*, June 20, 2020.

49. Other high-profile killings by MPD during this period include Justine Damond and Thurman Blevins.

50. Maher, *A World Without Police*, 81–82; Min-Seok Pang and Paul

Pavlou, "Armed with Technology: The Effects on Fatal Shooting of Civilians by the Police," Bureau of Justice Assistance; Lindsey Van Ness, "Body Cameras May Not Be the Easy Answer Everyone Was Looking For," *Stateline*, January 14, 2020. For a refutation of the most commonly used study used to support body cameras, see Ben Brucato, "Policing Made Visible: Mobile Technologies and the Importance of Point of View," *Surveillance and Society* 13, no. 3/4 (2015): 455–73.

51. Mission statement of Chicago Police Department Education and Training Division, pulled from official CPD website; accessed February 28, 2025.

52. Erin Snodgrass, "The Chicago Police Department has killed more children since 2013 than any other local law enforcement agency, according to police accountability data," *Business Insider*, April 15, 2021.

53. Murakawa, "Three Traps of Police Reform," 143–44.

54. Houston had a Community Services Division in the 1970s that implemented this program, and, in 1982, it was redoubled and exported. See Lee P. Brown, "Community Policing: A Practical Guide for Police Professionals," *Perspectives on Policing*, no. 12 (September 1989).

55. James Baldwin, "Fifth Avenue, Uptown," *Esquire*, July 1960.

56. Woods Ervin, Ricardo Levins Morales, Zola Richardson, Jonathan Stegall, "The Fantasy of Community Control of the Police," *The Forge*, February 4, 2021.

57. Jayda Van, "Who Controls Chicago's Cops?," *Rampant*, July 27, 2021.

58. This quote is from *Jacobin Magazine* founder and current president of *The Nation* Bhaskar Sunkara, in *The Socialist Manifesto: The Case for Radical Politics in an Era of Extreme Inequality* (London: Verso Books, 2020), 14.

59. Annika Norée, "Fatal Police Shootings in Sweden," *Bergen Journal of Criminal Law and Criminal Justice* 9, no. 2 (2021): 82–95.

60. Amelia Cheatham and Lindsey Maizland, "How Police Compare in Different Countries" *Council on Foreign Relations*, March 29, 2022.

61. Ibbi Chune quoted in Alexander Burlin, "Sweden's Shameful Record on Racism Shows Why We Need Black Lives Matter," *Jacobin*, June 6, 2020.

62. Taylor, "We Should Still Defund."

63. For a more expansive look at some examples of these types of demands see Kaba and Ritchie, *No More Police*, 131–36, and Taylor, "We Should Still Defund."

64. Cedric G. Johnson, *After Black Lives Matter: Policing and Anti-Capitalist Struggle* (London: Verso Books, 2023), 341.

65. Johnson, *After Black Lives Matter*, 250–53, 334.

66. Regarding "abolition communism," see the introduction of this book.

notes 259

67. Johnson, *After Black Lives Matter*, 48–49. For all its faults, Johnson's text does make good arguments about some of the liberal framing around "defund," and I agree with him that the "abolition of the wage relation" is our goal.

68. Gilmore, *Abolition Geography*, 451.

69. Assata Shakur, *Assata: An Autobiography* (New York: Lawrence Hill, 1987), 190.

70. Guy Aitchison, "Policing and Coercion," in *Abolishing the Police*, ed. Koshka Duff (London: Dog Section, 2021), 139.

71. Charmaine Chua, Travis Linnemann, Dean Spade, Jasmine Syedullah, and Geo Maher, "Police Abolition," *Contemporary Political Theory* 23, no. 1 (2024): 116.

72. This concept was first used by André Gorz in his 1967 book *Strategy for Labor* and other essays from the same period. The concept is used by many prominent abolitionist texts such as Kaba and Ritchie's *No More Police*, Ruth Wilson Gilmore's *Golden Gulag*, and Patrisse Cullors's *An Abolitionist's Handbook: 12 Steps to Changing Yourself and the World* (St. Martin's, 2022).

73. Gilmore, *Golden Gulag*, 242.

74. Amna Akbar, "Demands for a Democratic Political Economy," *Harvard Law Review* 134, no. 1 (November 2020): 90–119.

75. Chua et al., "Police Abolition," 116.

76. Rachel Herzing and Justin Piché, *How to Abolish Prisons: Lessons from the Movement against Imprisonment* (Chicago: Haymarket Books, 2024); Nisha Atalie, Gerardo Marciano, Rachel Cohen, "'It Failed Because You Made It Fail': The Story of Todo Para Todos," *Rampant*, September 21, 2023.

77. Kaba and Ritchie, *No More Police*, 243. Also see Dan Berger, Mariame Kaba, Dan Stein, "What Abolitionists Do," *Jacobin*, August 24, 2017.

78. Julia Lurie, "They Built a Utopian Sanctuary in a Minneapolis Hotel. Then They Got Evicted," *Mother Jones*, June 12, 2020.

79. Maher, *A World Without Police*, 145.

80. Kaba and Ritchie, *No More Police*, 247.

81. Maher, *A World Without Police*, 155.

82. See, for example, Herzing and Piché, *How to Abolish Prisons*, 141.

83. See for example, "The creation of new institutions that lay claim to the space occupied by the prison can eventually start to crowd out the prison so that it would inhabit increasingly smaller areas of our social and psychic landscape." Angela Y. Davis, *Are Prisons Obsolete?* (New York: Seven Stories, 2003), 107–8. Or "To build community is to make police

unnecessary, irrelevant: obsolete,"Maher, *A World Without Police*, 155.

84. André Gorz, "Reform and Revolution," in *Class, Party, Revolution*, ed. Greg Albo, Leo Panitch, Alan Zeuge (Chicago: Haymarket Books, 2018), 111.

85. Miski Noor and Kandace Montgomery, foreword to *No More Police*, ed. Kaba and Ritchie, xv.

86. Micah Herskind, "This Is the Atlanta Way: A Primer on Cop City," *Scalawag*, May 1, 2023.

87. Ian Birchall, *Bailing Out the System: Reformist Socialism in Western Europe: 1944–1985* (London: Bookmarks, 1986), 23.

88. Zachary Levenson and Teresa Kalisz, "States and Stakes: Relational Theory and the Politics of Class Struggle," *Verso* blog, November 13, 2019.

89. Chua, et al., "Police Abolition," 119.

90. Jamie Alinson, "The Actuality of Counter-Revolution," *Salvage*, January 28, 2023.

91. Ernest Mandel, *From Stalinism to Eurocommunism* (London: NLB, 1978), 195.

92. This definition of "revolutionary situations" is from V. I. Lenin, "The Collapse of the Second International," *Collected Works, vol. 21* (Moscow: Progress Publishers, 1977), 213–14.

93. Daniel Bensaïd, "The Notion of the Revolutionary Crisis in Lenin," *Viewpoint Magazine*, September 5, 2014.

94. Lenin, "Collapse of the Second International," 214.

95. Sheila Cohen, "The Red Mole: Workers Councils as a Means of Revolutionary Transformation," in *Ours to Master and to Own: Workers' Control from the Commune to the Present*, ed. Dario Azzellini and Immanuel Ness (Chicago: Haymarket Books, 2011); Victor Wallis, "Workers Council and Revolution" in Ness and Azzellini, *Ours to Master*; Donny Gluckstein, "The Workers Council Movement in Western Europe," *International Socialism Journal* 2, no. 18 (Winter 1983): 1–29.

96. Stuart Hall, "For A Marxism Without Guarantees," address, *Australian Left Review Marx Centenary Symposium*, April 1983.

97. Daniel Bensaïd, *An Impatient Life: A Memoir* (London: Verso Books, 2015), 19.

98. Chua, et al. "Police Abolition," 126.

99. Tobi Haslett, "States of Incarceration with Zhandarka Kurti and Jarrod Shanahan," interview in *Brooklyn Rail*, October 2022. Also see Duncan Hallas's 1971 essay "Towards a Revolutionary Socialist Party."

100. Quoted in Neil Davidson, "The Actuality of Revolution," in *Revolutionary Rehearsals in the Neoliberal Age*, ed. Colin Barker, Gareth Dale, and Neil Davidson (Chicago: Haymarket Books, 2021), 325.

index

Notes are indexed as page numbers followed by "n" and the note number.

abolition: anticapitalism as central to, 4–5; capitalist state as chief obstacle to, 8, 14, 112, 184, 204–7; as changing everything, 6, 102, 181; as class war, 200, 204–7; as creation, 102; possibilities created by, 200–2. *See also* police abolition

abolition, strategies for: autonomist abolition as, 203–4, 210–12; procedural abolition as, 202, 204, 207–9; role of a party in, 215–16; social revolution as, 212–13, 214–15

After Black Lives Matter (Johnson), 199, 259n67

Aitchison, Guy, 201–2

Akbar, Amna, 202

Alexander, Marissa, 96

All Cops Are Bastards (ACAB), 10

Anthracite Coal Strike, 67–68

anti-Black racism: as central to police, 101, 105, 142–43; as central to US capitalism, 2–3, 142–43; life expectancy and, 3; of slave patrols, 31–32, 33, 35–36. *See also* police brutality; police killings; racism

anticapitalism: as central to

abolition, 4–5, 158, 176–77; as sharpened by police, 175–77

antipolice movements: 1960s Black movement as, 72; Arab Spring as, 145–47, 162, 166; Free Derry as, 149–53; as necessarily anticapitalist, 177; Oaxaca Uprising as, 159–60; Paris Commune as, 174; in response to creation of police, 52–53; Russian Revolution as, 171–74; social injustices and, 13, 72, 176–77; Township Uprising as, 153, 154–55, 156, 157. *See also* police abolition

Arab Spring: as antipolice movement, 145–47, 162–64, 166, 167; community care as central to, 165; lead-up to, 145–47, 162–64, 251–52n57; police alternatives created by, 164–66, 168–69; workplace strikes during, 166

Austin, Stephen F., 56

autonomist abolition, 203–4, 210–12. *See also* abolition, strategies for

Aziz, Malik, 137

262 **Their End Is Our Beginning**

Bailey, Lindsey, 93
Baldwin, James, 1, 131, 195
Balto, Simon, 69–70
Barbados Slave Codes, 31–32
Barker, Colin, 117, 120–21, 141–42
Baughman, Shima, 83
Beckles, Hilary, 33
Bensaïd, Daniel, 211–12, 214–15
Berger, Dan, 133
Bevins, Vincent, 5
Birchall, Ian, 208
Bittner, Egon, 82, 142, 182
Black Codes, 37
Black Panther Party, 135–36
Bland, Sandra, 63, 232n2
Block, Fred, 113
bordering regimes, 186–87. *See also* capitalist state
Border Police Union, 132
Border & Rule (Walia), 186
Bouazizi, Mohammed, 163
Bow Street Runners, 30, 39
Bratton, William, 84, 87
Bridewell Prison, 21
Broken Windows Theory, 84–85, 87–88
Brown Long, Cyntoia, 96
Brucato, Ben, 11, 34, 37, 41, 181–82

Camp, Jordan, 87–88
Capital (Marx), 51
capital flight, 117, 209
capitalism: contradictions of, 51–52, 114; labor power as necessary for, 120–21; police as universal feature of, 5–6, 119–21; socialism as antithesis to, 6; system of states as necessary for, 117, 119–20, 141–42; unemployment as necessary for, 126; use

of term, 221–22n12. *See also* capitalist state
capitalism, development of: chattel slavery as central to, 22–23, 30–32, 33–34, 36; class societies prior to, 18–19; colonialism as central to, 22–23; in Europe, 19–22, 224n15, 224n16; urbanization as central to, 23–24. *See also* police, development of
capitalism, tools to maintain: crime as, 79–81; police as, 4, 49–50, 51–52, 60–61, 68; racism as, 2–3
capitalists: capitalist state and, 111, 114–17; competition between, 114; as lacking class consciousness, 113
capitalist state: capitalists and, 111, 114–17; as chief obstacle to abolition, 8, 14, 112, 184, 204–7; electoral politics and, 109–13; multiplicity as defining of, 118–19, 184–85; as necessary for capitalism, 117, 119–20, 141–42; necessity of confrontations with, 177, 178–79, 204–7, 211–14, 216; as police state, 12–13, 112, 119–21, 143, 181–83; racism as political project of, 13, 112, 124–28, 142–43; structural features of, 116–19; violence as central to, 112, 121–23. *See also* capitalism
Carmichael, Stokely, 135
Casey, Arthur, 57
Catanzara, John, 138–39
chattel slavery, 22–23, 30–32, 33–34, 36
Chicago Beer Riots (1855), 58–59
Chicago Police Department (CPD):

Index 263

creation of, 59; killings of children by, 191, 193, 258n52; racial profiling by, 85; work slowdown by, 90

Chua, Charmaine, 202, 203, 210

Chune, Ibbi, 197

class as social relationship, 129–30. *See also* working class

Clinton, Bill, 89

collective bargaining by riot, 41–42, 45–47. *See also* strikes

colonialism: as central to development of capitalism, 22–23; as central to development of police, 50–51, 54–55, 56–57, 68–69

Colquhoun, Patrick, 78–81, 183

Commissioners of Police (Scotland), 26

The Communist Manifesto (Marx), 5, 111

community policing, 136, 194–95, 258n54. *See also* police reforms

The Condition of the Working Class in England (Engels), 75, 77

Connolly, James, 214

Correia, David, 68, 131

crime: as class-based, 12, 63–64, 79–81; conditions that lead to, 103–4; falling rates of, 103; police as bad at solving or preventing, 12, 81–85, 236n81; as race-based, 77–78, 104, 234–35n51; statistics as biased, 85–86; as tool to maintain capitalism, 79–81; as unrelated to harmful acts, 74–78

Crisis Assistance Helping Out On The Streets (CAHOOTS) program, 93

Daley, Richard J., 72

Dalotel, Alain, 174

Davidson, Neil, 118

Davis, Angela, 5

de Blasio, Bill, 138, 139

democracy, farce of, 109–12. *See also* capitalist state

Derry Citizens Defence Association (DCDA), 149–50

Detroit Rebellion, 71–72

Dickerson, William, 32

divest/invest framework, 202. *See also* abolition, strategies for

Douglass, Frederick, 36

Draper, Hal, 115–16

dual power, 166, 167

Du Bois, W. E. B., 109

Dunbar-Ortiz, Roxanne, 56–57

du Pleiss, H. B., 157

Dutch East India Company, 23

Duverger, Maurice, 110–11

Edwards, Frank, 105

Egyptian Popular Committees (PCs), 164–66

Egyptian Revolution (2011), 145–47

electoral politics, 109–113. *See also* capitalist state

Eley, Geoff, 186

Empowering Communities for Public Safety (ECPS), 195–96. *See also* police reforms

Engels, Friedrich: on capitalists, 114; on police, 109; on relationship between working class and police, 53, 77; on social murder, 75; on the state, 113

Erakat, Noura, 118–19

Farrell, Audrey, 83

264 Their End Is Our Beginning

Fielding, Henry, 30
Fields, Barbara, 37
Finlayson, Niani, 97
The First Black Slave Society (Beckles), 33
Fox, Ruben, 36–37
Fraternal Order of Police (FOP), 132–33
Free Derry (1969, 1972): as antipolice movement, 149–53; community care in, 151–52, 153, 178; two periods of, 148

Gafsa Rebellion (2008), 162–63
Gainer, Ryan, 1–2
Gaines, Korryn, 9
Gates, Daryl, 71
Gilmore, Ruth Wilson: on capitalist discipline, 80; on class war, 200; definition of abolition by, 6, 102, 181; on imperialism, 101–2; on mass incarceration, 73, 74, 127; on necessity of abolishing capitalism, 5; on prisons and slavery, 37; on racism, 76, 127, 128
Giuliani, Rudolph, 87
Go, Julian, 69
Gordon Riots, 38–40
Gorz, André, 202, 205
Gottschalk, Marie, 71
Gramsci, Antonio, 215–16
Guariglia, Matthew, 136

Hadden, Sally, 32, 34–35
Haitian Revolution, 43, 56
Hall, Stuart, 124, 141, 214
el-Hamalawy, Hossam, 164, 165, 178
Harring, Sidney, 49, 61, 182

Harteau, Janeé, 193
Hartman, Saidiya, 34
Haslett, Tobi, 215
Heatherton, Christina, 87–88
Hillen, Liam, 150
Hinton, Elizabeth, 71, 73–74, 192
Hobsbawm, Eric, 41
Hopkins, E. Jerome, 190
How Europe Underdeveloped Africa (Rodney), 22
Hughson, John, 17

Ibrahim (Egyptian labor activist), 145
imperialism, boomerang effect of, 101–2, 118–19
incarceration rates, 2–3, 121, 122
INCITE!, 95, 97–98
instrumentalist theory, 112–13
Ismail, Salwa, 164

James, C. L. R., 23
Jefferson, Thomas, 27
Johnson, Cedric, 199, 259n67

Kaba, Mariame: on abolishing capitalism, 5; on fighting against police states, 8, 148, 204; on police alternatives, 94; on police reforms, 3; *Resisting Police Violence in Harlem* by, 70
Kelley, Robin D. G., 5, 80, 130
Kelling, George, 84
Kerner Commission (1967), 190–91. *See also* police reforms
killer cop contests, 131
King, Martin Luther, Jr., 71
Koen, Charles, 71
Kueng, Alex, 137

Index

Lacy, Akela, 100–101
La Mare, Nicolas de, 25
Lankford, Adam, 100
Larson, Sean, 126, 127–28
Law Enforcement Assistance Act (LEAA), 70–71
Lectures on Jurisprudence (Smith), 26
Lemaire, Jean-Charles, 24–25
Lenin, V. I.: on abolition, 145; on police and capitalist state, 111–12, 172, 243n16; on revolutionary mass action, 212; on soviet power, 170; on task of social revolutionary, 7
Lexow Committee (1894), 190. *See also* police reforms
Lightfoot, Lori, 138–39
Linebaugh, Peter, 79
Lipow, Arthur, 110
The London Hanged (Linebaugh), 79
London Metropolitan Police: demonstrations against, 52–53, 230n152; development of, 50, 53, 235n62; local adaptations of, 54–56, 57–58
Lovett, William, 17
Lynch, Patrick, 138, 139

Maher, Geo, 203, 204
managerial class, 129–30
Mandel, Ernest, 211
Marx, Karl: on abolition, 181; on abolitionist movement against chattel slavery, 7; on capitalists, 114; on chattel slavery, 23; on communism, 223n18; on development of capitalism, 19, 21; on labor, 126; on Paris Commune, 174; on police, 51; on the state, 113, 123

mass incarceration: as class war, 127; police expansion and, 73–74; as racialized, 37; rates of, 2–3, 121, 122
mass migration, 186, 255–56n15
mass shootings, 99–102, 240n146, 240–41n149
McCann, Eamonn, 149, 150, 151, 152, 153
McNally, David, 80–81, 124
McNeil, Angus, 54
Merritt, Keri Leigh, 35, 36
middle class. *See* managerial class; police
Minneapolis Police Department (MPD), 193, 257n49
Mitrani, Sam, 57–58, 59
modern police. *See* police
Mokhele, Tsietsi "Stompi," 155–56
Mokoena, Reid, 158
Morgan, Edmund, 37
multipolar world order, 184–85
Munif, Yasser, 168, 169
Murakawa, Naomi, 77, 189, 194

Neale, Jonathan, 188
Neocleous, Mark: on assumptions about policing, 11; on police and capitalist state, 26, 79, 80, 112, 119
New York Police Department (NYPD), 84–85, 89–90
Nicholls, George, 49
Nichols, Tyre, 4
Nieftagodien, Noor, 154
non-reformist reforms, 202, 259n72. *See also* abolition, strategies for; police, alternatives to
Noonan, Patrick, 156

Oaxaca Uprising (2006): as antipolice movement, 159–60; end of, 161–62; external solidarity for, 161; police alternatives created by, 161; teachers' strike origins of, 158–59
Occupied Territory (Balto), 69–70
Ó Dochartaigh, Niall, 149
Omnibus Crime Control and Safe Streets Act, 73
opioid crisis, 64
organized abandonment, 124–26, 127

Paris Commune (1871), 174
Parker, William, 71
Parkland school shooting (2018), 100
Parliamentary Acts of Enclosure of 1760–1830, 21
Pashukanis, Evgeny, 77, 173
Peel, Robert, 50, 195, 230n139, 235n62
"perfect victim" narrative, danger of, 9
Peter I (tsar), 25–26
Peterloo Massacre (1819), 45–47, 51
pin-mapping, 68–69, 87–88
Pizarro, René González, 159, 160, 161
police: ACAB as material analysis of, 10; anti-Black racism as central to, 101, 105, 142–43; as authority of capitalist state, 181–83, 188–89; bordering regimes and, 186–87; compared to military, 121, 133–34; demographics of, 135, 242–43n10; etymology of term, 24–25; as modern invention, 17; slave

patrol as core logic of, 11; tensions between politicians and, 138–41; as universal feature of capitalism, 5–6, 119–21; use of term "modern," 223–24n4; violence as primary tool of, 2, 11, 81, 82, 121
police, alternatives to: abolition as necessary for, 178; community care as, 151–52, 153, 165, 178, 203–4; created by Arab Spring, 164–66, 168–69; created by Oaxaca Uprising, 161; created by Township Uprising, 155–57; for domestic violence, 98; in Free Derry, 151–52, 153; lack of, 103–4; meeting needs and, 94, 98; for mental health emergencies, 93. *See also* procedural abolition
police, development of: alongside development of capitalism, 10–11, 51–52, 60–61; colonization and occupation as central to, 50–51, 54–55, 56–57, 68–69; Europe's precursors to modern, 27–30; insurrections and uprisings as central to, 38–42, 44–47, 52–53, 58–60, 67–68; racialization as central to, 35–37, 50; slave patrol as precursor to modern, 30–33, 33–36, 45, 227n73; through experimentation by ruling class, 47, 49, 60–61; urbanization as central to, 48–49, 58. *See also* capitalism, development of
police, myths about: as crime solvers, 12, 65–66, 81–85, 236n74, 236n81; diversity as solution to

Index

267

brutality, 135–38; as keeping us safe, 92–93, 95–98, 99–102, 105–7; preventative policing as, 78–81, 85–89; as preventing chaos, 89–91, 174–75. *See also* crime

police, purpose of: as core of capitalist state, 12–13, 60–61; in early capitalist Europe, 25–26, 29–30; maintaining capitalism as, 4, 49–50, 51–52, 60–61, 68; patrol and crowd control as, 49–50, 82, 105; threat of violence as central to, 2, 49, 82, 112, 181–83; violence as central to, 2, 11, 81, 104–5, 241n161

police abolition: as a beginning, 10, 183, 216; as central to socialism, 6–7; as creative act, 3–4, 147; definition of, 3–4; demands of, 198–99; end of capitalist state as necessary for, 7–8, 14, 184, 204–7, 211–14; necessity of, 4, 105–7, 143, 213–14, 216. *See also* abolition; antipolice movements

police as class enemies: class positioning of, 128–30, 134–35; by design, 11, 65–68, 112, 130–32, 142; white supremacy and, 139. *See also* police brutality; police killings

police associations and "unions," 131–33

police brutality: anticapitalism as sharpened by, 175–76; domestic violence and, 96; legal justification for, 194; against protesters, 149, 154, 164, 168,

170–71; sexual violence and, 97; in Sweden, 197. *See also* anti-Black racism; police killings

police expansion: as bipartisan, 115; mass incarceration and, 73–74; post-World War II, 69–70; prior to World War II, 67–69; in response to insurrections and uprisings, 70–74; through increased budgets, 70–71, 122–23, 189, 191; through police reforms, 189

"Police Force Size and Civilian Race" (Williams), 86–87

police killings: after enactment of reforms, 193–94, 257n49; of children, 70, 101, 191, 193, 258n52; of domestic violence victims, 97; as encouraged and defended, 131, 132–33; in innocuous situations, 4, 106, 145; during mental health crises, 1–2, 9, 92–93, 240–41n149; "no-knock" warrants and, 63–64, 232n3; "perfect victim" narrative and, 9; of protesters, 7, 154; rates of, 105–6, 122; in Sweden, 196–97. *See also* anti-Black racism; police brutality

police propaganda, 81, 140, 236n74

police reforms: community policing as, 136, 194–95, 258n54; dangers of, 3; enactment of, 192–93; impossibility of, 3, 14, 143, 184, 197–98; legitimization and normalization by, 191–92, 193; police expansion through, 189; review boards as, 195–96; use of committees and commissions for, 190–91

268   **Their End Is Our Beginning**

Powell, James, 70
preventative policing, 78–81, 85–89
procedural abolition, 202, 204,
207–9. *See also* abolition, strategies for; police, alternatives to
Punishing the Poor (Wacquant), 88
Purdue Pharma, 64
Purnell, Derecka, 97

Quincy, Josiah, 66

racism: definition of, 76, 124, 127–28;
as political project of capitalist
state, 13, 112, 124–28, 142–43;
as tool to maintain capitalism,
2–3. *See also* anti-Black racism
Reed, Dexter, 9
*Regulation of the Main Municipal
Administration of 1724* (Peter
I), 25–26
Resisting Police Violence in Harlem
(Kaba), 70
Ritchie, Andrea, 8, 94, 148, 204
Robinson, David, 48
Rodney, Walter, 22
Romney, George, 72
Rozario, Win, 9
Rueedi, Franziska, 155
Russian Revolution (1917): abolition
accomplished by, 172–73; as
antipolice movement, 171–72;
end of, 173–74; worker strikes
as central to, 170–71

Sackler family, 64
Saeed, Khaled, 145
school shootings. *See* mass shootings
Schrader, Stuart, 82
Scott, Julius, 42
Seals, Darren, 134, 247n82

Seattle General Strike (1919), 175
Seigel, Micol, 65
slave patrols: anti-Black racism of,
31–32, 33, 35–36; as core logic
of policing, 11; creation of,
30–33; impact of urbanization
on, 42–45; as precursor to
modern police, 30–33, 33–36,
45, 227n73
Smith, Adam, 26
Smith, Ashley, 185
Smith, Jacob H., 69
Smith, L. C., 68
social crises: as overlapping, 184–87;
police as state solution to,
188–89
socialism: antiracism as central to,
6–7; as antithesis to capitalism, 6; definition of, 6; police
abolition as central to, 6–7; use
of term, 222–23n18
social revolution, 212–13, 214–15.
See also abolition, strategies for
Soweto Uprising (1976), 154
Spade, Dean, 215
Spanish Revolution (1936–37), 175
Sparrow, Jeff, 102
Stetler, Russell, 149–50
Stop Cop City movement, 7
strikes: collective bargaining by riot
and, 41–42, 45–47; as part of
antipolice movements, 158–59,
166, 170–71
Support Team Assisted Response
(STAR) program, 93
Survived & Punished, 96
Syrian Local Coordinating Committees (LCCs), 168–69
Syrian Revolution (2011), 167–69

Index

269

Tambo, Oliver, 157
tanseeqiyat, 168–69
Taylor, Breonna, 63–64, 125, 175–76, 232n3
Taylor, Keeanga-Yamahtta, 72, 82, 105, 198, 221–22n12
Terán, Manuel Esteban Paez, 1, 7
Texas Rangers, 56–57, 231n171. *See also* slave patrols
Thompson, E. P., 129
Togliatti, Palmiro, 215–16
Tooze, Adam, 182–83
Tortuguita, 1, 7
Township Uprising, South Africa (1984): as antipolice movement, 153, 154–55, 156, 157; lead-up to, 153–54; police alternatives created by, 155–57; results of, 158
Treatise on the Police (La Mare), 25
A Treatise on the Police of the Metropolis (Colquhoun), 79
Trotsky, Leon, 112, 131, 134
Tunisian Uprising (2010), 163–64
Ture, Kwame, 135

urbanization: as central to development of capitalism, 23–24; as central to development of modern police, 48–49, 58; impact on slave patrols of, 42–45
US Border Patrol, 57, 231n171
US military, 122, 133–34
Uvalde school shooting (2022), 99–100, 101

Vaal Uprising. *See* Township Uprising, South Africa (1984)
vagrancy laws, 21, 36–37, 66
Van, Jayda, 196

Vargas, Richard, 86
Venkatesh, Sudhir Alladi, 127
Vesey, Denmark, 44
violence: as central to capitalist state, 112, 121–23; as central to purpose of police, 2, 11, 81, 104–5, 241n161; police use of threat of, 2, 49, 82, 112, 181–83; as primary tool of police, 2, 11, 81, 82, 121. *See also* police brutality; police killings
Vollmer, August, 68–69, 190

Wacquant, Loïc, 88
Walia, Harsha, 119, 186, 255–56n15
Watts, Stephon, 92
Watts Rebellion, 71
Wedderburn, Robert, 21–22
Weiner, Rebecca, 188
What Is to Be Done? (Lenin), 7
Whitehouse, David, 44
Wickersham Commission (1929), 190. *See also* police reforms
Williams, Alexander, 63
Williams, Eric, 23
Wilson, James Q., 84
Wilson, O. W., 69–70
Wood, Ellen Meiksins, 129
working class: broad definition of, 128; as defined by social relationship, 129–30; police as enemies of, 11, 65–68, 112, 130–32, 142; resistance by, 11, 38–42, 44–47, 58–60, 67–68. *See also* antipolice movements
wrongful convictions, 83

Zetkin Collective, 185–86

About Haymarket Books

Haymarket Books is a radical, independent, nonprofit book publisher based in Chicago. Our mission is to publish books that contribute to struggles for social and economic justice. We strive to make our books a vibrant and organic part of social movements and the education and development of a critical, engaged, and internationalist left.

We take inspiration and courage from our namesakes, the Haymarket Martyrs, who gave their lives fighting for a better world. Their 1886 struggle for the eight-hour day—which gave us May Day, the international workers' holiday—reminds workers around the world that ordinary people can organize and struggle for their own liberation. These struggles—against oppression, exploitation, environmental devastation, and war—continue today across the globe.

Since our founding in 2001, Haymarket has published more than nine hundred titles. Radically independent, we seek to drive a wedge into the risk-averse world of corporate book publishing. Our authors include Angela Y. Davis, Arundhati Roy, Keeanga-Yamahtta Taylor, Eve Ewing, Aja Monet, Mariame Kaba, Naomi Klein, Rebecca Solnit, Mohammed El-Kurd, José Olivarez, Noam Chomsky, Winona LaDuke, Robyn Maynard, Leanne Betasamosake Simpson, Howard Zinn, Mike Davis, Marc Lamont Hill, Dave Zirin, Astra Taylor, and Amy Goodman, among many other leading writers of our time. We are also the trade publishers of the acclaimed Historical Materialism Book Series.

Haymarket also manages a vibrant community organizing and event space in Chicago, Haymarket House, the popular Haymarket Books Live event series and podcast, and the annual Socialism Conference.

Also Available from Haymarket Books

All Our Trials: Prisons, Policing, and the Feminist Fight to End Violence (Revised Edition)
Emily L. Thuma, foreword by Sarah Haley

Defund: Conversations Toward Abolition
Calvin John Smiley

No Cop City, No Cop World: Lessons from the Movement
Edited by Kamau Franklin, Micah Herskind, and Mariah Parker

Not Your Rescue Project: Migrant Sex Workers Fighting for Justice
Chanelle Gallant and Elene Lam, afterword by Robyn Maynard, foreword by Harsha Walia

Perfect Victims and the Politics of Appeal
Mohammed El-Kurd

Set the Earth on Fire: The Great Anthracite Coal Strike of 1902 and the Birth of the Police
David Correia

Skyscraper Jails: The Abolitionist Fight Against Jail Expansion in New York City
Zhandarka Kurti and Jarrod Shanahan

Unbuild Walls: Why Immigrant Justice Needs Abolition
Silky Shah, foreword by Amna A. Akbar

About the Author

brian bean is a Chicago-based socialist organizer, writer, and agitator originally from North Carolina. They are one of the founding editors of *Rampant* magazine. Their work has been published in *Truthout, Jacobin, Tempest, Spectre, Red Flag, New Politics, Socialist Worker, International Viewpoint*, and more. They coedited and contributed to the book *Palestine: A Socialist Introduction*, also from Haymarket Books.

About the Illustrator

Charlie Aleck is a queer, First Nations artist (Nuu-chah-nulth) based in Chicago.